Baedeker

ALGARVE

Hints for using the Guide

Following the tradition established by Karl Baedeker in 1844, sights of particular interest, outstanding buildings and works of art are distinguished by either one ★ or two ★★ stars.

To make it easier to locate the various places listed in the "A to Z" section of the Guide, their co-ordinates are shown in red at the head of each entry: e.g., Faro D 13/14

Coloured lines down the right-hand side of the page are an aid to finding the main heading in the Guide: blue stands for the Introduction (Nature, Culture, History, etc.), red for the "A to Z" section, and yellow indicates Practical Information.

Only a selection of hotels, restaurants and shops can be given; no reflection is implied therefore on establishments not included.

The symbol ⓘ on a town plan indicates the local tourist office from where further information can be obtained. The post-horn symbol indicates a post office.

In a time of rapid change it is difficult to ensure that all the information given is entirely accurate and up-to-date, and the possibility of error can never be entirely eliminated.

Although the publishers can accept no responsibility for inaccuracies and omissions, they are always grateful for corrections and suggestions for improvement.

Preface

This guide to the Algarve is one of the new generation of Baedeker guides.

These guides, illustrated throughout in colour are designed to meet the needs of the modern traveller. They are quick and easy to consult, with the principal places of interest described in alphabetical order, and the information is presented in a format that is both attractive and easy to follow.

This guide covers the Portuguese coastal region of the Algarve as well as interesting places in the hinterland, i.e. the historic province of the Algarve which is today identical with the district of Faro.

The guide is in three parts. The first part gives a general account of the Algarve, its topography, climate, flora and fauna, environmental problems, population, economy, history, famous people, art and culture. A selection of quotations and a number of suggested routes lead into the second part, in which places and features of tourist interest are described. The third part contains a variety

Idyllic spots in the hinterland of the Algarve coast; Monchique and Alcoutim on the Guadiana

of practical information. Both the sights and the practical information are listed in alphabetical order.

The new Baedeker guides are noted for their concentration on essentials and their convenience of use. They contain numerous specially drawn plans and colour illustrations; and at the end of the book is a large map making it easy to locate the various places described in the "A to Z" section of the guide with the help of the co-ordinates given at the head of each entry.

Contents

Baedeker Specials

The Algarve has

Azulejos
on the Palácio de Estói

Extensive slopes clad with cork groves, fig and carob trees, yellow-flowered mimosa, lush almond and peach orchards, meadows red with poppies, and everywhere the trilling of cicadas and the sweet fragrance of orange blossom – spring in the Algarve must surely be one of the loveliest things of which those wearied by winter in less favoured climes might dream. But it isn't just in spring that the Algarve proves itself one of Europe's most popular holiday destinations. With 3000 hours of sunshine a year this delightful region, famous for its lovely beaches and sandy bays encircled by picturesque rocks, attracts visitors throughout the year.

In recent decades, though, the people of the Algarve have had to confront the all too obvious disadvantages such blessings of nature can bring. All along the coast tourist centres have sprung up to accommodate visitors hungry for the sun. In many places development has run riot, with consequences plain to see. Large parts of the coast are now in international hands and the foretaste of paradise lost for ever.

But amazingly, only a few miles from the ugly concrete dormitories, another magic survives, scarcely receiving a mention in travel brochures. Even today along the coast there are long sandy beaches and idyllic little coves with not a soul in sight. And a completely different Algarve lies waiting to be discovered in the hinterland, a peaceful, undulating garden-like countryside, a world away from the noisy, glitzy hustle and bustle of the seaside resorts.

Rock landscape
impressive coastal scenery near Lagos

Serra de Monchique
woodland scenery in the hinterland

Many Faces

As well as beaches and a frequently still enchanting rural atmosphere, the Algarve has delightful little towns, each with its own unique character – beautiful Tavira, its hipped-roofed houses reflected in its waters; the royal frontier town of Vila Real de Santo António, laid out with elegant symmetry on the bank of the Rio Guardina; Olhão with its sugar-cube houses and whimsical atmosphere; the cosmopolitan Faro, happily preserving its charming historic centre; the old Moor capital Silves; Lagos, city of noble past and agreeable present; and last but by no means least, the cluster of houses at Sagres, seeing which it is hard to believe that, in the 15th and 16th c., this most south-westerly tip of continental Europe was the hub of epoch-making events when Portuguese seafarers traversed the oceans on ambitious voyages and colonised more and more of the world.

Stone chimney
symbol of the Algarve

Virtually every one of these little towns grew out of ancient settlements. Phoenicians, Celtiberians, Romans and Moors all appreciated the Algarve's fortunate location, and left behind traces of their highly developed cultures.

And finally a word about the people. The Portuguese are renowned for their friendliness and warmth of welcome. They accept with good grace the unending foreign invasion, treating each individual tourist with traditional courtesy.

Holidaying in the Algarve guarantees not just a sunny climate, but a stay amongst people of sunny disposition too!

Fishermen in Olhão
there is always time for a chat

Albufeira
one of the largest tourist centres of the Algarve

Nature, Culture History

Facts and Figures

Location
: The Algarve, the most southerly of Portugal's eleven historic provinces, extends east–west between latitudes 36°58′ and 37°35′N and longitudes 7°25′ and 9°W. It thus lies in the extreme south-west corner of the Iberian peninsula and of Europe.

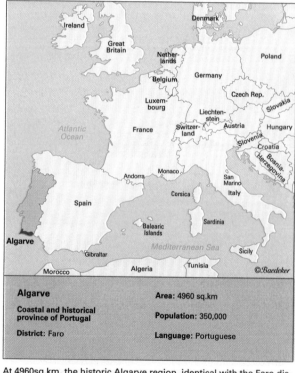

Algarve	**Area:** 4960 sq.km
Coastal and historical province of Portugal	**Population:** 350,000
District: Faro	**Language:** Portuguese

Area
: At 4960sq.km, the historic Algarve region, identical with the Faro district of today, represents less than one twentieth of Portugal's total land area. In shape it is a trapezium, about 135km wide, stretching from the Atlantic in the west to the Rio Guadiana forming the frontier with Spain in the east. The distance from the southern coast to the northern border with the Alentejo is 27km at the narrowest point and a good 50km at the widest.

Importance
: Its situation, isolated and exposed in the far south-west corner of the European mainland, has had a determining influence on the Algarve's

◄ *The picturesque fishing village of Ferragudo, near Portimão* history. For centuries it enjoyed close links with North Africa. Friendly trade relations, an influx of North African peoples into this part of southern Europe, and periods of occupation by one side or the other, have left an indelible mark on the cultural identity of the region. The ambitious ocean voyages of discovery and conquest by the Portuguese in later times, in which the western Algarve in particular played a crucial role, were born of the area's harsh economic realities. Even the Algarve's present popularity with tourists is due chiefly to its geographical location and resulting mild, already North African, climate.

The name Algarve goes back to the time of Moorish rule. The Algarve was then part of the Emirate of Córdoba and, lying on the very western edge of their empire, was called by the Arabs Al-Gharb (= "the West"). Under the Portuguese this became "O Algarve", "o" being the Portuguese masculine article "the".

The name

The boundaries of the historic Algarve coincided with those of the administrative distict of Faro today, of which the town of Faro is the chief administrative and regional centre. The district (distrito) is further divided into sixteen sub-districts or councils (concelhos) and 77 parishes (freguesias).

Administrative divisions

Topography

The Algarve is bounded on three sides by water: in the west and south by the Atlantic and in the east by the Rio Guadiana which forms the border with Spain. To the north it is sheltered by two substantial mountain ranges, the Serra de Monchique (north-west) and the Serra do Caldeirão (north and north-east). The region can loosely be divided into three: a narrow coastal strip (litoral), the foothills (baroccal) and the sparsely inhabited mountains (serra). Some parts of the former are highly developed for tourism, most of the latter as yet lies completely off the tourist track.

General

The landscape of the Algarve is exceedingly varied, something the ordinary travel brochure scarcely hints at. Even the coastline shows tremendous variation, with steep rocky shores contrasting with flat, dune-like sandy beaches. North of the coastal strip a swift transition occurs to the somewhat more hilly hinterland which, in winter and spring in particular, becomes clothed in green and ablaze with flowers. In the central and eastern sections stretches a gentle, fertile horticultural landscape with plantations of almond, fig and olive trees. Westwards, as the influence of the Atlantic makes itself increasingly felt, the hinterland becomes more and more barren until, in the very far west, scrub and Mediterranean-type macchia take over the landscape. The mountains are dominated by forests of eucalyptus, chestnut and holm oak, while higher up hardy cistus shrubs are to be seen almost everywhere.

A submerged mountain range, a continuation of the coastal mountains, exerts a critical influence on mainland Portugal. Just 65km south of the Algarve coastline the sea floor plummets to depths of about 4000m, while 250km or so south-west lies the Gorgine Bank, a submarine ridge the height of which varies as much as 5000m. Here, under the ocean, the Eurasian and African continental plates collide, causing frequent tectonic movement. The Gorgine Bank was the epicentre of the catastrophic earthquake which struck the Algarve coast in 1755 wreaking dreadful havoc.

Tectonic movement

Among its many attractions the Algarve boasts one very special geographical feature, the spectacular, legend-shrouded Cabo de São Vicente, the extreme south-westerly point of the European mainland

Cabo de São Vicente

Topography

where the continent of Europe ends in a wide rock plateau some 60m high dropping abruptly into the Atlantic.

West coast/
Costa Vicentina

The Costa Vicentina, taking its name from Cabo de São Vicente, extends north of the Cape and eastwards nearly as far as Lagos. The whole west coast northwards of the Cape comprises rugged, rocky cliffs rising to heights of 150m above the sea and interspersed with larger and smaller sandy bays. Along this stretch of coastline the waves come rolling in with all the force of the Atlantic, pounding against the rocks and breaking into surf on the beaches in the bays. Conditions are generally similar, though somewhat ameliorated, along the southern part of the Costa Vicentina, east of Cabo de São Vicente. Beyond Lagos the might of the Atlantic perceptibly diminishes, with the consequence that many of the more sheltered bays harbour picturesque villages and little coastal towns.

In 1988 a 90km stretch of coastline on the Costa Vicentina, extending northwards far into the Alentejo, became a conservation area known as the Parque Natural do Sudoeste Alentejo e Costa Vicentina. One of the most unspoilt coastal regions in Europe, the 74,788ha Parque provides an important habitat for a range of flora and fauna of a kind otherwise found in only one or two places in the world, including some 200 species of bird. Many migratory birds, some very rare, also find an excellent breeding ground here. Additionally some 60% of Portugal's reptiles and 65% of its amphibians are found in the Costa Vicentina area. 110 different species of fish have been identified in the waters of the Costa.

Rocky Algarve

The western section of the southern coast of the Algarve, extending from Cabo de São Vicente eastwards almost to Faro, is known as the Rocky Algarve or "Barlavento" (= the windward side). Here are steep cliffs and little sandy coves interspersed with longer sandy beaches dotted with picturesque rocky outcrops. Countless caves and grottoes, solitary stacks and intriguing rock formations give this region its scenic charm.

Sandy Algarve

The eastern section of the coast, the Sandy Algarve or "Sotavento" (= lee side), extends roughly from Vale do Lobo, west of Faro, to the Guadiana estuary. Much less exposed to the Atlantic than further west, it comprises on the one hand long stretches of wide sandy beaches and on the other an extensive network of lagoons. Reminiscent of tidal shallows, the large lagoon system to the west and east of Faro is protected by low, elongated island dunes lying close offshore.

Parque Natural
da Ria Formosa

The Parque Natural da Ria Formosa, which incorporates the lagoon to the west and east of Faro, covers a total area of about 18,400ha, roughly 4000ha of which are saline, with little channels and watercourses, saltpans, shellfish beds and fish ponds. The lagoon is separated from the open sea by a chain of islands some 60km long, stretching from Praia de Faro to Manta Rota west of Tavira, and broken in places by shallow natural, and in one or two cases artificial, channels such as those connecting Tavira, Faro and Olhão with the Atlantic. Continuous deposition of sediments means that, in course of time, the lagoon is becoming increasingly closed off, its natural outlets to the sea gradually silting up or shifting eastwards. With only a small influx of freshwater from the hinterland and continual replenishment by the tides, the saline content of the lagoon is very high. The combination of relatively warm shallow water, soft clayey bottom, and high salt and oxygen content produced by the regular exchange of water, creates a quite extraordinary habitat for an immensely rich and varied fauna and flora. The Ria Formosa was made a conservation area in 1987.

Serra

The mountains of the northern Algarve form a protective barrier separating the region from central Portugal and keeping at bay any incur-

Impressive rocks with caves and grottoes along the coast near Lagos

sions of cold air from the north. In consequence the foothills and southern coast enjoy climatic conditions which are already distinctly North African. The extensive Serra do Caldeirão rises to 589m. The highest summits though, Fóia (902m) and Picota (773m), are both in the Serra de Monchique. The most common rocks are argillaceous slate and sandstone, the latter widely used as a building stone in the Algarve. In the Serra de Monchique there are hot springs of volcanic origin, exploited for, among things, therapeutic purposes. Numerous small rivers rise in the mountains of the Algarve hinterland, flowing southwards towards the coast. Replenished by rain in winter and spring, they ensure a just about sufficient water supply. Towards the end of the 1950s several reservoirs were constructed in the foothills.

The Rio Guadiana (from the Arabic "Uadi-Ana" = Ana's river), forming the eastern border with neighbouring Andalusia, is the Algarve's principal river. Some 830km long, it rises in the La Mancha region of Spain. Navigable in Roman times to beyond Mértola, only the lowest 48km between Pomarão and Vila Real de Santo António are navigable today and then only by smallish vessels. Here the river is anything from 100 to 500m wide with an average depth of barely 5m.

Guadiana

Climate

The Algarve boasts one of the most dependable climates in the world, with some 3000 hours of sunshine a year. Protected by the mountains from the influence of cool northern air, conditions on the coast are similar to those on the coast of North Africa. High sunshine values are complimented by a warm, dry Mediterranean-type regime on which the Atlantic exerts a moderating effect, producing pleasant mild temperatures even in winter.

General

13

Climate

Spring in the Algarve hinterland

Temperatures

The warmest months are June, July, August and September. During this period the mean daily temperature climbs to 28°C, but with an ever-present light sea breeze it is not unbearably hot. In winter on the other hand it is almost never really cold, temperatures rarely dropping below 10°C, an exception being Cabo de São Vicente where values are the lowest in the Iberian peninsula (6.2°C).

Nevertheless holidaymakers should be sure to pack something warm to wear. The breeze can give a fresh feel to even the warmest summer evening, and with winters never very cold, rooms often have no heating so it can be distinctly cool indoors at this time of year.

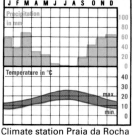

Climate station Praia da Rocha

Water temperatures

Atlantic sea temperatures are generally below those in the Mediterranean; in summer the water heats up to about 22°C, dropping in winter to only 15°C. Sea temperatures in the western Algarve tend to be somewhat lower than further east where the influence of the Atlantic becomes progressively weaker and that of the Mediterranean begins to make itself felt.

Precipitation

Rainfall averages range between 350 and 600mm a year, being generally higher in the mountains of the hinterland than on the coast. November as a rule is the wettest month. In recent years however rainfall has been considerably below average, leading to acute water shortages.

Flora and Fauna

Plant lovers should visit the Algarve in early spring. Even as early as December the brown, sunburnt landscape is beginning to turn green again. Then in January and February the almond trees are the first to burst into blossom.

The Algarve hinterland, the Serra de Monchique in particular, harbours a huge variety of species; but on the undeveloped stretches of coast too there are many different kinds of plants to be discovered. Of special interest here are the Ria Formosa and Costa Vicentina conservation areas. Across this whole region an unusually varied flora and fauna has been able not only to develop but also sustain itself, relatively undisturbed, in a succession of extensive interconnecting areas.

Additionally, many exotic plants from different parts of the world thrive in the Algarve. The age of discovery in the 15th and 16th c. saw many species of plant brought back from overseas, since when they have taken root and spread. For centuries even before that, plants were brought to southern Portugal from all over the Mediterranean by the Romans and Moors.

Olive
(Olea Europaea)

The gnarled, slow-growing olive is a very common sight in the Algarve, as throughout the Mediterranean region. Brought to Portugal by the Moors, olive trees can live as long as 2000 years. Known to have been cultivated since the earliest times, the olive was considered a symbol of wealth. The tree comes into blossom in May and June. For the fruit to ripen a long dry summer is needed; as they ripen they change colour from green to black. The harvest begins in November and continues until March. Presses are used to extract the oil.

Carob
(Ceratonia siliqua)

Also a familiar feature in the Algarve landscape is the carob tree, which for some time growers have been attempting to cultivate systematically. The region's high sunshine values make for ideal conditions. The tree develops large brown pods which are very nourishing and make good animal fodder.

Strawberry tree
(Arbutus unedo)

Strawberry trees, another common species in the Algarve, often seen growing on the roadside, are a kind of erica. Only 2–3m tall, they have leathery leaves. They take their name from their fruit, which looks a bit like a strawberry and from which "medronho", a clear schnapps with a high alcohol content, is made.

Orange
(Citrus sinensis)

Orange trees are special in that they blossom and bear fruit simultaneously. Blossom time is between February and June, in which months too the fruit starts to grow. The small white flowers emit an incredibly aromatic fragrance which, in the right weather conditions, wafts across the whole of the eastern Algarve where most of the orange groves are found.

Lemon
(Citrus limonium)

Lemon trees are less often cultivated in plantations than oranges. They have larger leaves than the orange, and their blossom is slightly pink at the tips.

Fig
(Ficus carica)

The fig tree is distinguished by its attractively shaped leaves with their five symmetrical "fingers". The green or dark mauve fruits with a soft pulpy inside are produced in spring and autumn.

Pomegranate
(Punica granatum)

The thorny pomegranate tree is a native of the eastern Mediterranean. It bears red blossom between May and September. Pomegranates have a very hard, leathery skin enclosing a mass of seeds, each in a fruit-like casing. Because of its numerous seeds the pomegranate is a symbol of fertility.

Japanese medlar
(Mespilus japonica)

The Japanese medlar was introduced to Portugal about 200 years ago. Today the cherry-sized yellow fruit (nêsperas) with large brown stones are sold in every market.

The Legend of the Almond Blossom

Try and imagine the Algarve without almonds. No snow-white sea of blossom in January or February. No fallen petals whirling in the breeze. On the markets no almonds for sale. No sweet, no salted, no roasted, no burnt almonds. And to crown it all: no marzipan delicacies.

Yet at one time the Algarve was just such a place, hardly an almond to be seen. That was before a certain Moor emir fell in love with a Swedish girl called Gilda. She packed her belongings and came to him in the warm sunshine of the Al-Gharb, where they married and should have been happy ever after – so at least a fairy-story would claim.

But something depressed the Swedish girl even in the first winter. In the second winter too she was silent and withdrawn. And in the third she became very sad, staring for hours at the castle's luxuriant green surroundings and never uttering a word. The emir was at his wits end. Head in hands he pondered long and hard. Every passer-by was asked for advice. At last he took the maid into his confidence. She of course had known all along what the trouble was. Her young Swedish mistress, she said, was simply homesick, her longing for northern climes worsening by the year; it scarcely bore thinking about how things would be the following winter.

Almond blossom comes early in the Algarve

The love-torn emir at first despaired, but quickly showed himself a man of resource. Another day spent brooding, another night – and then inspiration. Sparing no trouble and no expense he had thousands of almond trees brought secretly from his homeland to the Al-Gharb. Ship after ship arrived and unloaded the little *Prunus amygdalus* trees. They were planted in next to no time without the unhappy Gilda noticing, she was much too busy feeling homesick after all.

So it was a complete surprise when, the following year, the many thousands of almond trees bloomed and the emir, taking his young bride by the hand, led her onto the castle wall from where they gazed out over an endless expanse of white almond blossom. Look, the snow of the Al-Gharb, said the proud and generous-hearted emir. And the astonished girl? She is said to have been made truly happy by the sight of the snow-white blossom and the wilting petals drifting gently down.

The cork-oak plays an important role in the Portuguese economy, Portugal being the world's largest cork producer. Cork trees develop a layer of dead cells around the trunk as a way of reducing water loss and counteracting fluctuations of temperature. This layer of cork, approximately 3cm thick, can be peeled off for processing. The tree must be 20 years old before cork stripping begins. The cork layer grows back and stripping can be repeated every six years on average.

Cork-oak
(*Quercus suber*)

Like the cork-oak the holm-oak is also an evergreen. It can be recognised by its dark green leathery leaves with whitish felt-like undersides. Holm-oaks are still sometimes to be found growing in large stands. When solitary they can form very lush crowns.

Holm-oak
(*Quercus ilex*)

In Portugal the eucalyptus, frequently seen in the more mountainous areas, encounters an ecosystem very different from that in which it thrives in its native Australia. Able with its long roots to extract water from great depths, this newcomer is a significant factor in the devastation of large parts of the Portuguese countryside. Growing extraordinarily quickly and requiring substantial quantities of moisture, its systematic cultivation for the paper industry has caused great tracts of land to dry out. Even after the trees are felled it takes about 60 years for an area made desert by the eucalyptus to recover its ecological balance.

Eucalyptus
(*Eucalyptus globulus*)

In gardens or on verges Judas trees are often seen, their branches clad in April with pretty pink blossom; only afterwards do the distinctive, heart-shaped leaves form. Later in the year the trees can be recognised by their long pods. Judas is said to have hanged himself in one such tree.

Judas tree
(*Ceris siliquastrum*)

The *Acacia dealbata*, widely known as mimosa, is also very attractive, blossoming into a myriad yellow bobbles in February and March. It has rather unusual, very fine, pinnate leaves which curl up when touched.

Mimosa
(*Acacia dealbata*)

From May to early July the jacaranda or palisander tree is covered in wonderful violet-blue blossom, only a very few leaves forming thus early in blossom time. The Portuguese often plant jacarandas by the roadside or in car parks.

Jacaranda
(*Jacaranda mimosifolia*)

The exceedingly decorative umbrella pine is noted for its widely spreading crown. It grows in small pine groves or more often standing alone, when its luxuriant umbrella top offers welcome shade. The large cones contain edible seeds tasting like hazelnuts.

Umbrella pine
(*Pinus pinea*)

The araucaria or Norfolk Island pine comes from New Caledonia. In Portugal it is often planted in parks. It is immediately recognisable by its distinctive shape, its brush-like needles growing in echelons one on top of another.

Araucaria
(*Araukaria excelsa*)

Native to the Canary Islands from whence it has spread throughout the Mediterranean, the Canary date palm is one of the most common palms seen in the Algarve. It can be recognised by its small orange-yellow fruit (non-edible) hanging in long clusters between the palm fronds.

Canary date palm
(*Phoenix jubaea canariensis*)

While today it is almost impossible to imagine Portugal or the Mediterranean countries without the agave, it was only brought to Europe from America at the time of the voyages of discovery. Agaves produce a distinctive flower cluster on a tall stalk growing as high as a tree. After flowering the leaves die off, but the root survives to generate anew.

Agave
(*Agavae americana*)

Flora and Fauna

Mimosa . . .

. . . and Jacaranda blossom

Cistus
(*Cistus
ladanifer*)

Cistuses are among the more common shrubs found in the Algarve. At higher altitudes these low bushes form a sea of yellowy-white flowers from the end of March to June. The petals look slightly crumpled and the leaves have a sticky appearance.

Fauna

While uncontrolled over-development has caused widespread destruction of coastal habitats, the still relatively unaffected serra and nature reserves ensure the survival of many different species of wildlife, some quite rare.

Birds

Particularly in the more sheltered parts, herons, ospreys, snipe, oyster-catchers, kingfishers and plovers are seen. Storks come right into the towns to find nesting sites. The marshland near Castro Marim is renowned for its many flamingos. The woodlands are home to the azure-winged magpie, and orchards to the rufous warbler. The cliffs provide breeding places for rollers and bee-eaters.

Butterflies

Of the 200,000 species of butterfly identified world-wide, some 1600 are found in Portugal. Only about 300 of these inhabit the Algarve, among them the emperor moth, egger moth, death's head hawkmoth, red admiral, hummingbird moth, swallowtail, large blue and brimstone. Conditions on the whole tend to be inimical to butterflies; many parts of the region are densely populated and the more sheltered areas are near the sea where the vegetation is generally unsuitable. Though an abundance of species are found further north, few butterflies succeed in crossing the barrier formed by the mountains of the Alentejo and northern Algarve.

Mammals

Domestic species account for most of the mammals found in the Algarve, donkeys, goats and sheep being the most common. A few animals do survive in the wild, almost all of them in the mountains (wild boar, deer, foxes).

Lizards are very prolific and can often be seen sitting on walls basking in the sun. They disappear as quick as lightning the minute they sense movement around them. Moorish geckos have suction pads on the ends of their strange-looking toes, enabling them to scale smooth vertical walls. In sheltered parts there are chameleons, which protect themselves from predators by changing the colour of their skin to blend in with the light and background conditions. There are also snakes in the Algarve, some of them poisonous.

Reptiles

Some parts of the Algarve coast support a much greater variety of molluscs than others, the sandy beaches of the eastern section being poorly endowed compared with the chalky cliffs and rock strewn beaches further west, which offer a wider range of habitats. The most common shells are venus and razor shells, mussels, cockles, oysters and murexes.

Shells

Environmental Problems · Conservation

Tourism with all its far-reaching consequences, bush and forest fires every year, and a worsening water shortage today seriously threaten the Algarve.

General

In recent years the expected rainfall has failed to materialise even in winter and spring, so that throughout the Algarve as well as in the Alentejo adjoining to the north, an acute shortage of water is evident. Already by spring the water level in the reservoirs has fallen substantially. During the summer and autumn months a dearth of water is noticeable throughout the plant world. The cultivation of eucalyptus for the paper industry exacerbates the problem because the eucalyptus, introduced from Australia, draws great quantities of moisture from deep down in the ground. Since this is one of the most profitable branches of the Portuguese economy, the country faces an acute dilemma.

Lack of water

In tourist centres the water shortage is not yet too apparent; the fountains continue to bubble, the many golf course greens are kept copiously watered, and supplies to holiday accommodation are guaranteed. For many months of the year however the local population lives in daily expectation of interruptions to their supply.

Throughout the summer and autumn months, every part of Portugal runs the risk of woodland or forest fires, often burning completely out of control. The foothill region of the Algarve's Serra de Monchique is particularly prone. In addition to the general dryness due to lack of rainfall, and the fire risk posed by refuse burning, monocultivation, especially of eucalyptus and pine, is a further factor in the increased incidence of fires. EU subsidies encourage these forms of reafforestation at the expense of mixed woodland. Often whole areas are set alight deliberately, clearing the ground for eucalyptus plantations. Some fires burn for several weeks. Firefighting planes, most of them brought in from Spain, are used to try and stem the flames, water being drawn, in the case of this particular region, from the broad Rio Arade estuary. Because this is very salty, the land remains uncultivatable for many years afterwards. It is normally about two years before any shrubs take root following a fire; trees take even longer.

Forest fires

Tourism and its effects represent a massive problem for the Algarve. Until 50 years ago the litoral was still largely undeveloped; then great sections of the coastline were built on, destroying the habitats of countless plant and animal species and transforming the landscape almost overnight.

Tourism

The annual invasion of holidaymakers puts an enormous seasonal strain on the environment. In the peak season, refuse, sewerage and water consumption soar and traffic is swollen by great numbers of rental cars. In 1986 this prompted publication of a "National Plan for the Development of Tourism" which, though mainly concerned with promoting the tourist industry, also lays down guidelines for environmental and nature conservation.

Environmental awareness

For a long time environmental awareness in Portugal remained at a low level. Large areas of the country were or appeared unspoilt, and there was little to prompt public concern. Tourism among other things has changed all that, demonstrating clearly the perils of taking the environment for granted. Portugal's entry into the EU in 1986 was also a turning point; suddenly funds became available for industrial development and road-building, while at the same time a series of EU environmental directives came into force. In 1987 a legal framework for the protection of the environment was introduced, the first in Portuguese history. This was followed in 1989 by creation of a Department for the Environment, and in 1990 of a full Ministry. The Portuguese media however are as reticent as ever in reporting environmental problems and scandals. The task of raising public awareness thus falls mainly on independent environmental protection agencies, the best known and most powerful of which are Amigos da Terra, APEA (Associação Portuguesa dos Engenheiros do Ambiente), GEOTA (Grupo de Estudos de Ordenamento do Território e Ambiente), QUERCUS ("oak" – Associação Nacional de Conservação da Natureza) and the LPN (Liga para a Protecção da Natureza), the latter founded in 1948. In the Quinta de Marim near Olhão a nature conservation centre has been set up bringing schoolchildren face to face with environmental issues.

Conservation areas

A total of sixteen areas of various sizes have been declared nature reserves, of which the Costa Vicentina in the west, the lagoons of the Ria Formosa west and east of Faro, the banks of the Guadiana north of Castro Marim, the marshland south of Castro Marim and the banks of the Rio Arade north of Portimão are the largest. Then there are the Ponta da Piedade near Lagos, the lagoons in the estuary of several rivers at Alvor, parts of the Serra de Monchique, the Rocha da Pena mountains between Alte and Salir, one or two places with hot springs in the hinterland, and duneland near Monte Gordo.

Population

Statistics

Portugal has a population of some ten million. Of these roughly 350,000 live in the Algarve, which in area comprises about one twentieth of the country; by comparison, more than two million live in Greater Lisbon. The average density in the Algarve is 70 per sq.km (excluding the tourist influx in the summer months). The most sparsely populated regions (fewer than 20 inhabitants per sq.km) are in the north-eastern Algarve between Salir and Alcoutim, in the west between Aljezur and Vila do Bispo and in the mountains east of Monchique. In contrast the entire coast east of Luz (near Lagos) is very densely populated (more than 100 inhabitants per sq.km) with the exception of pockets west of Faro and east of Tavira.

The Algarve is experiencing a population explosion, reversing past trends when the only places in Portugal deemed attractive for living and working were Lisbon and the industrial area of Setúbal. The population of the serra has dropped steadily since 1930. On the coast there was quite an influx from 1940; thereafter numbers fell, only rising again after 1960.

Language

The official language is Portuguese. There are no recognised dialects, though the Portuguese spoken in the Algarve does differ slightly in pronunciation. Algarvios tend to colour their vowels a little differently and swallow their end syllables more than is the case elsewhere. In Portuguese generally, a relatively large number of Arab words have been preserved, and these can be recognised in some Algarve place-names. Almost all words beginning with "al-" are of Arab origin, including of course the word "Algarve" itself; also names of towns and villages such as "Albufeira", "Aljezur", "Alvor", "Alcantarilha" and "Algoz", and words like "almoço" (lunch) and "almofada" (pillow).

More than 95% of Portuguese are Roman Catholic, the other 5% being Protestant, Muslim or Jewish. Constitutionally there is no established church in Portugal and no tithes are levied. The extent to which Catholicism is practised varies widely in different parts of the country; in the Algarve observance is limited in comparison with further north. But even in the Algarve, feast days in honour of the local patron saint are major events in the calendar. Here, as throughout Portugal, celebrations are noticeably more in the style of folk festivals. Though generally commencing with mass and a procession, they soon dissolve into very worldly forms of entertainment – dancing, folk music, eating and drinking. A very well-known and popular pilgrimage or "romaria", attracting people from far and wide, takes place annually, two weeks after Easter, in Loulé. The patron saint's statue is carried in procession through the steep streets, after which there is a mammoth folk festival.

Religion

Since 1974 great emphasis has been laid nationally on providing a sound basic education. Throughout the period of Salazar's dictatorship, literacy remained well below average (in 1970 29% of all Portuguese over the age of 15 were unable to read or write). By 1994 the figure, though down, was still 13%, including a large proportion of older people and women. Even today signatures are often made with a thumb mark.

Today compulsory schooling in Portugal lasts nine years from the year in which the child reaches the age of six. There is then the option of a further three years secondary education in a comprehensive school augmented by a range of additional courses. Students now have the opportunity to attend university in the Algarve, at Faro.

Education

In recent years the Algarve has witnessed accelerating disintegration of the old family-based social structure which, until not so long ago, saw large families of several generations living together under one roof. Now young men and women become independent much earlier, thanks largely to tourism and the job opportunities it brings. There are an increasing number of small families. Women often have to shoulder the responsibility for housework as well as a career, and in this respect the equal rights movement appears no stronger in Portugal today than before.

Family structure

Within Portugal the Algarve is a special case, deriving its income chiefly from tourism. The growth of tourism brought about a general restructuring. Large numbers of people live and work on the coast, while rural areas, especially the remote mountain regions, are deserted or have very ageing populations. In such places poverty and unemployment are widespread. The poorest part of the Algarve is the Alcoutim district in the north-east. Tourism has also resulted in a two-tier population with disparate standards of living. Many younger people find work in one or other branch of the tourist industry, achieving a degree of prosperity as a result. Meanwhile older Algarvios or those in traditional occupations such as farming and fishing, have seen their already low standard of living reduced still further. In this respect the Algarve is not atypical, the same phenomenon becoming increasingly apparent throughout Portugal. A younger generation with good urban jobs enjoy standards of living comparable with those in Central or Western Europe; in contrast, older rural folk in particular often exist below subsistence level.

Social problems

21

Albufeira: the Portuguese always find time for a friendly chat!

Political system

When in 1974 Portugal's dictatorship was swept away in the "Carnation Revolution", a socialist constitution was introduced under which the country became a republic and a parliamentary democracy. In 1982 the constitution was amended, watering down the more radical socialist measures; in 1990 legislation restoring private ownership came into force, removing them completely. The head of state is the President, who is elected for a five-year term. A new parliament is elected every four years. The President appoints the Prime Minister, guided by the polls.

Political parties

The two largest parties are the Partido Social Democrático (PSD), founded in 1974, and the Partido Socialista (PS). In spite of its name the PSD is broadly liberal-conservative in outlook. The PS, founded in 1943 by Mário Soares while in exile in Germany, is social-democratic. Among the more influential smaller parties are the Partido Popular (PP), which developed from the Christian-Democratic CDS, and the Partido Comunista Português (PCP), founded in 1921 following the Russian October Revolution and later banned by Salazar. The abbreviation CDU sometimes seen blazoned on walls stands for a communist coalition. The Green Party (Os Verdes or Partido Verde), established in 1982, is politically marginal, as is the Partido Popular Monárquico (PPM) which, while also green, favours restoration of the monarchy.

Media

There is no regional daily paper published in the Algarve. As elsewhere in Portugal, people read the "Diário de Noticias" or the "Público". Popular weekend publications are the "Visão", the "Expresso" and the "Independente". Portuguese television currently has four channels: the state RTP 1 and RTP 2, the private company SIC and a religious channel TVI. The state radio station is the RDP.

Economy

Today tourism is the mainstay of the Algarve's economy, the great majority of the population being employed in the hotel, holiday or building trade. A minority of Algarvios continue to make a living from farming, fishing and fish processing. Until the late 1960s these were the region's primary sources of income; since then their importance has markedly declined.

General

Algarve industry, chiefly small-scale fish and cork processing, has never been of great significance nationally. Portugal's main industrial zones are located further north. Even building materials, the profitability of which owes much to the building boom in the Algarve, are manufactured in central and northern Portugal.

Portugal became a member of the EC (now the European Union) in 1986, hoping with financial aid gradually to improve the country's economic performance and bring it closer to the EU average. Ten years later however Portugal still ranks alongside Greece, Spain and Ireland as one of the poorest member countries. EU funds are targeted on modernising Portuguese industry, developing an infrastructure, improving the internal transport system and building warehouses. Today new roads are under construction all over Portugal, including the Algarve. Entry into Europe has also brought new problems, especially for agriculture. Because Portuguese fruit and vegetables do not meet EU standards, there is no real market for them in Europe. Indeed large quantities of foodstuffs are imported into Portugal from other member states.

Joining the EC

Fishing, together with farming, was long the leading industry of the Algarve. Since time immemorial the tuna and sardine harvests in particular have been vitally important to the economy of this coast. Today the Algarve still accounts for about 20% of the total Portuguese catch. The main fishing ports are Olhão (19,000 tonnes per year) and Portimão (17,000 tonnes per year); among the smaller ports is Vila Real de Santo António (4400 tonnes per year). Vessels leave Olhão for ocean fishing grounds off the African coast and the cod banks of Newfoundland. In the lagoons around Faro and Alvor and in the vicinity of the Rio Arade estuary near Portimão, considerable quantities of mussels are harvested. In the 1950s measures were taken to modernise the fishing industry, including the introduction of trawlers for sardine fishing. Now however Portugal's fishing fleet is out of date and unable to compete with their European rivals, especially the Spanish. Poorly equipped boats restrict Algarve fishermen to coastal waters, where sardines are the principal catch. While enough of these are netted to meet local demand, some other types of fish have to be imported and are expensive.

Fishing

Fish processing too is in sharp decline. Since 1974 this branch of the industry, centred mainly on Portimão and Olhão, has received virtually no subsidies, forcing many plants to close. The situation in Portimão tells the story: up until 1974 there were 61 canning factories in business, today there is only one.

Fish processing

In the barrocal and serra, where the normally favourable climate allows as many as four crops a year, a high proportion of the population used to be employed in farming. But since the late 1980s agriculture throughout Portugal has been severely affected by EU entry, in addition to which southern Portugal has experienced a catastrophic shortage of rain. Drought (and in some places poor soil), antiquated methods of cultivation and uneconomic use of labour result in produce below EU standards and relatively high in cost. EU agricultural subsidies are currently targeted on "set aside" (non-use of land)

Farming

23

The last few trawlers of the former fishing fleet of Portimão

and early retirement, the preconditions for which many small farmers in the Algarve cannot meet. Consequently farmers in areas near the coast often find it more profitable to sell their land for development. Another problem, likely to become apparent only some years hence, is that only 25% of those currently engaged in agriculture are under 35, while a similar proportion are over 65. This suggests that in future agricultural production could be threatened by a shortage of labour.

Fruit

Statistics for the fig harvest illustrate the decline in farming. Between 1953 and 1962 annual fig production was 16,000 tonnes, today it is only 1000 tonnes. One reason is that fig trees are being felled to create larger farm units or room for citrus plantations. Citrus production has risen accordingly from 16,000 tonnes between 1953 and 1962 to 150,000 tonnes today. In general, output of figs, almonds, olives and carob has sharply declined. Existing trees are neglected or crops remain unpicked, there being too few people left in rural areas to do the work. Virtually no new trees are being planted. Olive oil production is down by 75% compared with the 1950s. Only carob production has held up relatively well, new research having shown how the pods can be utilised commercially. But even here output, which in the 1950s was 40,000 tonnes, is down to 30,000 tonnes today.

Wine production is also in decline in the Algarve. At one time many Algarve farmers produced wine, but small vineyards are nowadays barely profitable and not always able to satisfy quality controls. Table wine though is regarded as still having a future. Well-known labels are "Algar Seco" from the Lagos region, "Moscatel" from Lagos, and "Dom Paio" from Tavira.

Vegetables

Sweet potatoes, tomatoes, beans, cucumbers, peppers, green salad and herbs are all grown. Greenhouse cultivation is common, providing protection from the sun's burning rays and, in the winter months, from storm and rain damage.

Orange trees on the sides of the Serra de Monchique

The eucalyptus is of major importance to the Portuguese economy; in the Algarve whole hilltops are seen planted with young trees. The wood is processed to produce cellulose. Because of the comparatively lax regulatory regime, the ecologically problematic cellulose industry is firmly established in Portugal, mainly on the Tejo. Both the industry and its raw material, the eucalyptus, are environmentally damaging. The fast-growing trees extract large quantities of moisture from the soil, causing it to dry out.

Forestry

The growing of cork is becoming less and less important. Though Portugal is still the world's largest producer, the cork industry has been badly hit by competition from man-made alternatives.

Tourism is now without question the pillar of the region's economy. About 50% of all visitors to Portugal holiday in the Algarve; in contrast only 25% head for Lisbon and its surroundings, while the rest make for the northern Atlantic coast and Portuguese islands. No other part of the country experiences mass tourism on anything like the same scale. In the 1980s alone tourism in the Algarve grew by 15% a year. In 1983 there were 75,000 hotel beds; today the figure is nearer 250,000.

Tourism

Over the years the coast of the Algarve has proved especially popular with the British. The number of German tourists is also rising steadily (500,000 in 1994, an increase of 12% on the previous year). The majority of visitors however are Spaniards, many of whom come just for the day and mainly to shop. Towns such as Vila Real de Santo António and Tavira in the eastern Algarve are the chief beneficiaries of this Spanish invasion.

Building has escalated to such an extent in the Algarve in recent years that it has attracted considerable adverse criticism. In future, quality not quantity is to be the watchword, the hope being that this will limit further damage to the landscape, wildlife and nature reserves. In 1994 a six-year plan was drawn up controlling the development of

Cork-oaks: Portugal is the largest producer of cork in the world

tourism throughout Portugal, financed by the government, EU and private sector. A third of the available funds will be invested in the Algarve.

Transport

Roads

At the beginning of 1994 Portugal introduced a form of MOT test. Lorries, taxis and ambulances are required to be checked annually by IPO (Inspecçoës Periódicas Obrigatórias), private cars every two years. By 1997 tests should have been carried out on all vehicles.

As part of a scheme to improve transport links with Spain, the motorway-style IP 1 (Via do Infante) through the Algarve has been recently upgraded. For the foreseeable future it is likely to remain the fastest route between Lisbon and southern Spain via the Algarve.

Air

The international airport at Faro opened in 1965; in 1989 a new terminal was completed. Today the airport extends over 144ha, with a 2.4km runway. Passenger traffic is expected to increase from 2.5 million in 1989 and 3.3 million in 1991 to 4 million by the year 2000. Between 1980 and 1991 the number of arrivals and departures rose from 9881 aircraft a year to 25,162.

History

Cave paintings and rock drawings testify to the presence of a Stone Age culture (from 20,000 B.C.).

Stone Age

A considerable number of remains survive from the Copper Age (from 5000 B.C.). Burial sites dating from the period have been discovered particularly in the Alentejo, neighbouring the Algarve to the north, but also in the Algarve itself.

Copper Age

Iberians arrive in the peninsula probably from North Africa, settling in the Algarve.

From 2200 B.C.

Phoenicians probably trading amber and copper on the Portuguese coast set up the first trading posts.

From 1000 B.C.

Celtic peoples coming from the north and settling in Portugal mingle in subsequent centuries with the Iberians to become Celtiberians. Some 30 to 40 Celtiberian tribes, the Lusitanians, form the largest ethnic majority on the Iberian peninsula. Fortified settlements ("castros" or "citânias") are built on easily defended hilltops.

From 700 B.C.

Greek merchants set out for the Portuguese coast where they establish trading posts.

From 500 B.C.

Carthage extends its sphere of influence beyond North Africa to include the Iberian peninsula too.

c. 450 B.C.

During the Second Punic War Roman strategy in the Iberian peninsula is directed mainly against the Carthaginians; the Romans are also concerned to defend their frontiers against the Celtiberians in the north and Lusitanians in the west.

218–206 B.C.

War between the Romans and Lusitanians results in Lusitania being incorporated into the Roman province of Hispania Ulterior.

197–179 B.C.

The Roman occupation is strongly resisted by the Lusitanians whose leader, Viriatus, "the man with the bangle", is later lauded in literature and art as a national hero. Resistance peters out following Viriatus's murder in 139.

147–139 B.C.

The province of Hispania Ulterior is finally subdued by Caesar during his campaigns.

61–45 B.C.

Augustus divides Hispania Ulterior into the two Roman provinces of Baetica, roughly covering the area of present-day Andalusia, and Lusitania. Lusitania extends along the Algarve coast to the Duoro in present-day northern Portugal and east into present-day Spain. Vulgar Latin, spoken throughout Roman territory, later evolves into Portuguese. In the Algarve the Romans build bridges in Tavira and Silves, and north of Faro large baths and a spa are constructed. Cabo de São Vicente, the most south-westerly cape on the European mainland, becomes a sacred site called "Promontorium Sacrum" on account of its exposed position. The Romans are also already extracting salt from seawater for preserving fish. Finally they establish a network of roads, the course of many of which still survive in places (the present N 125 running east–west along the coast of the Algarve was originally built by the Romans; also the road from Faro through Tavira and Mértola to Beja was a major Roman highway).

27–15 B.C.

History

From A.D. 200	The Christianisation of Lusitania is thought to have begun at an early date, the existence of Christian communities being attested in the 3rd c. A.D.
From 410	During the great movement of the Germanic peoples, Vandals and Alans migrate as far as southern Portugal.
418	The Visigoths advance into the Algarve. They occupy Faro and establish a bishopric there. They erect the first Christian church and practice an explicit form of Mariolatry.
From 711	Following their victory over Roderick, the last of the Visigoth kings, the Moors overrun (713–18) the whole of the Iberian peninsula except the mountainous regions in the north – Asturias, for instance, remains in Visigoth hands. The area of present-day Portugal becomes part of the Moorish Emirate (later Caliphate) of Córdoba. Xelb, present-day Silves, is the capital of the Moorish province of Al-Gharb. The Moors bring a highly developed culture to the Iberian peninsula. They possess a wealth of scientific knowledge especially in the fields of medicine, geography, nautics and astronomy. They establish a system of irrigation which remains largely unchanged over the centuries and Algarve land is successfully cultivated. Citrus, fig, almond and olive trees are introduced. Trade with Arab North Africa flourishes. The Algarve prospers; Xelb is a rich and much admired city of 40,000 inhabitants. Under Moorish rule peoples of different religions live peaceably side by side; in the towns there are Arab, Jewish and Christian quarters. In the south of the Iberian peninsula Moorish rule lasts for 500 years.
922	The Vikings launch an incursion north up the Rio Arade intending to attack the wealthy provincial capital of Xelb; they are encircled and halted only a short distance up the estuary.
1035–65	Under King Ferdinand I the Great of Castile and León the Christian reconquest of Portugal truly begins, with the Christians retaking territory from the Moors.
1112–1385	Starting with León-Castile, control of more and more of the peninsula is gradually wrested from the Moors. A Portuguese state is established. Now as before Portugal is required to resist Castilian claims.
1139	Afonso Henriques, having secured Portugal's independence from León-Castile, is crowned king. With the help of German, English and Flemish crusaders he is able to seize Lisbon. His successors extend their territory by further conquests in the south.
1189	Under Sancho I, some noted crusaders, among them Friedrich Barbarossa and Richard the Lionheart, assist in recovering parts of the west Algarve including Silves and Albufeira. A bishopric is established in Silves and a Flemish priest appointed bishop.
1191	With reinforcements from Seville and Córdoba the Moors succeed in recapturing towns they have lost in the Algarve.
1240–49	During the reigns of Sancho II and Afonso III the Moors are finally defeated, losing control of all the Algarve towns. The reconquista is complete. Disputes continually erupt with neighbouring Castile. Under Portuguese rule trade between the Algarve and North Africa ceases. An economic, cultural and religious restructuring occurs throughout the region. Jews and Arabs are either driven out or forced into slavery. Only a few mudéjars, Arab artists and craftsmen are permitted to stay and work in the country. The Moorish agricultural system is taken over. The Portuguese also benefit from the Arabs' scientific knowledge.

The Algarve towns are annexed to the kingdom of Portugal with the result that Portugal becomes the first European nation state to attain its full territorial limits, limits which have remained unchanged to this day.

1250

Dinis I establishes the Order of Christ at Castro Marim.

1319

Magellan's ship "Victoria"

João I founds the Avis dynasty. In the 200 years of its existence Portugal becomes the leading maritime and colonial power in Europe. The country amasses enormous riches. The major voyages of discovery and conquest occur at this time. Though the spirit of adventure is one reason for journeying across the world's oceans, the explorers are motivated more by economic considerations. Among other things they seek an alternative to the Arab-controlled overland route to the spice-rich countries of Asia. Together with Lisbon the Algarve is a centre of expansionist activity. Lagos becomes one of the premier Algarve ports.

1385–1580

Following the discovery of the Senegal estuary in the reign of Afonso V the first slaves are auctioned in Lagos. The slave trade, like the spice trade, becomes a major generator of wealth. It is not abolished until the 18th c.

1444

Manuel I lays the foundations of Portugal's commercial power, establishing trading posts in the East Indies, East Asia, South Africa and Brazil. Lisbon becomes a focal point of world trade. The crown, nobility and merchants enjoy undreamed of riches; but the unparalleled colonial expansion imposes so great a strain on the Portuguese people that population figures drop rapidly in a very short time.

1485–1521

Vasco da Gama, setting out from the Lisbon port of Belém, sails round the Cape of Good Hope and becomes the first European to reach India by sea. Belém has replaced the ports of the Algarve as the principal departure and arrival point for ocean voyages.

1497/98

The Algarve has 54,000 inhabitants.

1527

Establishment of the Inquisition. Jews, Judaeo-Christians, atheists and witches are persecuted, as are any Christians whose ways of life, attitudes or convictions the Inquisition finds inimical. The Inquisition is not abolished until 1820.

1540

Lagos becomes the provincial capital of the Algarve. The bishopric is transferred from Silves to Faro.

1577

The young King Sebastião sets out from Lagos on a crusade against Morocco, only to be killed, together with most of the Portuguese army, at the battle of Alcácer Quibir.

1578

With no successor to the throne the Avis dynasty ends. Philip II of Spain, a grandson of Manuel I, claims the Portuguese throne, occupy-

1580–1640

ing the whole of Portugal by force. During the interregnum Portugal loses some of its colonies in southern Asia and South America. Spain finances its colonial wars in part by taxes levied on the Portuguese people. In 1640 a successful rising by the Portuguese nobility results in Portugal regaining its independence.

1640–1701
The Duke of Bragança, one of the nobles involved in the rising, is crowned king as João IV, the first of the Bragança dynasty. Throughout this time the country becomes ever poorer on account of a failure to develop economically.

The period following 1640 is overshadowed by the wars of restoration between Spain and Portugal. The frontier towns on the Guadiana are the scene of numerous armed conflicts between the two countries. Britain provides military aid, so consolidating British influence over Portugal. In 1688 Spain finally acknowledges Portugal's independence.

1706–50
Under its spendthrift King João V, who sides with Austria in the War of Spanish Succession, Portugal becomes totally impoverished despite its vast holdings of Brazilian gold and diamond mines; as a result financial dependence on Britain increases.

1750–77
The reign of King José I represents the heyday of enlightened absolutism. His chief minister, the Marquês de Pombal, carries through a series of reforms inspired by Enlightenment and Mercantilist ideas.

1755
On November 1st 1755 a devastating earthquake strikes the Algarve coast and Portuguese mainland. The capital Lisbon is almost completely destroyed. There is likewise great damage throughout the Algarve, even extending to Monchique in the mountains. Furthermore the coastal towns and villages are hit by a 20m-high tidal wave. Several ports and river estuaries are blocked by sand. Further tremors are experienced the following year, the last on August 20th 1756.

1756
Faro replaces Lagos as provincial capital of the Algarve. At this time 85,000 people inhabit the province.

1774
The Marquês de Pombal rebuilds the flood-destroyed town of Vila Real de Santo António on the Guadiana, using the reconstruction of Lisbon as his model.

1777
After the death of José I, most of the Marquês de Pombal's reforms are reversed during the reign of Maria I; Enlightenment thinking is stifled with the aid of the Inquisition.

1807
Napoleon's troops occupy Portugal. The royal family flees to Brazil. In the Algarve opposition to the occupation is widespread.

1820
Liberal revolution, starting in North Portugal. It marks the beginning of conflicts between liberals and absolutists throughout Portugal, culminating in the Miguelite Wars.

1832–34
Miguelite Wars. Adherents of the liberal Pedro IV oppose the reactionary monarchists, who support the regime of Pedro's absolutist brother Miguel. In the Algarve the notorious Remexido and his promonarchist guerrillas create a reign of terror. Albufeira is beseiged in 1833 and then set to the torch. The Miguelites are defeated in 1834. Miguel leaves Portugal.

Mid 19th c.
Industrialisation begins in Portugal, starting relatively late and proceeding only slowly. In the Algarve fish processing and the cork industry play a leading role.

Opening of the Lisbon–Faro railway line. The population of the Algarve reaches 230,000.　1889

After several abhortive uprisings a civilian and military revolution succeeds in Lisbon. Manuel II, last king of the Bragança dynasty, flees to Great Britain. On October 5th a republic is proclaimed. Subsequent years are characterised by internal political strife and numerous changes of government.　1910

The democratic system, which has just begun to stabilise, is abruptly terminated by a military putsch.　1926

The "Estado Novo" era begins. President António de Oliviera Salazar, previously finance minister and founder of the Fascist União Nacional, establishes a dictatorship.　1933

In the Second World War Portugal remains neutral though on May 6th 1943 diplomatic relations with Germany are severed.　1939–45

During an earthquake in the Algarve a large number of houses are destroyed.　1969

Popular resistance to the dictatorship increases. The restrictive nature of the regime and the senselessness and cost of the colonial wars in Africa become ever more evident. On April 25th the dictatorship is overthrown in the "Carnation Revolution" in Lisbon, a military coup supported by a majority of the population. A socialist constitution is declared. Frequent changes of government and the formation of numerous coalitions result. The basic political orientation is pro-western.　1974

Portugal becomes a full member of the EC (now the European Union).　1986

The Algarve now has a population of 340,000.　1991

Following the parliamentary elections of October 1st, António Guterres of the Socialist Party (PS) becomes Prime Minister, taking over from the Liberal-Conservative Anibal Cavaco Silva.　1995

The election of the Socialist Jorge Sampaio as the new Portuguese President consolidates the noticeable swing to the left evident in recent years.　1996

Famous People

The following famous people all had connections of one sort or another with the Algarve, whether as the place of their birth or death, or because they lived or worked there.

João de Deus
(1830–96)

The well-known writer and educationalist João de Deus was born in the little town of São Bartolomeu de Messines. Son of a shopkeeper, he grew up in modest circumstances in the Algarve. At the age of nineteen he went to Coimbra, enrolling at the faculty of law where he studied for ten years. He was 30 when he found temporary work as a journalist in Beja and Évora in the Alentejo. In 1868 he became elected representative for the Silves district in which his home village was situated; but feeling unequal to the task and claiming he could achieve nothing through his political work, he soon resigned his seat.

His first book of poems "Flores de Campo" was published in 1869. By then resident in Lisbon, he joined the literary circle in the celebrated Café Martinho. He was valued as a poet whose lyrics are characterised by unaffected emotion. His best poems are contained in the last of his anthologies "Campo de Flores", which appeared in 1893. His satirical poems are less well known.

From 1877 he became increasingly interested in education, developing a method similar to that of Montessori; his theories inspired the building of 29 nursery schools in Portugal. Though lauded by some his ideas also met with considerable hostility.

Bartolomeu Dias
(c. 1450–1500)

As a knight of the Order of Christ, Bartolomeu Dias had a decisive role in the Portuguese voyages of discovery and conquest in the 15th c. He achieved world-wide fame as the first modern European to navigate the southern tip of Africa.

Commissioned by the Portuguese king to find a sea route to India, Dias set sail from Portimão in 1487. He rounded the Cape in 1488 without at first realising it, being engaged at the time in battling a fierce storm. It was only on the return journey that it became clear he had rounded the southern tip of the African continent. He called the Cape "Cabo Tormentoso" (Cape of Storms). It was João II who more optimistically christened it "Cabo da Boa Esperança" (Cape of Good Hope), an expression almost certainly of his confidence that, with the reconnaissance of this southernmost point of Africa, a significant milestone had been set for the discovery of a sea passage to India.

In subsequent years Bartolomeu Dias was involved in other important sea voyages. When Vasco da Gama set sail in July 1497 en route for India, Dias accompanied the expedition as far as Cabo Verde in West Africa. In 1500, aboard his own vessel, Dias participated in the voyage of his fellow countryman Pedro Álvares Cabral which led to the discovery of Brazil. While sailing around the southern tip of Africa a storm broke near the Cape of Good Hope. Dias's ship got into difficulties and he died within sight of the cape he had reconnoitred.

Gil Eanes
(born c. 1400)

Gil Eanes, who came from Lagos and whose dates are not known with any exactitude, made a name for himself in 1434 by sailing round Cape Bojador. It was widely believed in the Middle Ages that beyond this West African promontory lay a bubbling, boiling sea which swallowed up any ships venturing there. Henry the Navigator however became convinced on the basis of his explorations that the ocean beyond Cape Bojador was no different from the waters off the Portuguese coast. Gil Eanes let himself be similarly persuaded and set sail into the unknown, his faith being rewarded with success. Returning safely from this exploratory voyage, he then set sail again, landing some 300km further south on the West African coast. There he encountered signs of human habitation though not the inhabitants of the region themselves. In 1444 he took part in an armed expedition to Lanzarote. Because of his ground breaking exploits Gil Eanes is considered the pioneer of Portuguese exploration and conquest on the west coast of Africa and especially of the first circumnavigation of the African continent.

João II earned himself a place in history as "John the Perfect", having guided his country's development with a sure touch at the time of the voyages of discovery and conquest, and having prepared Portugal for its role as one of the foremost maritime and trading powers. The Avis king died in 1495 in the Algarve.

João II (1455–95)

João was born on May 3rd 1455, the son of Afonso V and Isabel. A marriage was arranged for him with his cousin Leonor, a sister of Manuel I. Whereas his father, whom he succeeded in 1481, remained deeply rooted in the Middle Ages both in thought and style of rule, João II proved open to Renaissance ideas. The young king governed the country strictly, bending the nobility and clergy to the will of the Crown. He purposefully fostered the voyages of discovery, and during his reign Portugal began to develop into one the leading sea powers. He established the "Junta of Mathematicians and Astronomers" specifically to advance theoretical knowledge of seafaring use. Both the discovery of the mouth of the Congo and the rounding of the Cape of Good Hope were achieved with his financial support. It was also during his reign however that Christopher Columbus discovered America, his voyage funded by the Spanish Crown – which even today in Portugal is clearly remembered with bitterness. It arose from the Portuguese obsession at that time with discovering a sea route to India. Columbus repeatedly urged João II to consider his suggestion of an alternative route to the spice islands. When the king referred the Genoese's plans to his scientific advisers for their opinion, they concluded variously that the westward passage proposed by Columbus could not lead to India and "Cipango" (Japan), or that it would prove substantially longer than the eastward one. While the Portuguese accepted that unknown lands probably existed to the west, they did not consider financial backing for Columbus's enterprise justified. So when in 1492 Columbus finally made his chance discovery of the American continent, Portugal could claim no share of the glory. To this day Portuguese historians persist in attempts to establish some family connection or even to show Columbus to be of Portuguese descent, so that their country may claim a part in the discovery of the New World.

Another painful episode in the life of João the Perfect was the premature death of his son and successor, killed in a riding accident on the banks of the Tejo near Santarém.

In 1495 João travelled to the Algarve for a cure at the Monchique spa. He died shortly afterwards aged 40 in Alvor near Portimão and was buried in Silves Cathedral. His remains were later transferred to Batalha.

Lídia Jorge, a native of the Algarve, is one of Portugal's best known writers. An only child, she was born near Albufeira in the small town of Boliqueime, where she spent her childhood and youth. At nine she went to secondary school in Faro where she was confronted for the

Lídia Jorge (born 1946)

first time with life in a small city. On leaving school she went to Lisbon to study Romance languages and literature. During the colonial wars she spent some years in the former Portuguese colonies of Mozambique and Angola. She now teaches in a secondary school in Lisbon.

With the appearance in the 1980s of her novels "O Dia dos Prodígios", "O Cais das Merendas", "Notícia da Cidade" and "A Costa dos Murmúrios", Lídia Jorge has achieved a lasting place in contemporary Portuguese literature. She takes as her recurrent theme the political and social situation in Portugal following the Carnation Revolution, the changes and absence of change experienced by the country since 1974. In "O Dia dos Prodígios" (The Day of the Miracle) she describes life in sleepy Vilamaninhos, an imaginary village in the Algarve where the people hope for better things in the wake of the revolution. Many of the characters and events have their roots in the writer's childhood.

Sebastião José de Carvalho e Mello, Marquês de Pombal (1699–1782)

The Marquês de Pombal, chief minister and proponent of enlightened despotism, left the mark of his philosophy on the Algarve when he completely rebuilt the town of Vila Real de Santo António near the mouth of the Guadiana.

Born into Lisbon's minor aristocracy, his first experience was in the diplomatic service as an envoy to London and Vienna where his brief also included economic matters. In 1750 José I appointed him minister for foreign affairs, and in 1756 chief minister.

Pombal proved adept at using his powers in office singlemindedly to promote his own ideas, showing few qualms about the means employed to achieve his longer-term aims. He saw his most important tasks as reorganising the state finances, reforming education, promoting trade and industry (to free Portugal from the economic hegemony of Britain) and the abolition of slavery. He passionately opposed the Jesuits and the minor nobility whose inherited privileges stood in the way of his reforms.

He also had an outstanding role in the reconstruction of Lisbon following the devastating earthquake of 1755; and when some years later Santo António da Avenilha in the Algarve was destroyed in a catastrophic flood, he masterminded its replacement, completing a whole new town, Vila Real de Santo António, chequerboard in plan, in just five months, drawing on the very latest models of town planning which he had employed in rebuilding Lisbon's Lower Town.

After the death of José I the Marquês fell from favour; in 1781 pressure from his many enemies brought about his banishment to Pombal where he died the following year.

Dom Sebastião (c. 1554–78)

The reputation and importance of this Portuguese king owe more to myth than to the man.

Dom Sebastião was born in 1554, shortly after his father died in an accident. As a result, on the death of his grandfather João III, Dom Sebastião succeeded to the throne. A brother of João III acted as regent until the boy, known since birth as "The Longed For", reached the age of fourteen; thereafter the young king ruled in his own right. Described as arrogant and a religious fanatic, one of his main ambitions was to bring North Africa under Christian rule. In 1578 he set out from Lagos to fulfil his mission. Before leaving he attended a final mass held in the open near the harbour, afterwards boarding ship. Shortly thereafter he marched into Morocco. At Alcácer Quibir there was a disastrous battle which cost the lives of 80,000 men. Back in Portugal people refused to believe that the young king was among the fallen, retaining for some time a hope for his return. But "The Longed For" never did reappear; instead a succession of pretenders emerged claiming to be the missing king.

Since that time a legend has grown up around Sebastião, elevating him to a knightly figure whose homecoming is still awaited especially when times are bad. Were he but to appear, everything would be all right. A new term – Sebastianism" – has even been coined to denote not only the passive fatalism and laissez faire attitude allegedly widespread in Portugal but also the typically Portuguese "saudade" (nostalgia); both reflect a backward-looking element in Portuguese dreams and hopes, and a deep-lying sense of resignation, recurrent themes in Portuguese literature, art and music.

José Joaquim de Sousa Reis, leader of a guerrilla group active in the Algarve in the 19th c., is known in Portuguese history by the name "Remexido".

José Joaquim de Sousa Reis (died 1838)

Born in the village of Estômar near Portimão, de Sousa Reis lived for many years in São Bartolomeu de Messines. During the absolutist reign of Miguel I, under whom every liberal reform introduced by his brother and predecessor Pedro IV was reversed, de Sousa Reis commanded a Miguelite force in the Algarve. This was a period when the political climate of the entire country was dominated by the struggle between liberal elements and Miguel's supporters. In 1833 liberal forces landed at Cacela in the eastern Algarve, seizing control of large parts of the region. In the civil wars which followed, Remexido directed operations against them in the western Algarve. Algarve towns were fiercely fought over with control passing back and forth. On May 26th 1834 the so-called Miguelite Wars were ended by the Treaty of Évoramonte though friction continued beneath the surface for some time.

In 1836 Remexido took up arms again, gathering about him members of his former band; he carried out attacks on Algarve towns and villages in defiance of the liberal regime. On August 23rd 1836 he was responsible for an appalling massacre in the infantry barracks at São Bartolomeu de Messines where a number of soldiers were murdered. Remexido's guerrillas hid out in inaccessible parts of the Algarve hill country; even special military units sent by Maria II at the request of the town of Silves proved impotent at first.

Eventually, in May 1838, well-equipped government troops were despatched into the Algarve uplands. José Joaquim de Sousa Reis was tracked down east of São Marcos da Serra and taken prisoner. He was sentenced to death in Faro and summarily shot on August 2nd 1838.

Cape St Vincent, the south-westernmost tip of Portugal and of continental Europe, takes its name from São Vicente.

São Vicente (died 304)

Little is known about the life of the saint. It is not known when he was born though sources refer to Zaragossa as his birthplace. As deacon there he worked in close co-operation with Bishop Valerius. During the reign of Diocletian he was brought before the governor Decius, taken to Valencia and incarcerated. In 304 he was sentenced to death, allegedly being laid, whilst still alive, on a red-hot grill. During his martyrdom the room is said to have suddenly become filled with light, a carpet of flowers appeared and angels' voices were heard. He was buried in Valencia.

Subsequently canonised, a hundred or so years later a cult began to be associated with his name. Portuguese tradition has it that in the 8th c. an unmanned skiff bearing the saint's corpse was washed up on the headland which now bears his name (Cabo de São Vicente). His only companions, it is said, were two crows. A more credible account is that Christians fleeing Valencia during the Moorish invasion took the saint's body with them. Having landing at the cape the Romans called

Promontorium Sacrum marking the most south-westerly point of the European mainland, a chapel was erected there in the saint's honour. Arab writings mention a "crow chapel", and the headland itself is referred to as "crow cape" (from whence also derives the Portuguese name for the high point of the promontory, Monte Corvo, "crow mountain").

In the 12th c., having retaken Lisbon from the Moors in 1147, Afonso Henriques had the saint's bones removed there. At first they were preserved in the forerunner of the present Igreja de São Vicente, later being transferred, in a shrine inlaid with mother-of-pearl, to Lisbon's cathedral, the Sé.

Today São Vicente is venerated in Portugal as the patron saint of seafarers and vintners. He is also the patron saint of Lisbon, depicted on the city's arms together with a boat and two crows. The Portuguese are not however alone in their devotion to the saint; the Spanish too venerate him and, in a Romansque church dedicated to St Vincent in Ávila, in Spain, there is what is said to be his grave.

Art and Culture

Art history

General

The Algarve has relatively few art historical treasures of note, having been decimated, as was Lisbon, by the 1755 earthquake. A great many buildings were either completely destroyed or so badly damaged that little from previous centuries survived, often just fragments.

Until the mid 13th c. the Algarve's development mirrored that of neighbouring Andalusia. In 1250 however the Algarve was incorporated into the kingdom of Portugal, after which its culture and the culture of Andalusia diverged. As a result, the 500 years of Moorish rule have left few enduring marks on the landscape, their legacy being seen more in various aspects of daily life and work, such as language and agriculture, than in architectural heritage.

However the Algarve also differs in important respects from much of the rest of Portugal. The Moors having been driven from the north that much sooner, most of the early churches in northern Portugal date from the Romanesque period. In the Algarve on the other hand, Moorish rule continued into the 13th c. and the earliest Christian churches are Early Gothic in style. The building stone used shows interesting variations, in some cases red sandstone from the Serra de Monchique, in others yellow sandstone from the coast.

Romans

The most important relics of the Roman period are found at Milreu near Faro. They include the remains of a Roman patrician villa, thermal

The impressive Roman fish mosaics at Milreu

37

Art history

baths and shrines. Roman mosaics have been uncovered at Vilamoura, and Roman salination plants on the Quinta de Marim reserve near Olhão. The bridges at Tavira and Silves are of Roman origin but rebuilt.

Moors

Though virtually all the castles in the Algarve were built originally by the Moors, a courtyard in the Castelo dos Mouros at Silves is the only substantial reminder left today. Fragments of wall forming part of fortications at Salir, and a few items in the archaeological museum at Silves (a cistern and one or two small finds) complete the scant Moorish legacy.

Gothic

The earliest Christian church, a well preserved Early Gothic chapel (13th c.), can be seen near the village of Raposeira. The 1755 earthquake almost completely destroyed the cathedrals in Silves and Faro, leaving little of the Gothic fabric standing. In Silves the main doorway, former choir and crossing are still clearly discernible; in Faro the bell tower has defied the centuries.

Manueline

Manueline, so called after Manuel I, is a distinctive Portuguese ornamental style which developed in the early 16th c. The prosperity flowing from Portugal's overseas conquests brought a cultural flowering which found expression in architecture as well as other ways. This being the period of transition between the Gothic age and the Renaissance, Manueline buildings incorporated both Late Gothic and Early Renaissance elements while simultaneously drawing on contemporary events of national importance in their ornamentation. Specific recurrent motifs were used: the cross of the Order of Christ, the crown and "M" for Manuel, the king whose hand guided Portuguese conquests; ropes and hawsers in stone, miniature caravels, anchors, and the armillary sphere (a nautical instrument), symbolising the sea and seafaring; stylised corals, shells, tropical plants, leaves and flowers denoting new-forged links with distant tropical lands. Very occasionally architecture took inspiration from foreign cultures, the Torre de Belém in Lisbon being a good example. The leading architects of this period were Diogo de Boytaca, Diogo de Arruda, Francisco de Arruda and João de Castilho.

Grand buildings representing the pinnacle of the style grace Lisbon, Batalha and Tomar rather than the Algarve. But its close association with the voyages of discovery means that many, albeit more modest, examples are found in the districts, towns and villages directly involved in Portugal's maritime exploits and overseas conquests. Accordingly, a comparatively large number of the Algarve's small churches have Manueline stylistic elements. Typically, entrance doorways, and less commonly the arches between nave and choir, display Manueline decoration. Splendid examples of Manueline ornamentation can be seen in the churches at Alvor, Alte, Monchique, Luz de Tavira, Estômbar and Odiâxere. Silves still boasts a Manueline wayside cross.

Renaissance

Generally speaking the Renaissance style never really became established in Portugal. This was partly because of Manueline, which had a retarding effect on new developments, and partly because, by the mid 16th c., not only was money for ambitious architectural projects noticeably more scarce, but also, with the passing of the Golden Age, there was no longer cause to erect magnificent buildings. Isolated Renaissance features, mostly entrance doorways, survive in a handful of Algarve churches, e.g. the Igreja da Misericórdia in Tavira, the Igreja de São Pedro in Faro, and the Igrejas da Misericórdia in the castle courtyards at Mexilhoeira Grande and Castro Marim.

Baroque

Towards the end of the 17th c. the gold mines for which the Portuguese had long searched in Brazil were finally discovered and money once

The interior of the Baroque Church of São Lourenço at Almansil ▶

again flowed into the coffers. Under the extravagant King João V, numerous churches and palaces were built in Portugal in the first half of the 18th c.; at the same time existing churches acquired Baroque altars and chapels. Churches in the Algarve are rich in Baroque furnishings. The Igreja do Carmo in Faro is pure Baroque. The Baroque Igreja de São Lourenço in Almansil is renowned for its azulejo walls, and the Igreja de Santo António in Lagos for its sumptuous "talha dourada" decoration.

Azulejos

Ceramic tiles, "azulejos", adorn the walls of chapels, churches, palaces and railway stations throughout Portugal, sometimes covering entire house façades. Moorish in origin, the name derives from the Arabic "az-zuleycha" meaning mosaic pieces. They were first imported from southern Spain at the beginning of the 16th c. At that time, to keep the various different colours separate before firing, the Moors relied on indentations in the surface of the tile. Green, blue, black, rust and white are the dominant colours on azulejos of this period.

After the Moors were driven out of southern Spain, the first azulejo factories were established in Portugal. Thanks to the majolica technique taken over from the Italians, tiles could now be produced with a flat surface instead of relief. They were given a white tin glaze on which designs were painted using metaloxide pigments. In the 17th c. a distinctive Portuguese style evolved, influenced by porcelain painting of the Ming dynasty and by Delft tile makers. Whole floors were carpeted with tiles in shades of blue, white and yellow. Clearly-defined patterns such as the "Ponta de Diamante" with its stylised cut diamonds also began to appear. Then, in the 18th c., the large tile pictures typical of the Baroque period came more and more into fashion. The walls of churches, the interior and exterior walls of palaces, staircases, fountains and banks, were all decorated with tile pictures. The Igreja de São Lourenço in Almansil is an outstanding example of a church interior completely tiled in the Baroque manner.

In the early 19th c. when Portugal was convulsed by civil war, the production of azulejos virtually ceased. By the middle of the century, however, they were enjoying a revival. Following the Brazilian model, tiles now began to be used, both externally and internally, for the decoration of ordinary middle-class houses and commercial, municipal and other public buildings. The practical advantages of tile façades were far more widely appreciated, and the use of paint on large expanses of wall became less common. Tile-making flourished once again during the Art Nouveau period, after which enthusiasm noticeably waned. In recent decades new interest has been shown in the tradition surrounding Portuguese azulejos; decorated with contemporary as well as old established motifs, they have begun to be used again in the construction of public buildings.

Talhas douradas

Equally distinctive of Portuguese Baroque are the wood sculptures, gilded in fine gold leaf, known as talhas douradas, predominantly seen in church interiors. The wood was usually oak and the gold came from Brazil. Talhas douradas served, in essence, to display the wealth which flowed into the country again after the discovery of the Brazilian gold mines. Initially confined mainly to picture frames, they were later also incorporated into designs for pulpits, high altars and even walls. In the Algarve the Igreja do Carmo in Faro has talha dourada decoration; but the best example of this style of church furnishing is the Igreja de Santo António in Lagos.

18th and 19th centuries

Almost every building in the Algarve, whether private house, public building or church, dates from after the 1755 earthquake. Some of those destroyed were rebuilt, others replaced by something completely new. At the end of the 18th c. the then Bishop of the Algarve, Francisco Gomes do Avelar, committed himself to rebuilding much of the ecclesiastical stock. The Italian architect Francisco Xavier Fabri, responsible for many buildings in Lisbon, was invited to the Algarve where his contribution to the work was substantial. Of new buildings constructed after the earthquake, the Palácio de Estói deserves special mention.

Portugal in the second half of the 18th c. represents something of a special case in the history of town planning. The 1755 earthquake caused widespread devastation, complete towns being utterly destroyed. Lisbon's Lower Town had to be rebuilt from scratch. Those responsible followed a blueprint laid down by the Marquês de Pombal (see Famous People), chief minister and leading exponent of enlightened absolutism in Portugal. At his instigation the Lower Town was systematically reconstructed to a rational, supremely orderly and functional chequerboard plan. The Marquês applied the same principles in designing the completely new town of Vila Real de Santo António in the Algarve, built on what was to all intents and purposes a virgin site.

Town planning

The face of the Algarve has fundamentally changed during the 20th c. Tourist development began in the 1960s, and by the late 1970s highrise blocks had mushroomed. The road bridge built over the Rio Arade near Portimão in the early 1990s is one of the more impressive modern structures.

20th century

Throughout Portugal there are squares and pavements laid with most attractive black and white mosaics. It seems that after the 1755 earthquake people hit upon the idea of turning the rubble from houses, palaces and churches into small rectangular stones and setting them in the pavements. Motifs and clearly defined patterns are often painstakingly worked in. The craftsmen who lay them are called "calceteiros". Mosaic laying used to be a common trade in Portugal; today the work is very poorly paid and there are very few calceteiros left. The pavement mosaics in the centre of Faro, Lagos, Albufeira and Portimão are a delight to the eye. The finest designs of all are on the Praça do Marquês de Pombal in Vila Real de Santo António; the radial pattern was laid out in 1879.

Pavement mosaics

In the Algarve as elsewhere, working windmills are a thing of the past, though the circular, whitewashed, slightly conical mills were once a common sight in the landscape. They had small triangular sails, often with clay vessels attached which made a whistling sound as the sails turned and told the miller the strength of the wind. Of the few remaining in the Algarve, the two finest are at São Brás de Alportel and Odiáxere.

Windmills

In Olhão and neighbouring Fuzeta in particular, distinctive cube-shaped one-, two- or three-storey fishermen's houses are found; all have the flat roofs or roof-terraces known as açoteias, used traditionally for drying fish, fruit, laundry, fishing nets and other fishing gear or simply for taking the air. Many of the açoteias have little look-out towers called mirantes, from where the fishermen's wives are said to have kept a look out for their men returning from the sea.

Açoteias

Chimneys, "chaminés", are a real feature of the Algarve, works of art rather than just smoke outlets, and utterly distinctive. They come in many different shapes and sizes, some round, some square, some with little hipped roofs, some with spires, some looking like tall birdcages, others like squat minarets. The vents in their sides make very varied patterns too. At one time every chaminé was individually constructed by hand; today they are mass produced.

Chaminés

Few paintings or sculptures of art historical interest are to be seen in the Algarve. The collection of the former diplomat and connoisseur

Painting and sculpture

41

Lagos: squares and streets surfaced with black and white mosaic

Ferreira d'Almeida, now attached to the archaeological museum in Faro, has one or two pleasing 19th and 20th c. Portuguese paintings but nothing of great worth.

The most notable modern sculpture is the statue of Dom Sebastião in the Praça Gil Eanes in Lagos. Erected in the early 1960s, it is the work of João Cutileiro, one of Portugal's most celebrated 20th c. sculptors.

Literature

General

Portuguese literature is not widely known elsewhere in Europe, though more is now being translated into other languages. Among the more familiar writers are Fernando Pessoa, José Saramago and Luís Vaz de Camóes. Literature from the Algarve or about the Algarve is exceedingly rare.

15th and 16th centuries

A number of Portuguese writers chronicled the age of discovery and conquest, their work being best known in that context. One or two voiced criticism of Portugal's adventurism overseas and the "conquistador" mentality, but always in veiled terms or minor works (the Inquisition threatened any writer adopting a too openly subversive stance). Among the greatest historians of the 15th and 16th c. are Fernão Lopes (1384–1460), Gomes Eanes de Zurara (c. 1410–73), João de Barros (c. 1496–1570) and Diogo de Couto (c. 1542–1616).

Best known of all Portuguese works and a source of fascination to many foreign writers especially in the 19th c., is "Os Lusíadas" by Luís Vaz de Camóes (c. 1524–80). To this national poet the age of discovery was a glorious era in almost every respect, a viewpoint not shared by Fernão Mendes Pinto (c. 1510–83) whose "Peregrinação" cast a more jaundiced eye over Portuguese exploits. More importantly, Pinto's work, unusually for that period, includes valuable descriptions of the countries about which he writes. Another very well known 15th/16th c. author was Gil Vicente (c. 1465–1540), famous as the founder of Portuguese theatre. A critical observer of his times, his so-called "autos", one-act dramas with music and dancing, brought him into conflict with the Inquisition.

In the early 18th c. Portuguese writers began to concern themselves with the ideas of the Enlightenment. A number of literary circles emerged seeking a revival of literature and the theatre. One author to make a name for himself was Manuel Maria Barbosa do Bocage (1765–1805), persecuted by the authorities on account of his emotive works and eccentric lifestyle.

18th century

The 19th c. produced a considerable number of writers many of whom remain popular with modern readers and some of whose works have been translated from Portuguese. Their books are mainly about Portugal, its people, and the various regions of the country. Among the most famous are Almeida Garrett (1799–1854), Camilo Castelo Branco (1825–90) and José Maria Eça de Queiróz (1845–1900), of whom the latter, with his "The Maias", "Cousin Basilio" and "The Illustrious House of Ramires", is the leading Portuguese exponent of the social novel.

19th century

The Algarve writer João de Deus (see Famous People) established a reputation throughout Portugal with his poems, distinguished by their unimpassioned emotionalism.

The most celebrated 20th c. Portuguese writer is undoubtedly Fernando Pessoa who, together with Almada Negreiros and Mário de Sá-Carneiro, inspired an avant-garde circle whose activities threw middle class Lisbon into a state of turmoil; they also used to meet in Faro in the Algarve (see Baedeker Special "Birthplace of the Man who Never Was").

20th century

José Saramago (b. 1922) has written numerous novels on themes from Portuguese history. His "Hope in the Alentejo" chronicles events in the Alentejo from the turn of the century until the Carnation Revolution in 1974. His novel "The Gospel according to Jesus Christ" was initially banned by the authorities as offensive to religious sensibilities. Lídia Jorge (b. 1946; see Famous People) is a native of the Algarve; her novel "The Day of the Miracle" describes life in an Algarve village against the background of the Carnation Revolution.

Music

While Portuguese rock and pop music have much in common with these same genres in other western countries, they also incorporate elements from Portuguese folk music. Among the most successful artists are the singers Fausto, Sérgio Godinho, Vitorino and José Afonso and groups such as Trovante, GNR, Delfins and Peste e Sida. Helped by Wim Wenders' "Lisbon Story", the Madredeus have become one of Europe's most popular groups. Dulce Pontes is another vocalist to win international acclaim, as also is jazz singer Maria João.

Rock, pop and jazz

Despite the royal patronage bestowed on Portuguese music by kings many of whom were keen musicians themselves, practically no work by a Portuguese composer is ever performed outside his native country. From the 12th c. when Christianity was finally restored, music in Portugal mirrored developments in the rest of Europe. Some composers have given Portuguese music a national flavour by introducing elements from folk music or by reinterpreting themes from Portuguese history. The most acclaimed composers are João Domingos Bontempo and Alfredo Keil (19th c.), and Fernando Lopes-Graça and Jorge

Classical music

Peixinho (20th c.). The pianist Maria João Pires has gained a world-wide reputation for her performances of classical music.

Fado

Fado is unique to Portugal. No one is quite sure of its origins. It is thought to have evolved either from the "lundum", an African slave dance brought to Portugal by way of Brazil, or from the Brazilian modinha, a form of sentimental song which, when it became popular in Portugal, acquired a more lyrical, yearning quality. Since the Portuguese like to attribute almost everything to the age of discoveries, some have also claimed on account of the "wave-like" melodies and deep sense of longing, that fado actually developed among the seafarers of the 15th c.

One thing is certain, namely that fado first made its appearance at the beginning of the 19th c. in the port area of Lisbon, where it was sung, or more accurately, performed (because fado is acted not just sung) in simple bars or casas de fado. Accompanied by one ordinary and one special twelve-stringed fado guitar (the "guitarra portuguesa"), the fadista, who can be male or female, evokes the mood of the song not only by voice but also posture and gestures. Women normally dress all in black and always wear a black stole which they wrap tightly round themselves as if for protection, especially when singing fados of a serious, melancholic nature.

Sometimes these are the purest laments, with more than a hint of the music of the Arab world. Their themes are lost or unrequited love, homesickness, a longing for distant places or a general malaise resonant with every conceivable human sorrow. Thus the fado is a setting to music of the supposedly widespread, typically Portuguese, "saudade", that passive fatalism reflecting an insatiable, boundless yearning – for a better past, a better future, something distant and unattainable like a lover in a far off land. It is captured in the gaze from the harbour wall across the restless waters of the Atlantic to the horizon and beyond. And this is indeed the dominant mood of fado, at least for the most part. But there is also, in sharp contrast, a very popular type of song which is witty, amusing and not infrequently bawdy. These often take the form of a coquettish duet and the audience, infused one moment with life's sorrows, is convulsed with laughter the next.

Great fadistas have always been very special to the Portuguese, celebrated and revered. In the 19th c. there was the legendary female singer, A. Severa, who died when she was only 26. Today it is Amália Rodrigues. Born in 1920, hers was a fairytale rise from simple flower-girl to renowned fado singer appearing on the world's great stages. Other famous 20th c. fadista include Alfredo Marceneiro and Carlos Ramos.

Most performances of fado in the Algarve are laid on specially for the tourists. In the holiday resorts there are no true casas de fado where authentic fado can be heard.

Folk Music and Dance

Festas

The many "festas" which take place in Portugal throughout the year offer the best opportunity for getting to know the country's folk music and dance. Virtually every public festival, especially religious ones, feature troupes of musicians and dancers who, decked out in traditional costume, perform the music and dances of that particular region or area. Much of what passes for folk music and dance in the Algarve is actually contrived for the tourist trade; it is a lucky visitor who happens upon a festival where the authentic music and dance of the Algarve are performed. Typical of the instruments used in Portuguese folk music are the guitar, sometimes the "viola de arame" strung with metal strings, pipes (pipas), bagpipes (gaitas de foles) and, in particular, a square, doublesided tambourine (adufe).

There are two kinds of dances: the "danças", intended for particular occasions, and the "bailes", specific to this or that area. Very popular in the Algarve is the "corridinho", a fast polka danced to the accompaniment of guitar, accordian and sometimes also flute, mandolin and castanets.

Suggested Routes

These routes focus deliberately on the less familiar Algarve hinterland with its very varied scenery and often picturesque little country towns and villages. The coast on the other hand hardly features at all. The coastal towns are of course worth visiting, but this is better done at greater leisure.

Faro is the starting point for the tour of the eastern Algarve, Albufeira for the circuit of the central Algarve, and Portimão for the route through the western Algarve. All three can be reached quite easily on the N 125 or IP 1 from any of the popular holiday resorts. Alternatively, since all the tours described are circular, they can be followed easily enough starting at any convenient point along the way. Headings in the margin and the map on pages 48–49 give an overview of the routes. Locations with a main heading in the A to Z section of the guide appear in bold.

Route 1: Eastern Algarve (190km)

Introduction

Adding up to a fairly long day's drive, this route explores the scenic contrasts of the eastern Algarve. Beyond São Brás de Alporte lies some very remote mountain country; and at the eastern extremity a delightful stretch of the Guadiana valley. The mountain roads tend to be very winding and progess therefore slow, leaving little time to visit the coastal towns on the final section of the route; they are perhaps best left for another day.

Faro

From ★★ **Faro** take the N 2 via Estói to São Brás de Alportel. At first there is a fair amount of traffic, but soon the road becomes quieter. Setting out in good time allows a brief stop right at the start of the tour to visit the palace gardens in ★ **Estói** and/or the Roman ruins at Milreu. Beyond Estói the route passes through a charming garden landscape continuing all the way to **São Brás de Alportel**, a pleasant small country town. At the large crossroads keep on the N 2 which now heads north towards Almodôvar and Lisbon. A little way along, at Pousada de São Brás, there is a fine view over the countryside. In due course the N 2 reaches the remote village of Barranco Velho, a few kilometres beyond which fork right onto a road through the mountains to Cachopo. The scenery on this stretch is exceptionally beautiful, as indeed it is south of Barranco Velho. The road follows a convoluted course through lonely hill country, passing few villages. Cachopo is worth a short stop. There is not much to see but it does drive home just how very isolated and out of the way Algarve villages can be. Afterwards head east on the N 124, now making somewhat quicker progress. The poorness of this part of the Algarve is all too evident from villages such as Vaqueiros, Martim Longo and Giões along the way.

São Brás de Alportel

Cachopo

Alcoutim

Continue until eventually arriving at ★ **Alcoutim**, a little town on the banks of the Guadiana. Here the fortress and the alleys beneath the fortress walls are well worth visiting, not to mention the riverside cafés with views across the water to Sanlúcar de Guadiana in Spain.

From Alcoutim a quite delightful, albeit narrow, road runs southwards parallel to the river, the banks of which are gently undulating on both the Portuguese and Spanish sides. For most of the way the road runs a little above the river, dropping down to the water from time to time. Guerreiros do Rio is a particularly charming village with a small historical and natural history museum. Joining the wider but no less quiet N 122 south of Odeleite, head next for Castro Marim from where the IP 1 invites a quick return to Faro. Those with time and energy to spare could take this opportunity to look around ★**Castro Marim** and perhaps visit ★**Vila Real de Santo António**. Returning to Faro by the coast road (N 125) there are several possibilities. Some time could be spent on the beach at Manta Rota, or at ★Cacela Velha, a little seaside spot with (almost) no tourists; alternatively ★**Tavira** and **Olhão** could be the final ports of call.

Odeleite

Vila Real de
Santo António

Olhão

Instead of returning to Faro by the busy coast road, a detour can be made from Tavira on the N 270 through very pretty countryside. At São Brás de Alportel turn left again for Faro.

Other options

Holidaymakers based in resorts on the east coast between Tavira and Vila Real de Santo António can shorten the tour slightly by taking the N 397 direct from Tavira to Cachopo. Even so, allow plenty of time, the road through the lovely Serra de Alcaria is very twisting and therefore slow.

Route 2: Central Algarve Hinterland (125km)

For most of its length this route passes through a delightful, largely cultivated landscape, dotted with picturesque villages and small towns, before ending with a visit to the ancient Moor capital of Silves. Along the way there is the opportunity for a walk on the Rocha da Pena.

Introduction

Leaving **Albufeira** take either the N 125/N 270 or the IP 1 eastwards to ★**Loulé**. If on the N 270, pull in just short of the town to visit the pilgrim

Albufeira

A traditional calling: fishermen in Albufeira

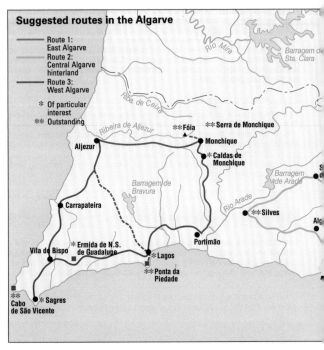

Suggested routes in the Algarve

━━━ Route 1:
East Algarve
━━━ Route 2:
Central Algarve
hinterland
━━━ Route 3:
West Algarve
* Of particular
interest
** Outstanding

chapel of Nossa Senhora da Piedade, a little way up from the road, on the south side (good view). Loulé's daily lunchtime market brings a real splash of colour to the area around the market hall. The old town centre is in any case well worth visiting.

Salir

From Loulé proceed north to ★ Salir, either direct or with a detour at about the half-way point to Querença, a village in a picturesque setting. Salir itself is one of the prettiest villages in the Algarve, occupying two hills from where there are charming views of the little farms and holdings which are the chief feature of the landscape.

Now follow the N 124 westwards. Anyone keen to stretch their legs and see some of the lovely baroccal scenery on foot rather than from the car, will enjoy the round walk of just 5km on the ★ Rocha da Pena (479m). Otherwise drive straight on to ★ **Alte**, one of the showpiece villages of the Algarve hinterland, with pretty white houses and on the east side an interesting church and spring.

Alte

São Bartolomeu de Messines

Next comes **São Bartolomeu de Messines**, a little country town where a brief stop is in order to explore the old centre (some may prefer not to stop here, so leaving more time for Silves). The almost deserted road then cuts across some very remote country, passing scarcely a single village. A short distance to the north lies the Arade reservoir, its water level pitifully low after the failed rains of recent years. Soon ★★ **Silves** comes into view away in the distance. Its red sandstone castle and wall are particularly impressive, dominating the townscape.

Silves

Immediately outside Silves, on the right of the road, stands a Manueline wayside cross protected by a roof. To do real justice to the town

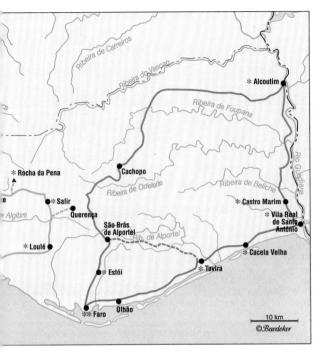

requires a fairly lengthy stop. There is the cathedral, chiefly notable for the number of Gothic features which survived the 1755 earthquake more or less unscathed; there is the imposing castle, dating back to the Moors, where visitors can walk along the walls around the courtyard; and there is the archaeological museum offering a good insight into the cultural history of the region.

For the last lap of the tour follow the N 269, a quiet country road, eastwards through tranquil countryside to Algoz, a typical Algarve village worlds removed from the bright lights and bustle just a few kilometres away on the coast. From there it is only 11km back to Albufeira.

Algoz

Route 3: Western Algarve (160km)

This tour of the Western Algarve encounters some exceptionally varied scenery. Foothills merge gradually into the Serra de Monchique where rises the highest peak in the Algarve. The serra in turn gives way to the barren landscape of the far west, quite different from anywhere else in the Algarve and counting among its wonders Cabo de São Vicente, the most south-westerly point of Europe. An early start is required if there is to be any time to enjoy the sights of Lagos. And if stops are to be made in some of the villages en route, Cabo de São Vicente should be dropped from the itinerary (shortening it to about 100km).

Introduction

Leaving **Portimão**, take the N 266 northwards towards Monchique. Soon the road enters relatively sparsely populated countryside and as

Portimão

49

View from Fóia, the highest point in the Serra de Monchique

it gains height one splendid view succeeds another. A few kilometres before Monchique a very special little place is reached – ★ Caldas de Monchique, a spa considerably smaller but rich in history and with much more atmosphere than Monchique itself. Anyone already wanting to rest need look no further than one of several charming cafés here.

Monchique

The small town of **Monchique**, regional centre for the ★★ **Serra de Monchique**, spreads up a hillside, its steep alleys inviting ascent and a backward glance down into the valley. Virtually every street in the north-west of the town proves a gateway to lovely mountain scenery and it is well worth allowing time for a walk.

Not to be missed either is the short detour (16km in all) to ★★ Fóia (902m), the highest peak in the Algarve. The summit, reached by a road starting in Monchique, commands a magnificent panorama of almost the entire coastline and a fine view inland towards the Alentejo to the north.

Returning to Monchique by the same road, head south again, branching left after only 3km onto the N 267 running west. At first it winds its way with numerous bends through most pleasing mountain scenery, but as it nears Aljezur the landscape becomes increasingly barren and monotonous, the influence of the Atlantic being more and more reflected in the vegetation.

Aljezur

Rather than spend time in **Aljezur** some may prefer to make a detour to the coast. Places like Praia de Monte Clérigo give a good idea of how the west coast of the Algarve differs from the more tourist-orientated south coast. About 6km south of Aljezur the N 120 veers inland offering a fast run direct to Lagos some 24km away. The alternative is to continue south-west on the N 268 with detours to the sea at either Carrapateira or **Vila do Bispo**. In due course the main road reaches

★**Sagres**. Just south of the town is the Fortaleza de Sagres, and 6km west ★★Cabo de São Vicente, the most south-westerly point of the European mainland. Standing on the cape gazing out to sea, it is easy to imagine what emotions the Portuguese seafarers of the 15th c. must have felt as they set sail on their voyages beyond the horizon.

Sagres

From Cabo de São Vicente return by the same route through Sagres to Vila do Bispo where branch off eastwards onto the N 125 which in these parts carries very little traffic. A few kilometres beyond the little town of Raposeira a historical gem stands hardly noticed by the roadside – the ★Ermida de Nossa Senhora de Guadalupe, the oldest surviving church in the Algarve.

Vila do Bispo

Finally ★**Lagos** is reached. The town centre is relatively small so visitors can choose between a more or less comprehensive tour, which might even take in the Igreja de Santo António and the museum, or a somewhat less arduous stroll through the streets in the centre of town. There are a great many cafés and restaurants in which to sit and rest. ★★Ponta da Piedade, about 2km south of Lagos, boasts perhaps the strangest rock formations in the Algarve. From Lagos it is then another 17km back to the starting point at Portimão.

Lagos

The tour of the western Algarve can just as well be done in reverse which has the advantage firstly that Lagos can be explored while still relatively fresh, and secondly that the day can be brought to an agreeable conclusion in the little spa of Caldas de Monchique, so full of character. The only disadvantage is that a decision has to be made early on as to whether to include Cabo de São Vicente or not.

Alternative route

**Sights
from A to Z**

Capital of the administrative district of Albufeira
Population: 17,000

Situation and importance

The town of Albufeira lies on the southern coast of the Algarve about 35km west of Faro. Albufeira is the first town of any size in the east of the Barlavento, and is situated on one of the bays surrounded by rocky cliffs which characterise this region. Once just a village, Albufeira remained relatively unaffected by the initial influx of holidaymakers in the 1960s and 1970s, but this idyllic situation did not last long, and by the end of the 1970s it, like many other places in the Algarve, attracted the attention of large holiday companies and quickly developed into one of the Algarve's major tourist centres. Together with the surrounding beaches, it is now dominated by tourism and the infrastructure that goes with it. All kinds of water-sports can be enjoyed here, as well as tennis, golf and horse-riding.

History

Albufeira can look back on a long and eventful past. The Romans settled here in the first half of the 2nd century B.C. – however, its ideal situation leads one to assume that there had been settlements here long before that. The Romans erected a castle on the cliffs, named their settlement Baltum and built salt-extraction works by the sea, salt being needed to preserve fish. In the 5th century B.C. the Visigoths came to the region, only to be driven out by the Moors in A.D. 716. They named the town Al-Buhara or Al-Buhera, from which the present name of Albufeira (meaning "lagoon") was derived. Albufeira became an important port as a result of trading with North Africa. Occupation by Christian troops in 1189 lasted a mere two years, and it was the middle of the 13th century before Albufeira was conquered by knights of the Order of Santiago and subsequently fell to the Portuguese. Trade with North Africa declined and the town lost its importance. In the 16th century the people of Albufeira successfully withstood repeated attacks by Moorish, British and French pirates. The earthquake of 1755 caused much devastation, and floods destroyed many houses near the coast. Civil war in the 19th century was Albufeira's next disaster; guerilla troops led by the infamous Remexido, a supporter of the absolutist King Miguel I, besieged the town and finally set fire to it.

Townscape

Albufeira still occupies an impressive amphitheatre-like situation on the slopes of the rocky bay. The wide beach is crowded with tourists, but also

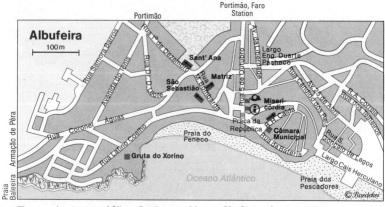

◄ *The massive towers of Silves Castle are evidence of its former importance*

54

fishermen moor their boats here and go about their daily business. However, modern buildings and tourism now dominate the scene and little remains of the old fishing village.

Motor traffic, which for a long time plagued the narrow streets, has been banished to the outskirts, and the town centre is now one large pedestrian zone. The streets are laid with typical Portuguese mosaics, and the little whitewashed houses give the centre of the town an appealing atmosphere. Souvenir and jewellery shops and boutiques abound, while in the evening Albufeira becomes an eldorado for lovers of night-life. Sounds and rhythms of all kinds emanate from the houses, and those who enjoy a pub-crawl will find many from which to chose. The same goes for restaurants and cafés; some streets seem to be full of them, especially the Rua Cãndido dos Reis. Less noisy and to be recommended is a stroll from the indoor fish market up the narrow Rua da Bateria and along the steep coast.

Sights

Before going on a tour of Albufeira visitors should enjoy the view over the bay and the old town centre from the viewing site above the beach to the east. This superb panorama is perhaps the most beautiful experience the little town has to offer. ★View

From here steps lead down to the beach and to the Largo Cais Herculano. After following the Rua da Bateria as far as the busy Rua 5 de Outubro, either continue westwards or join the crowds in Rua 5 de Outubro and the centrally located Largo Engenheiro Duarte Pacheco. Tour

Near the old Town Hall with the unusual metal construction on its tower stands the hospital. A plaque indicates that the entrance gate to the castle once stood here. Hospital

Rua 5 de Outubro – a popular pedestrian street in Albufeira

Albufeira

Igreja da Misericórdia	In nearby Rua Henrique Calado the little Igreja da Misericórdia is almost hidden in a row of houses. Only the Manueline door of red sandstone makes it stand out from the others.
Igreja Matriz	The Igreja Matriz was rebuilt after the earthquake by Francisco Gomes de Avelar, the then Bishop of the Algarve. In 1993 the whole building was renovated but has not really benefited thereby.
Igreja Sant'Ana	The Igreja Sant'Ana on the corner of Rua 1° de Dezembro by the Largo Jacinto d'Ayete, on the other hand, is an extremely pretty church. This typical, whitewashed Algarve building dates from the 18th c. and provides an almost rural element in its urban surroundings. Of note are the crossing cupola and the Baroque gables on all four sides.
Igreja de São Sebastião	This church still has a small Manueline side door from a previous church.
Largo Engenheiro Duarte Pacheco	The newly laid out Largo Engenheiro Duarte Pacheco is Albufeira's main square. This is the busy hub of the town, the meeting place of locals and tourists alike. It is lined with cafés, restaurants and snack bars, interspersed with postcard stands and fashion jewellers. The town's churches are portrayed on the fountain in the square, and a tile-picture provides a view of old Albufeira. Among the pretty herbaceous borders old Portuguese men sit under a rubber tree and survey the scene.
Gruta do Xorino	The Gruta do Xorino in the south-west of Albufeira is where the liberals fled when the town was besieged by the monarchist Miguelists in 1833. They reached the caves through an underground passage, and from there continued their flight by boat to Faro. Fishermen offer boat trips to the Gruta do Xorino from Albufeira's town centre; it is also possible to reach the caves by a path along the cliffs.

Beaches

Municipal beach	From Rua 5 de Outubro a tunnel leads to Albufeira's municipal beach. The tunnel was cut through the massive rock between 1932 and 1935. The engineer in charge of the project was Duarte Pacheco, who was Minister of Construction under Salazar. For a municipal beach this is perfectly acceptable, although in summer it is generally overcrowded. Above the beach is a short promenade lined with flags of all nations, where cafés provide a welcome change from the throngs below.
Beaches west of Albufeira	To the west of Albufeira lie several small beaches in attractive bays as well as the long Praia da Galé which extends as far as Armação de Pera. Everywhere can be found smallish or not so small catering establishments together with good facilities for water sports – diving, surfing, waterskiing. The Praia da Galé is preferred by surfers, while the best beaches for diving and snorkelling are those between Albufeira and the Praia do Castelo, namely, the popular Praia de São Rafael and the Praia da Baleeira.
Beaches east of Albufeira	Attractive smaller beaches in the east of Albufeira include Oura, Balaia and Maria Luisa, which form part of the tourist suburbs of Montechoro and Areias de São João. All beaches offer good water-sports and catering facilities.
Olhos de Água	Olhos de Água lies on the coast 7km east of Albufeira. The name stems from the freshwater springs which can be seen on the beach at low tide and which the local inhabitants describe as "water eyes". Although somewhat rocky in parts, the beach is very attractive but tends to become crowded in the high season.
★Praia da Falésia	The Praia de Falésia is another well-tended beach some 12km east of Albufeira. It is noted for its high rock-wall extending for several kilometres

The beaches of Albufeira are popular in summer

along the coast which shines colourfully when the light is favourable. There is plenty of room on the beach, even although on the cliffs is one of the Algarve's largest holiday parks, with apartments, bungalows and a hotel and covering an area of 35ha. Originally only a few small holiday homes were built here in 1973, followed by a huge hotel in 1978. The last bungalows were completed in 1992.

Surroundings of Albufeira

Tunes, situated some 10km north of Albufeira, is a sleepy village known only for its railway station. From the name it has been assumed that immigrants from Tunis in North Africa settled here.

Tunes

The village of Paderne lies 12km north-east of Albufeira in the midst of some beautiful, slightly hilly countryside. This picturesque spot offers a peaceful escape from the hustle and bustle on the coast. Known to the Moors as Badima, it was conquered by the Portuguese under Dom Paia Peres Correia in 1248. The parish church, founded in the 16th c., still shows some Manueline features from this period.

Paderne

Also of interest are the ruins of a Moorish castle about 4km south of the village; parts of the original walls and a watch-tower remain. The castle played an important defensive role when the region was won back from the Moors. Impressive, too, are the ruins of a small Gothic church built after the Portuguese conquest. A narrow bridge near the castle dates from Roman times, but was rebuilt in the 16th c.

Boliqueime, a village 10km north-east of Albufeira, has been somewhat spoiled by modern development. It was the birthplace of Cavaço Silva, who was prime minister of Portugal for a number of years. Lídia Jorge (see Famous People), one of Portugal's best known authors, also grew up here.

Boliqueime

Alcoutim

In her novel "The Day of the Miracle" she described everyday life in the sleepy village during the Salazar period and the hope that first sprang from the Carnation Revolution.

Guia

In Guia, 6km north-west of Albufeira, stands the Igreja de Nossa Senhora da Guia, built in the 19th c., the interior of which is decorated with attractive tiles.

Zoomarine Park

Near Guia lies the well-known Zoomarine Park, which attracts some 400,000 visitors a year and is laid out with small lakes, gardens and restaurants. Among the birds and animals to be seen are parrots which include some droll items in their repertoire and mainly – as the name implies – various marine animals. There are several ponds and aquaria with many varieties of fish, including sharks, as well as performing sea-lions, dolphins and seals. There is a large swimming pool suitable for children and adults, together with roundabouts, a giant wheel and cinema shows. Those who are less keen on the beach and the sea can easily spend a whole day here. Just to see the main attractions and the many animals will take at least four hours (open: daily 10am–6pm, to 8pm in summer, closed in Jan. and Feb.).

Algoz

Algoz is a typical little Algarve country town some 10km north-west of Albufeira and 15km east of Silves. It lies in the middle of some very beautiful countryside, some of which is almost completely unspoiled. While the traffic piles up on the N125 further south, there is very little on the country road which passes through Algoz and on to Silves. Although relatively close to the tourist coast Algoz has retained much of its originality. It is also worth making a short detour to the Ermida de Nossa Senhora do Pilar on a hill on the edge of town. From up here there is a splendid view of Algoz and its surroundings.

Alcoutim   north of A 19

Capital of the administrative district of Alcoutim
Population: 3500

Situation and importance

Alcoutim is beautifully situated in the north-east of the Algarve on the right bank of the Guadiana, which here forms the frontier between the Algarve and Spanish Andalusia. 40km further south the Guadiana enters the Atlantic. In the town the Ribeira de Cadavais flows into the Guadiana.

The town's charm lies in its seclusion; only a few tourists stray this far. Some do come by boat; when conditions are favourable excursion boats from Vila Real de Santo António (see entry) continue on to Alcoutim. Yachts and other craft moor alongside the pier.

There is only a modest degree of tourist infrastructure. Alcoutim and its western and southern surroundings form part of the most remote regions in the Algarve. Population density is low and poverty levels high as there is little work available.

Opposite the town to the east, on the Spanish bank of the river, lies the town of Sanlúcar de Guadiana – a tranquil picture, far removed from the military battles and enmity which existed between the two towns in centuries past.

History

Alcoutim was a river port back in Phoenician times, and it is thought that there was also a Celtic settlement here. In the 2nd century B.C. the town was Roman, when it was known as Alcoutinium. In A.D. 415 the Alans took Alcoutim, followed shortly afterwards by the Visigoths; the Moors ruled the town in the 8th century. In 1240 the Portuguese under Sancho II succeeded in taking Alcoutim, and in the early 14th century Alcoutim was handed over to the Knights of the Order of Santiago. In 1371 Portugal and

View of the Guadiana and the Spanish town of Sanlúcar from the castle ruins of Alcoutim ▶

Castille concluded the Treaty of Alcoutim; after a festive meeting on the river Fernando I and Henrique II of Castille signed the treaty which temporarily ended the wars between the two countries. In the 17th century Alcoutim again became the scene of battles between Spain and Portugal after Portuguese nobles had initiated the restoration of Portugal's independence from Spain by means of a revolt. It was 1668 before Spain finally recognised Portugal's independence, and until that date there were frequent attacks from both sides of the river. Alcoutim suffered its last political conflicts at the time of the Miguelist Wars in the 1830s, when liberals and absolutist Miguelists fought one another.

Townscape

Alcoutim with its shining white houses stretches beneath the castle as far as the river bank. A stroll through the little streets of this still unspoiled town will be well worthwhile. On the river bank and in the town itself there are some attractive squares, and several churches and the castle bear witness to the town's turbulent past.

Sights

★Castelo

Because of its location Alcoutim played an important strategical role early in its history. The present castle dates back to an 11th c. Moorish fort, but there were probably larger defensive walls here before that. It is known that in 1304 Dom Dinis I provided the town with funds to renovate the town walls and the castle.

The castle has not been used for military purposes since 1878. Since then it has served various needs, including being at one time an abattoir. In 1973 archaeologists began to take an interest in its history and undertook extensive digs and restoration projects based on the original plans. Today there is an exhibition of archaeological finds which is open to visitors, and the old foundations which were revealed during the digs can also be inspected.

Ermida de Nossa Senhora da Conceição

The Ermida de Nossa Senhora da Conceição lies higher up to the west of the castle site. A semicircular flight of steps leads up to this simple edifice. The chapel dates from the 16th c.; all that remains of the original is a Manueline doorway. The building was extensively restored in the first half of the 18th c., and the Baroque altarpiece from that period is particularly striking.

Igreja Matriz

The parish church is charmingly situated on the bank of the Guadiana. Between 1538 and 1554 the former small, single-aisled chapel was replaced, with help from the Santiago Order of Knights, with a triple-aisled church in Early Renaissance style; the Renaissance portal has been preserved. Inside the church, note the capitals and the baptistry with a 16th c. bas-relief.

Ermida de Santa António

The inconspicuous Ermida de Santa António also stands by the river. This little chapel with the archaic-looking circular window above the doorway dates from the 16th c.

Igreja da Misericórdia

The little Igreja da Misericórdia on the Praça da República was built at the beginning of the 16th c. but underwent numerous restorations and renovations in later years.

The site has been flooded on numerous occasions over the centuries. A mark on the outside wall shows the level reached by the waters during one of the worst floods in 1876.

Surroundings

Museu do Rio

From Alcoutim a road leads southwards along the bank of the Guadiana through some beautiful countryside. In the sleepy village of Guerreiros do Rio, which is idyllically situated on the banks of the river some 12km south of Alcoutim, the Museo do Rio has been opened in the former primary school. A small exhibition provides information on the history, fauna and flora and life of the people living by the river. The fishermen in Guerreiros offer boat trips on the Guadiana.

8km west of Alcoutim is the N124, and 25km along this road lies the village of Giões. On the edge of the village stands the 16th c. parish church which houses some attractive portraits of saints, including one of Nossa Senhora das Relíquias which dates from the 16th c.

4km east of Giões, near Clarines, can be found the remains of a pre-Roman settlement – today known as Cerro das Relíquias.

Giões

30km west of Alcoutim lies the isolated village of Martim Longo, which was settled in Roman times. Remains of 16th c. wall-paintings can still be seen in the parish church. The hills in the vicinity are ideal for gentle walks.

Martim Longo

In the middle of the Algarve mountains, some 10km south-east of Martim Longo, lie the houses of Vaqueiros. The most striking building in the village is the 16th c. church, which was renovated in the 18th c. Its attractively painted side-altars are of particular interest.

Vaqueiros

Cachopo is a pretty, secluded Algarve village which very few tourists visit. From Martim Longo, follow the N124 in a southerly direction. On the edge of the village can be seen the barns which are typical of this region and are reminiscent of Celtic round-houses.

Cachopo

Aljezur   A 3

Capital of the administrative district of Aljezur
Population: 5500

The small town of Aljezur lies in the west of the Algarve some 40km north of Sagres. The N120 from Lagos passes through Aljezur, continues north through the Alentejo region and on towards Lisbon. Far away from the busy holiday centres, Aljezur is an ideal destination for those wishing a different kind of holiday with less emphasis on comfort and a good tourist infrastructure and more on enjoying nature at its best. The climate is somewhat harsher than in the east of the Algarve, and the vegetation in particular differs from that in the south-east. It is markedly more barren, no pretty gardens but more in the way of low undergrowth and macchia bushes. The peace and quiet the region has enjoyed to date has been due in the main to the fact that the whole of the coastal strip south and north of Aljezur is a nature reserve. However, even in the Costa Vicentina nature park tourist projects are planned, albeit on a small scale.

Situation and importance

It is assumed that Aljezur was founded by the Moors. In 1246 it was conquered by the Portuguese Order of Santiago led by Dom Paio Peres Correia. Because of its secluded situation Aljezur never became of great importance.

History

The most attractive side of Aljezur is seen when entering it from the north after first crossing a small river, the Ribeira de Aljezur, and then reaching the town centre. The major public buildings, some banks and cafés and restaurants line the main street. Up on a hill lie the remains of a castle which dates back to Moorish times. Over the centuries it fell more and more into decay and was finally completely demolished in an earthquake and was never rebuilt. From here there is a superb view of the surrounding countryside.

Townscape

Surroundings

There are some excellent beaches near Aljezur, but some are difficult to get to and the wind and sea are rougher here than on the south coast of the

Beaches

Algarve. Strong currents mean that conditions vary from year to year. The isolated and extensive Praia de Carriagem, the semicircular Praia de Monte Clérigo and the Praia da Arrifana with the remains of an old fortress are scenically beautiful. Also very popular are the beaches near Carrapateira and that at Odeceixe in the north-west of the Algarve. Odeceixe itself is a pretty village. The beach lies 2km further west at the mouth of a small river.

Almansil   C 12

Administrative district: Loulé
Population: 6000

Situation and importance

Almansil (or Almancil), 13km north-west of Faro, has been somewhat spoiled by development. The busy N125 bisects the town and leaves it looking disorganised and torn. Nevertheless, with its numerous shops and banks Almansil is the shopping centre for the nearby luxurious holiday resorts of Vale do Lobo and Quinta do Lago. Above all, however, Almansil is well known for two reasons – the Igreja de São Lourenço is one of the most artistically and historically interesting churches in the Algarve, and the Culture Centre near the church has also made a name for itself with art and music-lovers.

Sights

★Igreja de São Lourenço

The Igreja de São Lourenço stands outside the town on the road to Faro, and is visible from afar. It is thought to date back to the 15th c., when a small chapel was first built here. From the outside the present Baroque church appears rather plain; only the dome above the choir really stands out.

The church is renowned for the extraordinary glazed tile decoration in the relatively small interior. Architecture and decoration blend together into one unit. The walls, vaulted ceiling and even the dome are all clad in blue and white *azulejos*. A warm contrast is provided by the high altar in *talha dourada* with a figure of St Lawrence. The six tile-paintings on the side walls depict scenes from the saint's life. In the front on the left is shown a conversation between St Lawrence and Pope Sixtus in which St Lawrence is complaining that he was unable to die a martyr's death. He then learned that he would become a martyr within the next three days. The following tablets show the martyrdom of the saint whom the authorities caused to be burned to death because he had given to the poor money intended for building a church.

The tile-paintings have been dated as 1730. At that time the production of large paintings in tiles was very popular in Portugal. Political events, town views, allegories and even Biblical scenes were portrayed on tiles. The azulejos in São Lourenço were the work of the Baroque artist António Oliveira Benardes, but it is not known in which factory the tiles themselves were made; possibly they were imported from Italy or Holland.

Centro Cultural São Lourenço

The Centro Cultural São Lourenço, a short distance down from the church, was fitted out in the early 1980s by a German firm. In the beautiful rooms – when restoring the building traditional Algarve architecture was preserved – is a gallery with seven rooms in which temporary exhibitions are held. Concerts and series of concerts, ranging from classical to jazz, are held in the culture centre with, now and again, avant-garde music included in the programme. There is also a sculpture garden and a patio where open-air performances are held.

Surroundings

★ Quinta do Lago

Quinta do Lago, the "country estate by the sea", is an extremely exclusive holiday resort 6km south of Almansil. Tasteful villas and bungalows have

The Church of São Lourenço contains splendid azulejos decoration

been built on this spacious area of land, some of them privately owned and some available for hire as holiday accommodation. Between the houses broad lawns have been laid out with small artificial waterways and decorative umbrella-pines. There are several golf courses and tennis courts, and the beach which is wide, relatively empty and clean, offers facilities for various water sports. The restaurants are first class. In 1989 Quinta do Lago was chosen as the venue for the NATO Assembly.

"Wolf's Valley", a few miles west of Quinta do Lago, is a similar luxurious holiday resort, with attractive villas with small gardens and swimming pools, broad lawns and pine trees. Here too there are golf courses and tennis courts and a wide range of similar leisure pursuits, but amusement-wise things are rather quiet. The little centre of Vale do Lobo is attractively laid out, and one can pass a pleasant hour or so in one of the cafés or restaurants – some with a view of the sea.

★Vale do Lobo

The beach between Vale do Lobo and Quinta do Lago is suitable for long walks, and there are some beach restaurants.

Alte

B 10

Administrative district: Loulé
Population: 500

Alte is an extremely attractive village in the Algarve hinterland, lying at the foot of the Serra de Caldeirão, north of Albufeira, at least 20km from the coast. The easiest access is by the quiet country road which leads from São Bartolomeu de Messines eastwards into the foothill region. The countryside around Alte is relatively unspoiled and hilly. The delightful "Algarve gardens" stretch this far; north of Alte the landscape becomes a little more

Situation and importance

The Ermida de São Luís in Alte

barren. Olives, figs, oranges, lemons and, above all, almonds thrive in the fertile soil; in spring luxuriant gardens come into bloom everywhere.

Alte is known for its festival held on May 1st each year, when the streets and lanes are decorated with flowers. There are flower processions through the streets and a grand dance festival which attracts folk-dancing groups and spectators from far and wide. Picnics are traditionally held in and around Alte on the first of May. Somewhat quaintly, perhaps, in February the "Festa dos Chouriços", or "Sausage Festival", is celebrated in honour of the village saint and patron saint of animals, São Luís.

★ Townscape

In recent years this picturesque little village has attracted increasing numbers of tourists. Coachloads of holidaymakers visit it, and it is to be hoped that its delightful and quiet image will not change too rapidly. Not only is Alte's situation captivating, the village itself with its whitewashed little Algarve houses, small lanes, flower gardens and planted containers at the gates is quite entrancing. Hibiscus, geraniums and oleander bushes bloom everywhere, and visitors can follow twisty and cobbled lanes through the village. Away from the hustle and bustle on the coast, a stroll through Alte will provide much information about rural life in the Algarve.

Sights

Igreja Matriz

In the village centre towers the Igreja Matriz, built in the early 16th c. Some features from that time remain, such as the simple Manueline doorway. The pretty village church is usually open, the entrance being on the right-hand side via the sacristy. In the three-aisled interior note the beautiful wooden ceiling and Manueline arch which separates the choir and high altar from the main nave. A glance up at the choir ceiling shows three bosses; the front one symbolises the Portuguese voyages of discovery, the central one in the shape of a moon symbolises discoveries in the Orient, and the rear blue one the sea-routes to India discovered by the Portuguese. There is an attractive pulpit with steps made of *azulejos*. In the Baroque side-chapels in the left and right aisles are portrayals of numerous popular saints – at the front in the left aisle are São Jorge, São Francisco and São Vicente, at the back John the Baptist, Mary and Christ, in the right aisle São Miguel with a pair of scales and São Sebastião. In the Capela de Nossa Senhora de Lurdes in the left aisle can be seen a black saint. This side-chapel is clad in rare tiles from Sevilla.

The road to the Fonte das Bicas leads past the Ermida de São Luís. This Baroque chapel with a simple façade is usually closed. It is dedicated to the patron saint of Alte.

Ermida de São Luís

The Fonte das Bicas is an absolutely idyllic little place on the eastern edge of the village. As well as verses by the poet Cândido Guerreiro (1871–1953), who hailed from Alte, there is a tile-picture of St Anthony.

At the taps, the *bicas*, the village people fill their plastic bottles with fresh spring water; people even come from far and wide, as it is believed by many that the water has healing powers and is said to be the reason why the inhabitants of Alte live so long.

Fonte das Bicas

A short distance along the river lies the Fonte Grande, the "great stream". Tables and benches invite visitors to picnic, while a kiosk supplies drinks. There is also a restaurant a few yards away.

Fonte Grande

Those wishing to extend their walk can continue out of the village and along by the river. After 2km is Queda do Vigário, the largest waterfall in the Algarve.

Queda do Vigário

Surroundings

The very peaceful village of Salir 15km to the east is as pretty as Alte. It lies on two hills, on the western one of which a few traces of a Moorish castle are still to be seen. The importance of these wall fragments lies in the fact that this is one of the few places in the Algarve with authentic Moorish remains. The little Castelo quarter with its tiny white houses and many flowers is quite idyllic. The larger part of the village lies on the second hill, dominated by the water-tower and plain village church. From the church square there is a fine view of the mountainous countryside where small-holdings abound on the rich red soil.

★Salir

Between Alte and Salir a little signposted road, which climbs to 479m, leads north off the N124 to the Rocha da Pena, a small mountain. A circular route 4.7km long starts at a round flowerbed with an old carob tree in the centre. The route climbs up past good viewing points and a small cave to which the Moors are said to have fled during attacks by Christian soldiers in the 13th c. This region has been designated a nature reserve, and a specially equipped centre a little way down the road features the flora and fauna of the Rocha da Pena. After the walk visitors can seek refreshment in the "das Grutas" bar at the setting-out point.

★Rocha da Pena

Alvor

C 5

Administrative district: Portimão
Population: 5000

Alvor is a tourist fishing village on the south coast of the Algarve. It lies about 1km inland, between Lagos and Portimão, on the wide Baia de Lagos (Bay of Lagos). To the west of Alvor is a lagoon formed at the mouths of four rivers where many of the villagers work as fisherfolk.

Situation and importance

Armação de Pêra

History

It is thought that Alvor dates back to the 5th c. In the Moorish period – when it was known as Albur – there was probably a castle here which was captured by the Portuguese in 1250 during the reign of Afonso III. Alvor gained a place in Portuguese history when King João II died here in 1495. His body was buried in Silves Cathedral and later transported to Batalha. Alvor was almost completely destroyed by earthquake and the resultant flood.

Townscape

Alvor is a prosperous place lying as it does between the two holiday centres around Portimão and Lagos, and although itself tourist-orientated it has retained its attractive appearance. The centre of the village with its small lanes features some low whitewashed fishermen's houses. There are a few restaurants, cafés and souvenir shops, but all in all it remains relatively rustic. Some streets lead down to the water. Particularly attractive is the harbour with its fish market and simple taverns and cafés along the bank. To the east of Alvor, however, near Torralta and by the Praia dos Três Irmãos there are some larger hotels.

Sights

Igreja Matriz

The Igreja Matriz is one of the village's highlights. Dating originally from the 16th c., it is a typical Algarve village church which retains some of its old architectural features. The Manueline main and side doors are worthy of note. Other Manueline features are to be found inside – the arch above the chancel is adorned with a turned stone ribbon, the delicate capitals on the six pillars consist of stone fishing ropes and plant ornamentation. The altarpieces are framed sparingly in *talha dourada*.

Praia de Alvor

Alvor's "own beach" is the kilometre-long, wide Praia de Alvor stretching to the west and east of the village. There are hotels on the Praia dos Três Irmãos further west.

Surroundings

Mexilhoeira

Mexilhoeira, 4km north-west of Alvor, has retained its rustic character. At its highest point stands the Igreja Matriz with a Renaissance doorway and a Manueline side-door. The bell-tower, too, has a small door decorated in Manueline style. The courtyard in front of the church, from where there is a superb view towards Alvor and the sea, is attractively planted with trees.

Armação de Pêra   C 8

Administrative district: Silves
Population: 3000

Situation and importance

Armação de Pêra, with its high-rise hotels and apartments, lies on the south coast of the Algarve between Portimão and Albufeira, some 45km west of Faro.

Surprisingly, just a few kilometres to the north lies countryside which, if not completely uninhabited, is still extremely attractive. Those approaching Armação de Pêra from the north along the N125 will initially not anticipate anything undesirable at all – until suddenly behind a hill the bizarre skyline of the town comes into view.

Townscape

Apartment blocks, huge hotels and other high-rise buildings still in course of construction together with giant cranes combine to give Armação de Pêra a sorry appearance to say the least. The long, broad beach stretching for several kilometres to the east of the town may compensate somewhat for all this. The small, painted fishing boats on the beach are most picturesque, and the promenade is passable.

The long sandy beach at Armação de Pêra

There is still a little of the old village to be seen – the remains of the 17th c. fort with the little Capela de Santo António. The most pleasant side of Armação de Pêra lies to the east of the coast road.

Surroundings

To the west lie rows of hotels and holiday accommodation. In part these are quite attractively laid-out apartment villages lying on the cliffs above beautiful sandy bays. Between large rocky headlands there are deep bays which the waters of the Atlantic have over thousands of years shaped into cliffs. Popular small sandy bays include the Praia da Cova Redonda and the Praia Maré Grands.

On a high rocky overhang 1km west of Armação de Pêra stands a little jewel – a marked contrast to its surroundings. The little Ermida de Nossa Senhora da Rocha has been built on a 35m-high cliff above the sea. Gleaming white, it stands out against the blue sea, and a *miradouro*, a viewing-point, juts out into the sea. From there one can clearly see the neighbouring headlands.
    The chapel shows traces of Early Gothic. The entrance between two columns leads into a small hall. The capital of one pillar is still well preserved, while the second has weathered over the centuries. A few candles always burn in the small anteroom – many Portuguese come here to pray to the Senhora da Rocha. The unusual hexagonal spire above the chancel can be seen from afar. There is a well nearby.

★Ermida de Nossa Senhora da Rocha

Below the chapel lie two narrow sandy bays, linked by a tunnel. Both beaches have fine sand and are relatively quiet.

Praia de Nossa Senhora da Rocha

Pêra, 2km inland from Armação de Pêra, is still a pretty village with practically none of the turbulent atmosphere of the coastal strip nearby. The

Pêra

The white Ermida de Nossa Senhora da Rocha silhouetted against blue sky and sea

villagers keep themselves to themselves. Beautiful, too, is the surrounding countryside with its small country houses and orange and lemon groves. In front of one of the two churches is a square from where there is a view of the sea.

Alcantarilha

The village of Alcantarilha, 3km north of Armação de Pêra, was founded by the Moors, and the name is Arabic for "small bridge". The busy N125 cuts through the village, but nevertheless there are some attractive nooks and crannies. The interior of the pretty parish church still displays some Manueline features. Adjoining the church is a charnel-house.

Porches

Together with Tavira, Moncarapacho and Loulé, Porches is a centre of Portuguese ceramic manufacture. The village lies on the N125 4km north-west of Armação de Pêra. Along the road are numerous sales centres offering ceramic articles of all kinds.

Between Porches and Alcantarilha will be found the bathers' paradise known as "The Big One" (see Practical Information, Water Parks).

Carvoeiro   C 7

Administrative district: Lagoa
Population: 4000

Situation and importance

Until quite recently the coastal town of Carvoeiro was a pretty fishing village, but more recently this idyllic spot has also developed into a wide-

The attractive modern development of the coastline at Carvoeiro ▶

spread tourist centre. Initially many Portuguese chose Carvoeiro as their summer resort, and then in the early 1980s an international building boom began. In spite of everything, however, the town has managed to retain something of its former atmosphere.

Townscape

The town centre above the little bay still consists of narrow streets and lanes. The houses are traditionally whitewashed, and new villas and small apartment houses have been built among the old fishermen's cottages. The buildings around the former village display an appealing degree of sympathy with their surroundings, and many of the holiday centres reveal hints of Moorish architecture in their construction. Carvoeiro has gained its fine reputation from its overall planning. However, building has now spread so that almost all the coastal strip around Carvoeiro has been built on. The infrastructure is more than adequate: cafés and restaurants abound and on the beach fishermen offer trips in small boats. From the sea there are fantastic views of the rocks and cliffs: the Atlantic has pounded them for thousands of years, carving bizarre shapes in the soft limestone.

Surroundings

★★ Algar Seco

Near Algar Seco, 2km east of Carvoeiro, in particular, visitors can admire some grandiose rock formations. In the course of time wind and weather have shaped a unique landscape. It is best to explore here on foot – walking through a labyrinth of plateaux, rock pillars, narrow openings and natural archways and past a pool which rises and falls with the tides. Below, the sea bubbles through hidden caves and grottoes. As the light changes so the limestone takes on a wide range of colours. Protected by walls of rock but with a view of the sea is a small café in the midst of this world of limestone.

Beaches

To the east and west of Carvoeiro are a few beautiful sandy bays; some of them, however, are difficult to reach. Access to the beach in the Vale de Centianes is by way of some steps near the Hotel Cristal. The little Praia do Carvalho is reached from Alfanzina, also by means of steps.

Castro Marim   B 19

Capital of the administrative district of Castro Marim
Population: 5000

Situation and importance

Castro Marim lies in the south-east of the Algarve, some 4km north-west of the border town of Vial Real de Santo António. The town lies on small hills which rise up out of the fenland plain of the Guadiana which flows past Castro Marim about 3km further to the east. Around Castro Marim are salt-works, and to the south lies a protected marshy region, the "Reserva Natural do Sapal de Castro Marim", with a rich variety of flora and fauna.

The name Castro Marim (castle by the sea) suggests that at one time there was a settlement directly by the sea and that the present-day hills could even once have been islands.

History

Archaeological finds have proved that there was a pre-Roman settlement of Castro Marim. The Phoenicians probably established a trading port here. The name of the town also suggests the presence of Iberian Celts; fortified Celtic settlements on the peninsula were known as *castros*. Both in Roman times – when it was known as Castrum Marinum – and under Moorish rule, Castro Marim was of importance because of its situation on a major link road. In 1319 Dom Dinis I declared the town the main seat of the Knights of Christ, the order which played such a decisive role in the Portuguese voyages of discovery and conquest. In 1356 the order moved its seat to Tomar, but for centuries afterwards Castro Marim remained a fortified town of strategic importance in guarding the frontier with Spain. In the 14th and 17th c. the fortifications were extensively enlarged. During the period

The Order of the Knights of Christ

At first glance it appears as if Castro Marim is the very cradle of the Knights of Christ. The order – which played a decisive role in the story of Portuguese expansion during the 15th and early 16th centuries – was founded in 1319 and set up its headquarters on a hill near the town. The members of the order stayed on the right bank of the Guadiana until 1356, when they moved to the former templar castle in Tomar.

This "flying visit" concealed an ingenious chess move. The Knights of Christ were no less than the former Templars, who had been suppressed in 1312. The Knights Templar had been founded in 1119 to protect pilgrims in the Holy Land and had played a definitive role in the medieval Crusades. Not only did the Pope support the order, he also bestowed sundry privileges on it. The standing and power of the Templars grew apace, and soon they were able to call large tracts of land their own. In Portugal they settled by the Rio Nabão and built the well-known fortress of Tomar with its temple church.

In France, too, the Templars acquired considerable influence and owned large areas of land – much to the annoyance and envy of Philip IV. In the early 14th c. he sought a means to suppress them. He accused the members of the order of heresy and of having links with Islam. The Pope, who was dependent on France, declared the accusations justified, and the Templar order was henceforth banned from all Christian countries.

In Portugal, however, the dissolution of the order was purely superficial. Soon after the suppression of the Order of Knights Templar the "Order of Christ" was founded. The members of the order were the same, they merely changed their name and the design of the cross on their white robes. What had previously been a red cross with eight points now had a smaller white cross set into the red. The possessions and property of the Templars passed to the Knights of Christ – in principle, everything remained as it was. Only their headquarters was moved for form's sake to the Algarve. After a few years, when everything had quietened down, there was nothing to prevent them moving back to Tomar.

When the order was founded its members had sworn to defend the Christian faith, fight Islam and help to expand the Portuguese sphere of influence. Now they had the opportunity to carry out these promises. In the centuries that followed the Knights of Christ exercised considerable influence on Portuguese history and eventually on the history of the world. Some of the major seafarers of the 15th and 16th centuries were members of the order – Bartolomeu Dias, Vasco da Gama, Pedro Álvares Cabral. Henry the Navigator was a Grand Master of the order from 1418. Several kings also belonged to the Order of the Knights of Christ, in particular Manuel I. The symbol of the time, the Cross of the Knights of Christ, was displayed on the sails of the caravels and on the dress of the mariners – and so became known throughout the world.

Its conversion to an order of monks in 1523 saw the beginning of the end. In 1789 the order was secularised and dissolved in 1910 when the Republic was proclaimed.

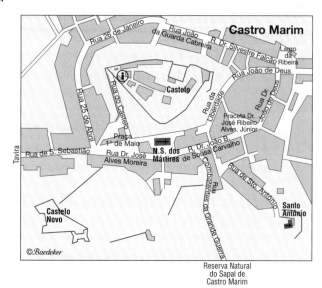

Reserva Natural
do Sapal de
Castro Marim

of the Inquisition Castro Marim was a much-feared prison camp. As a result of the destruction caused by the 1755 earthquake and the rebuilding of the nearby Vila Real de Santo António in 1744 Castro Marim lost much of its importance within a short space of time.

Townscape

The centre of Castro Marim lies between several small hills with castles on top. The town centre around the long and prettily laid out Praça 1° de Maio with its benches and plants and the Igreja de Nossa Senhora dos Mártires is very attractive.

Sights

Igreja de Nossa
Senhora dos
Mártires

From the Praça 1° de Maio steps lead up to the Igreja de Nossa Senhora dos Mártires. This church was built in the 18th c. by the Knights of Christ, and an example of their work is the side balustrade displaying typical Knights of Christ crosses. The beautifully harmonious dome is very striking.

★Castelo

Above the little town centre stands the extensive castle complex which can be reached in a few minutes from the Praça 1° de Maio. Originally 13th c., it was extended by the Knights of Christ after 1319. Within the fortified walls lie the ruins of an older Moorish castle, square in plan with circular towers at the corners. Also part of the complex is the Igreja de Misericórdia with a pleasing Renaissance doorway. From the castle walls there is a superb view of the town and the newer castle opposite and also over the Guadiana towards Spain.

Within the castle walls can be found the information office for the Sapal nature park (see below); here, too, are sundry exhibits relating to the history of Castro Marim.

Castel Novo

The Castel Novo or Castelo de São Sebastião stands above the town centre to the south. It was built in the 17th c. during the Wars of Restoration between Spain and Portugal.

The main square of Castro Marim

On a third hill to the east stands the Igreja de Santo António containing some interesting portrayals of the saint.

Surroundings

To the south between Castro Marim and Vila Real de Santo António lies the marshy nature reserve of Sapal de Castro Marim. This is the breeding ground of oyster-catchers, herons, storks and ospreys; many species of fish also live in the waterways. The plant life in this largely unspoiled region is also very diverse. Guided tours are available (details can be obtained from the information office in the castle).

Reserva Natural do Sapal de Castro Marim

Estói   C 14

Administrative district: Faro
Population: 600

Estói is a village typical of the eastern Algarve hinterland. The main buildings and some pretty houses are grouped around the church. It is known chiefly for its palace and for the Roman excavations nearby.

Situation and importance

Sights

The 17th c. parish church appears almost too large for this little village. Dedicated to São Martinho, it was badly damaged in the 1755 earthquake. In the early 19th c. the then bishop of the Algarve, Francisco Gomes do Avelar, had the church rebuilt to plans by Francisco Xavier Fabri, the Italian

Igreja Matriz

architect whom he had invited to south Portugal after the earthquake to give expert advice on rebuilding the damaged cultural possessions of the Algarve. The internal structuring of the church was carried out mainly in the 1840s by local craftsmen. The church's most valuable possession is the 55cm-high monstrance of gilded silver. The 17th c. figure of St Vincent with the Raven on the right-hand altar was saved from the damaged church.

★ Palácio de Estói

Immediately north of the church lie the parklands belonging to the Palácio de Estói (open: Mon.–Sat. 9am–noon and 2–5pm). The palace lies in some wonderful surroundings with extensive orange plantations, and it is worthwhile taking a walk along the palace wall to the north-west. Two *noras*, typical old Algarve fountains, can be seen; however, these are no longer functioning.

The Palace of Estói was built as a small Rococo palace at the end of the 18th c. by the Visconde de Carvalha. Later it passed into the possession of another nobleman, and since 1989 it has been owned by the municipality of Faro. There are plans to restore it and to use the rooms for concerts. For the time being, however, it is not open to visitors, but the surrounding park (albeit not very large) is open. Laid out in the 18th and 19th c., the gardens are on several levels. Through the present main entrance – originally a side entrance – an attractive avenue of palms leads initially to the terrace on the middle level with a small pavilion and a pool, in the centre of which stands a group of Italian statues. The square is decorated with several tile-pictures of allegorical and mythological scenes. Leda with the Swan is particularly fine. Busts of some Portuguese politicians and writers, including the Marquês de Pombal, Luis de Camões and Almeida Garrett line the walls.

Steps lead down to a somewhat overgrown part of the garden. Here, too, there is a wall with attractive blue-and-white *azulejo* paintings. The "Casa da Cascata", standing out amid the lush greenery, is clad in mosaics from nearby Milreu. A statue of the Three Graces, modelled on the famous group

Azulejos decoration on the steps of the Palácio de Estói

by the Italian Antonio Canova, will also catch the eye. An avenue of old trees links this part of the garden with the former main entrance.

From the middle level steps lead up to a gate which is unfortunately locked. From here there is a view of the somewhat sober façade of the palace with an open staircase on both sides. In the background can be seen the tower of the palace church.

Surroundings

On the western outskirts of Estói, alongside the road to Santa Bárbara de Nexe, lies the Milreu archaeological site (open: Tues.–Sun. 10am–noon and 2–5pm). Digs have been going on here for more than a hundred years since they were started by the historian and archaeologist Estácio da Veiga in 1877.

★ **Milreu**

In Roman times Milreu was a summer residence for wealthy families from Faro, then known as Ossonoba. Sometimes Milreu is also called by the Roman name Ossonoba. In the course of the excavations the foundations of a Roman villa and remains of thermal baths have been discovered. They are believed to date from the first century A.D.. Relatively well preserved are the walls of an early Christian basilica which was built on the foundations of a Roman temple. A later small chapel was also built here.

Remains of a Roman road divide the area into a northern and a southern half. To the south of the Via Roman stands a semi-circular walled ruin. Here the Romans erected a shrine which was unique in that it was constructed like a Roman ambulatory temple – an exceptional feature on the Iberian Peninsula. Extraordinary, too, is the fish frieze of coloured tesserae which was first discovered by German scientists from the Archaeological Institute in Madrid in 1971. The find was sensational for two reasons – first, the decoration of an exterior wall is very rare, secondly, this discovery refuted the earlier theory that there was a shrine to Venus near Milreu. It has now been agreed that here a sea-nymph was revered as a tutelary goddess.

Nymphæum

High inside the temple lies the podium with the cella, in the centre of which there was once a pool. In the entrance area another, semi-circular pool was found.

In the 5th c. A.D. the Visigoths erected a Christian church in the walls of the Roman shrine. A font and the remains of a mausoleum dating from that period have been preserved.

On the north side of the Via Romana lies the excavation site of the patrician house which a rich Roman probably had built. It has the typical ground-plan of a Roman villa, with a peristyle, or pillared courtyard, around which

Villa

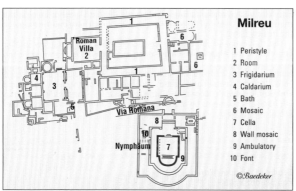

Milreu

1 Peristyle
2 Room
3 Frigidarium
4 Caldarium
5 Bath
6 Mosaic
7 Cella
8 Wall mosaic
9 Ambulatory
10 Font

©Baedeker

The most important Roman remains in the Algarve – the Ruins of Milreu

living, dining, and recreation quarters were grouped. Still to be seen are some mosaic floors where the archaeologists again stumbled upon fish and sea-creature motifs. The most important items found in the villa, a bust of Hadrian and one of the Empress Agrippina Minor, are now in the Archaeological Museum in Faro. A bust of the Emperor Gallienus is kept in the museum in Lagos.

Thermal baths

To the west of the villa were the hot baths with a changing room (apodyterium), a warm bath (caldarium) and a cold bath (frigidarium). Remains of underfloor heating in the warm bath and the boiler-room belonging to it were also discovered. Also well preserved is a relatively small pool also decorated with fish mosaics.

Santa Bárbara de Nexe

The little village of Santa Bárbara de Nexe lies 6km west of Estói in the midst of some beautiful fruit-growing country. From here there is a view of the nearby hills.

The 15th c. parish church has three aisles and is one of the few smaller churches in the Algarve which are open every day. It is charmingly sited above the village street and has a pretty forecourt. The chancel is divided from the nave by a Manueline pointed arch decorated with stone-rope and coral designs. Spanning the choir is a Manueline ceiling with stone-rope and Gothic network decoration. Some side chapels – the middle one in the left-hand aisle contains an attractive statue of Santo António – are embellished with *talha dourada*.

Faro   D 13/14

Capital of the administrative district of Faro
Population: 30,000

Faro is the capital of the historic province of the Algarve and also of the district of Faro, thus making it the administrative and economic centre of the Algarve region. It is a port and to a moderate degree an industrial town, as well as having had its own university for some years now.

Faro lies in the south-east of the Algarve in the north of an extensive system of lagoons – several islands which here form the coastline lie offshore. 10km west of the town centre is the Algarve's international airport, where the whole year round chartered and scheduled flights from a number of European countries land each day, bringing holidaymakers to the south of Portugal. In spite of this fact Faro is not really a tourist centre itself. Most visitors merely arrive and depart from here, but spend their holiday elsewhere in the Algarve and may just make a day trip into the town.

Faro has had a very varied history. The town is presumed to have been founded by the Phoenicians, who set up a small trading post on the south coast of Portugal. Under Roman occupation – when it was called Ossonoba – Faro developed into an important administrative town and the port also grew in importance. To the north of Faro there was at that time apparently a kind of summer residence, and in Milreu (see Estói, Surroundings) remains of a Roman shrine and of a villa with baths can still be seen. In A.D. 418 the

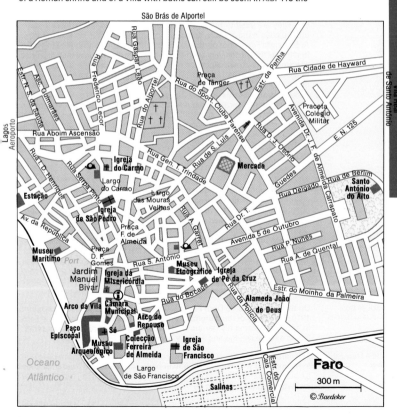

Faro

Visigoths conquered the south Portuguese port, and Faro became an episcopal see for the first time. The Visigoths began to build a Christian church
dedicated to the Virgin Mary. Because of the cult of the Virgin Mary which
played such a major role at that time, the Visigoths named the town Santa
Maria de Ossonoba. From 714 to 1249 Faro was Moorish, and the capital of
the province of Al-Gharb (Algarve) at that time was Xelb, now Silves.

King Afonso III of Portugal conquered Faro in 1249. That year saw the end
of Moorish rule in south Portugal, and in 1250 the Algarve towns were
affiliated to the Kingdom of Portugal. In 1577 the Portuguese transferred
the episcopal see from Silves to Faro. Subsequently the town was twice
largely destroyed – in 1596 following an attack by the Count of Essex and in
1755 by the great earthquake which also completely laid Lisbon to waste. In
1756 Faro was named the capital of the province of the Algarve. In the early
19th c. the town again had to suffer foreign occupation when Napoleonic
troops invaded in 1808. Since the middle of the 20th c. Faro has developed
into the major centre in south Portugal.

Name of the town | It is thought that the town's present name may date from the Moorish era;
in the 11th c. Ben Said Hárum founded a principality here, and the word
"Faro" may well be a corruption of his name. On the other hand, there is
clearly a possible link with the Portuguese word *farol* (a lighthouse).

★Townscape | Generally speaking, in Faro the Portuguese go about a normal everyday
life. They are used to tourism it is true, but the town is not, like so many
other places in the Algrave, exclusively dominated by the holiday industry.
At first sight Faro is not particularly appealing. Upon entering the town the
first things the visitor sees are dismal commercial areas and then high-rise
apartments. The town centre, on the other hand, is extremely inviting. Most
houses date from the 18th and 19th c. and a large part of the inner town is a
pedestrian and shopping zone. Here there are some good stores as well as
numerous street cafés and restaurants in which to unwind. The sidewalks
are paved with typical Portuguese black and white mosaics. Everywhere
there are small or not so small squares with attractive trees or parks.
Particularly idyllic is the historic core of the town around the old cathedral,
lying a little way from the pedestrian streets and surrounded by a town
wall.

Sights

Tour | A tour through Faro will give a general impression, following which the
visitor can devote time to a particular sight or place of interest. The setting-
out point can be the central Praça de Dom Francisco Gomes by the harbour
basin. From here proceed via the Jardin Manuel Bivar park to the historic
centre with the Cathedral and the Museu Arqueológico. Leave the old town
walls through the Arco do Repouso, continue to the Praça da Liberdade
with the Museu Etnográfico and finally to the Praça Ferreira de Almeida.
This is the business centre of Faro. After resting in one of the many cafés or
restaurants, simply enjoy a stroll through the little streets or go on a
shopping expedition. The tour could then be followed by a visit to the Igreja
do Carmo and/or a walk to the Museu Maritimo in the harbour.

Praça de Dom
Francisco Gomes | On the busy Praça de Dom Francisco Gomes stands an obelisk erected in
1910 in memory of the diplomat Ferreira d'Almeida, who was born in Faro
in 1847 and during his period in office as minister of naval affairs established a naval college and actively promoted the fishing industry.

Jardin Maunuel
Bivar | The Jardin Manuel Bivar to the south of the square is much more peaceful.
In the gardens with their pretty flower beds, tall palms and jacaranda trees
sit mainly elderly Farenese citizens reading, writing, having forty winks or
just watching the world go by.

The symbol of Faro: the Arco da Vila ▶

On the eastern side of the park stands the Igreja da Misericórdia, a 14th c. church which was rebuilt after the 1755 earthquake. The tourist information centre will be found on the opposite side of the adjoining Rua da Misericórdia.

★★ Centro Histórico

At the south end of the park can be seen the Arco da Vila. Built in the 18th c. by the Italian architect Francisco Xavier Fabri it has a bell-tower and a statue of the patron saint of Faro, St Thomas Aquinas. The gate leads into the extremely attractive historical centre of Faro which is partly enclosed by a 13th c. town wall. It is well worthwhile having a good look around here. Galleries, antique shops, cafés and restaurants can be found in the little streets, and those who visit in the spring will be able to see storks' nests built on many towers and ledges. The parent storks fly over Faro's old town while the beaks of the young can be seen poking out of the nests.

Largo da Sé, Paço Episcopal

In the spring, too, the Lago da Sé shows it most beautiful side. This magnificent square, which unfortunately serves as a car park during the day, is lined with orange trees which flower in March and April and give off a pleasant aromatic scent. On the north and west sides of the Largo da Sé lies the Paço Episcopal, the Bishop's Palace. When it was decided in the late 18th c. to incorporate a priests' seminar here the original building was extended by Fabri in the shape of the long west wing. After 1974 the building served provisionally as a reception centre for the *retornados*, those returning from the former Portuguese colonies. Since 1986 priests have again received training here. In 1940 a memorial was erected on the square in front of the building to Bishop Francisco Gomes do Avelar, who in the late 18th c. promoted the idea of a priests' seminar and campaigned vigorously for the rebuilding of the numerous churches destoyed in the earthquake. In the north-east corner of the Largo da Sé stands Faro's Town Hall (Câmara Municipal).

The bell tower of Faro Cathedral

The most striking building on the Largo da Sé is the Cathedral. A part of its ★ Sé
history can be seen from the outside – large sections of the original Gothic
church were destroyed in the earthquake in the 18th c. and rebuilt. Only the
tower and one window on the south side remain from the earlier church.
The Visigoths built a first Christian church in honour of Santa Maria –
probably on this site. Later there was thought to have been a mosque here
on the foundations of which – as so often happened after the Moors had
been driven out – the Portuguese again built a church.

Gothic, Renaissance and Baroque features can all be found on the cathedral. Its Gothic origins can be seen mainly on the entrance dooorways. The
north side is unusual in that there is no uniform area of wall, instead it is
made up of three side-chapels, the centre one of which has a dome.

The interior (open: Mon.–Fri. 10am–noon) of the church which was
rebuilt in the 18th c. is striking as a result of its light and almost hall-like
character. It has three aisles each separated almost imperceptibly from its
neighbour by three slender columns. The choir has a coffered barrel
vaulted ceiling. António Pereira da Silva, Bishop of the Algarve from 1704
to 1715, had his tomb built in the Capela de Santo Lenho on the right near
the chancel. The side walls of the cathedral are asymmetrical with three or
four side chapels of quite different dimensions. The tile-cladding in the
chapels is predominantly 18th c. The Baroque organ above the entrance to
the high choir is striking; it was painted by Francisco Cordeiro between
1716 and 1751.

Continue by way of the south-west corner of the Largo da Sé to the Arco da   Arco da Porta
Porta Nova, the second preserved gate in the old town wall. It was built in   Nova
1630 and restored in 1992. The Arco da Porta Nova leads directly to the sea.
Ferries to the offshore islands leave from here, and the railway line from
Vila Real de Santo António to Lagos runs past here.

From the Largo da Sé it is also worth making a detour through the arched
gateway at the end of Rua do Arco. A courtyard leads to the architecturally
tasteful "Arco" gallery.

East of the cathedral lies the little Praça Afonso III. A memorial to the king,   Museu
during whose reign the Moors were driven out of Faro and other Algarve   Arqueológico e
towns, has been erected on a lawned area in the centre.   Lapidar Infante
Dom Henrique

On the south side lies the relatively plain façade of the former Convent of
Nossa Senhora da Assunção, a house of Poor Clares endowed in 1518 by
Dona Leonor, the third wife of Manuel I, and completed in 1561 to plans by
the architect Diogo Pires. The small two-storey cloister is very attractive.
Since 1973 the Archaeological Museum has been housed in a part of the
building around the cloister (open: Mon.–Fri. 9am–noon and 2–5pm). On
display are some Roman finds – busts, gravestones, glass and coins – as
well as architectural fragments mainly from the Manueline period. The
most beautiful Roman exhibits are a bust of the Emperor Hadrian from the
2nd c. A.D. and one of the Empress Agrippina Minor from the 1st c. A.D., both
finds from Milreu. A Roman mosaic which was uncovered in Rua Infante d.
Henrique dates from the 3rd c.

Further rooms surrounding the cloister house the very comprehensive
private collection of the diplomat and art-lover Ferreira d'Almeida. Particular items on display are 19th c. paintings, including some portraits of
members of his circle of friends, 18th c. prints, old views of Lisbon and
Coimbra, porcelain, silver and glass. There is also a small museum section
in which paintings by mainly Portuguese artists are displayed, including
views of the Algarve from the first decades of the 20th c.

To the east of the convent stands the Arco do Repouso. Tradition has it that,   Arco do Repouso
after seizing Faro, Afonso III first rested here (*repouso* means rest or
repose). In the 18th c. a small prayer-chapel was built into this very beautifully restored gateway. Afonso III is portrayed on several tile-pictures on
the town wall outside the gate, including one showing the taking of the
town.

Cloisters of the former Convent of Poor Clares – now an archaeological museum

Igreja da São Francisco

Continue along Rua D. Teresa and Rua de Caçadores to the Igreja de São Francisco on the strangely inhospitable Largo de Francisco. This square changes dramatically, however, when Faro's annual markets are held here. The Igreja de São Francisco was originally 17th c., but was rebuilt following the earthquake. Military personnel at present occupy the adjoining former Franciscan monastery. The church is open only for fairs. Inside, the azulejo paintings with scenes from the life of São Francisco are very attractive. Another tile-painting shows the Coronation of the Virgin Mary.

Igreja do Pé da Cruz

On the Largo do Pé stands a little 17th c. church of the same name. It is thought to have been built on the site of a former synagogue.

Alameda João de Deus

Those seeking a little rest are recommended to walk to the Alameda João de Deus. This park is beautifully laid out with flower-beds, tall trees, ornamental ponds and a basket-ball pitch, and there are small kiosks in which to sit and enjoy a drink. The park is named after perhaps the best known Portuguese educationalist on whose model – related to the Montessori method of teaching – a large number of kindergartens were established in Portugal.

Museu Etnográfico Regional

Also worth a visit is the Museu Etnográfico Regional (open: Mon.–Fri. 9.30am–12.30pm) on the busy Praça da Liberdade. Anyone interested in knowing more about everyday life and culture in the Algarve before tourism took over and how the region looked in the early decades of this century will particularly enjoy seeing the photographs and everyday objects on display in this lovingly assembled collection. Especially interesting are the photographs showing old town views and landscapes which have now disappeared for ever. Preserved on film are Algarvios at work in the saltworks, in the fields, fishing, weaving baskets, washing clothes and transporting water. There is also a picture of a genuine donkey-

Portuguese Coffee-house Culture

A true coffee-house culture is probably the last thing you would expect to find in Portugal. And there isn't one either – at least not in the classical Austrian sense of the term. What you will find however, is a genuine coffee-house culture Portuguese-style. Cafés have always played an important role in Portuguese public life, something that is perhaps seldom found abroad. A certain set would meet in the café, people who felt themselves linked by age, profession, sport, political leanings or other factors. The men met in one café, the women in another. They drank a *bica*, a *galão* or a clear *medronho* and simply chatted or held more serious discussions. For the most part it was adherents of a certain political persuasion who came together in one café, while in another café on the next corner sat the "opposition". It was sufficient just to order a bica (a small cup of black coffee) in order to be allowed to occupy a table for a whole morning.

A piece of this culture still lives on in the "Aliança" in Faro. It is one of the oldest cafés in Portugal, having been established by the merchant José Pedro da Silva in 1908. At that time it was considerably smaller than it is today. Over the years additional rooms have been built on, and as a particular feature a sort of kiosk was built in which newspapers and magazines were sold and from which telephone calls could be made, and the remains of this still exist. Shortly after the turn of the century there were several good coffee-houses in Faro, but the Aliança is the only one to have survived. Its interior fittings and fixtures are no longer the originals, these having been destroyed by fire in the 1920s. However, the rooms have been beautifully restored; stucco decorates the ceilings, and the walls have again been clad in heavy wood panelling. From that date, too, are the wrought-iron tables with marble tops. Being the first café in Faro, the Aliança also served drinks on the pavement. At that time the Praça de Dom Francisco Gomes had a completely different atmosphere from that of today. It was the scene of much that went on in public life – demonstrations, parades and rallies were held in the square, and patrons of the Aliança had a "ringside seat".

In its history the Aliança has seen some illustrious guests. Cavaco Silva, for many years prime minister of Portugal, was a frequent visitor during his student days, and Simone de Beauvoir came here in 1942 as did Lídia Jorge. The poets Fernando Pessoa and Mário Sá-Carneiro and the multi-talented artist Almada Negreiros were also among its patrons, although they met mainly in Lisbon, but often travelled south. And of course Cândido Guerreiro, one of the few Algarve poets from the village of Alte, came here too.

When the "Aliança" came into contact with the artistic sets it – like the "Brasileira" café in Lisbon – provided the painters, graphic artists and caricaturists with space in which to exhibit. It is no doubt from this tradition that the "photo gallery" has developed, which today is very popular with visitors. On display are photographs of the Algarve as it no longer is. In a considerable number of now yellowing black and white photos visitors can get an idea of the sea-side towns and the inland villages as they were before the region changed in appearance.

cart used as an *aguadeiro*, or water-carrier, as well as several items of fishing and agricultural equipment. Last but not least, some rooms from Algarve houses have been faithfully reproduced.

Igreja de São Pedro

In the northern part of the inner town, in the little square of the same name, stands the Igreja de São Pedro. It was built in the 16th c. to replace a church to St Peter, when the development of this part of Faro led to the formation of a new community. A figure of São Pedro is carved into the Renaissance doorway. The interior is three-aisled, the choir being spanned by a barrel-vaulted roof, and in the first chapel in the right-hand aisle can be seen a tile-painting reassembled after the earthquake.

★Igreja do Carmo, Capela dos Ossos

Near the Igreja de São Pedro to the north is the Largo de Carmo. on which stands the Igreja do Carmo, a Baroque church built in 1719 and flanked by two low campaniles. In this church a meeting was held in 1808 to plan the revolt against the Napoleonic occupation of the town.

The interior is dominated by the over-extravagant use of *talha dourada* on the high altar and side altars. Simpler, on the other hand, is the sacristy where various statues of Christ are displayed in small wooden niches. Notice also the wooden ceiling of the sacristy with its 24 differently painted tablets.

The sacristy leads out to a cemetery and the Capela dos Ossos (Bone Chapel), dedicated in 1816, which is known far beyond the boundaries of Faro (open: Mon.–Sat. 10am–1pm and 3–6pm). The vaulted ceiling and walls are ''decorated'' with human bones and skulls. The chapel was built by monks, and the skeletons come from earlier graves in the cemetery.

Mercado

Outside the actual commercial district and to the east of the Igreja do Carmo lies Faro's indoor market which is open in the mornings. On sale are fish, meat, vegetables and fruit.

Capela de Santo António do Alto

On a small hillock on the eastern edge of town stands the Capela de Santo António do Alto. The adjoining museum, which houses a collection in-

Igreja do Carmo with . . .   *. . . the Bone Chapel*

cluding portraits of St Anthony and books about him, is closed at present. The view from the church courtyard is now blocked by new buildings, but down in the inner courtyard visitors can obtain a key and climb the church tower.

The Museu Marítimo Almirante Ramalho Ortigão (open: Mon.–Fri. 9.30am–12.30pm and 2–5pm) in the north-west corner of the harbour basin houses a collection of exhibits on the theme of "The Sea" in the widest sense. Various ships' models – from the caravelle to the steamship – are displayed, together with information about various methods of catching sardines, cod and squid or octopus, and visitors can also admire a small shell collection.

Museu Marítimo Almirante Ramalho Ortigão

Those who feel in need of a rest and refreshment after a tour of the town have plenty of opportunity to enjoy these in the centre of Faro. Among the many cafés and restaurants the Café Aliança on the Praça D. Francisco Gomes, on the corner of Rua 1° de Maio, is the richest in tradition. It is one of the oldest cafés anywhere in Portugal, having been opened in 1908 (see Baedeker Special "Portuguese Coffee-house Culture").

Café Aliança

Surroundings

The municipal beach is the Praia de Faro, about 10km by road from the town centre. It is reached along the same road which leads to the airport. Shortly before the airport turn right and proceed over a small bridge direct to the beach which is a kilometre in length from east to west.

★Praia de Faro

There is a ferry link from Faro to the Ilha da Barreta, a spit of land lying off the lagoon islands. The boats leave from the landing-stage near the Porta Nova (Centro Histórico).

Ilha da Barreta

Lagoa
C 7

Capital of the administrative district of Lagoa
Population: 6500

The little town of Lagoa lies 8km east of Portimão. Also 8km away, but to the north, is Silves, the old capital of the Algarve, and it is 5km from Lagoa to the coast at Carvoeiro. The busy N125 passes to the south of the town, so Lagoa has remained a typical little Portuguese town.

Situation and importance

The Lagoa region is well known as a wine-producing area. It is one of the last wine districts to have survived in the Algarve. A large proportion of the Algarve farmers used to earn their living from viniculture, but when with the onset of tourism land prices went up many of them took the opportunity to sell. In the countryside surrounding Lagoa relatively heavy red wines are produced. They include the dry "Algar Seco" and "Aguardente Afonso III", which is stored in oak casks and drunk as an aperitif. Lighter wines of certified origin and quality are sold under the "Lagoa" label, young country wines under the name "Porche's". Wines can be tasted and purchased at a wine merchant's on the edge of town (Adega Cooperativa de Lagoa, on the N125).

Wine-producing region

Not much is known about the history of Lagoa. Only the name gives a clue as to the earlier situation of the town; Lagoa means lagoon or inland sea and so it is assumed that there was once a stretch of water here on the banks of which a settlement grew up.

History

Lagoa is not a particularly attractive town. Nevertheless it is worth a brief visit, as here visitors can obtain an idea of what Portuguese everyday life is

Townscape

really like, something they will not find in the nearby tourist centres. On the Praça da República, a little way away from the hurly-burly of the main street, is a busy indoor market which is worth seeing.

Sights

Igreja Matriz

In the Igreja Matriz, the main façade of which dates from the 19th c., can be seen a statue of Nossa Senhora da Luz by the major Portuguese sculptor Machado de Castro. The church forecourt is planted with jacaranda and araucaria trees, and in the centre is a memorial to the soldiers who died in the colonial wars in Guinea, Mozambique amd Angola.

Torre-Mirante

In the building of the former Convento de São José near the parish church there is now a gallery in which temporary exhibitions are held. The Torre-Mirante, the bell-tower of the old convent with its characteristic narrow row of windows, spans the small street.

Surroundings

Estômbar

Estômbar is a small country town prettily situated on a hill 3km west of Lagoa. José Joaquim de Sousa Reis, who went down in Algarve history under the name ''Remexido'' (see Famous People), was born here in 1797. He was the leader of a group of monarchists who terrorised many places in the Algarve and in southern Alentejo in the struggles against the liberal forces during the civil wars of the early 19th c.

Estômbar church, situated on a slight hill, is very attractive. It has a Baroque façade with a well-preserved 16th c. Manueline portal.

Between Estômbar and Lagoa lies the ''Slide and Splash'' aquapark (see Practical Information, Aquaparks) which is particularly attractive to younger visitors.

The showpiece of the Church of Estômbar: the Manueline Doorway

Lagos

Capital of the administrative district of Lagos
Population: 11,000

The town of Lagos lies on the south coast of the Algarve in the western section known as the rocky Algarve. It is barely 40km from here to Cabo de São Vicente (Cape St Vincent), the south-westernmost point of the European mainland. The N125, part of which is an expressway, provides a rapid road link with Faro, 90km away, and the international airport, while the railway line which serves the whole coast as far as the Spanish frontier at Vila Real starts in Lagos.

Situation and importance

The Ribeira de Bensatum enters the Atlantic near Lagos; the river narrows just before its mouth and has been made into a channel. Lagos lies at the western end of a wide bay, the Baia de Lagos, which to the south-west is protected by the Ponte de Piedade and in the east extends as far as Portimão. In the north-east of the town the flat Meia Praia stretches over several kilometres, while the coastline south and west of Lagos, on the other hand, consists of bizarre rock formations and small, sandy rock encircled bays which make this region so attractive to tourists.

All the countryside around Lagos is tourist-orientated. To the east holiday centres continue to increase, although a few kilometres to the west of Lagos it is much more peaceful. Lagos is the last large town on the west of the Algarve coast. The hinterland becomes increasingly more barren; near Lagos there are still fig and almond trees, but further west the delightful garden-like Algarve landscape of the central and eastern parts increasingly gives way to scrubland.

The tourist infrastructure in and around Lagos is excellent. There are numerous apartment blocks, hotels, guest houses, private houses offering bed and breakfast as well as camp sites. Restaurants and cafés abound in

The attractive waterfront outside Lagos tourist centre

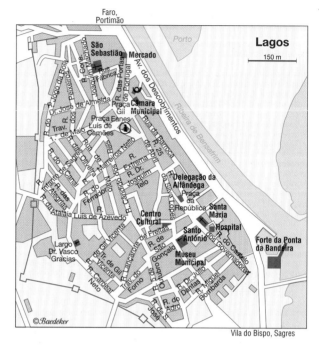

Faro,
Portimão

Lagos
150 m

©Baedeker

Vila do Bispo, Sagres

Lagos and near the beaches. With all that, however, some of the population still make their living from trade and fishing. The main fish caught are tuna and sardines. Near the fish harbour in Lagos there is a yacht station which was only completed in 1995.

History

Historically speaking, the town of Lagos is one of the richest in the Algarve. The Phoenicians established an important trading centre here as long ago as the 1st c. B.C. Lagos was predestined for a base of that kind; for traders from the Mediterranean who sailed the whole of the Iberian Atlantic coast Lagos Bay offered the first sheltered harbour when coming from the west and the last when coming from the Mediterranean. The Greeks and Carthaginians, too, used this favourable anchorage. In Roman times, from the 2nd c. B.C., the town was known as "Lacobriga". Under the Moors it was named "Zawaya", meaning fountain or lake. Under Abderraman the Moors began to protect the town with strong walls. In 1189 it was taken by Portuguese troops led by Sancho I and supported by German and English soldiers, and two years later it was recaptured by the Moors.

The town was finally taken by the Portuguese during the reign of Afonso III in the middle of the 13th c. From then onwards it was called Lagos, from the Portuguese "lago" (lake). Lagos was ceded to Bishop Dom Roberto as a territorial possession and developed into an important centre in south Portugal. In the 13th c. and again in the 14th c. under Afonso IV the town walls were rebuilt to withstand Moorish attacks. In the second half of the 14th c., under Pedro I, the town was given a new form of legal administration making it independent of Silves, which at that time was the more important town.

The town's real heyday was in the 15th and early 16th c. Lagos was the departure harbour and thus the centre for the great voyages of conquest and discovery which at that time made Portugal one of the major countries in Europe. Large numbers of shipyards were built where the famous Portuguese caravelles were constructed, their designs being drawn up in nearby Sagres under Henry the Navigator. In 1434 the navigator Gil Eanes (see Famous People), who was born in Lagos, set out from his home port on what was to be the first voyage by a European round Cape Bojador in West Africa. Great riches came to Lagos as a result of the numerous discoveries made, the booty plundered and the new trading links established. There was also trade in human flesh – the first slave auctions were held in Lagos in 1444.

Although the town was made the capital of the Algarve in 1577 it had by then already begun to lose much of its former importance. A large proportion of the Portuguese caravelles were no longer launched in Lagos but in Belém near Lisbon. The real decline of Lagos, however, went hand in hand with that of Portugal as a whole. For over 100 years Portugal and Spain had been the leaders in sailing the seas of the world, but failed to use the resultant riches to their best advantage. Money was spent building large numbers of prestigious buildings while the nation's general prosperity suffered. In 1578 King Sebastião I sailed from Lagos in an attempt to undertake a crusade in North Africa. He was killed in the first battle of Alcácer-Kibir and in the resultant dispute over succession to the throne Spain occupied the whole of Portugal.

During the 60 years when Spain ruled Portugal in the 16th/17th c. Lagos became a second-rate town. In 1755 the heavy earthquake caused much destruction and the resultant flood inundated the lower quarters of the town. One year later Faro superseded Lagos as the capital of the Algarve, and Lagos became little more than a provincial township. When tourism made an impact in the second half of this century Lagos regained some of its importance.

The outer districts of Lagos are unattractive, with skyscrapers and large blocks of flats. The immediate suburbs are also heavily populated and not very inviting. The centre of Lagos is far more attractive. Although geared to tourism it has retained its own particular charm. In many places the Old Town is still surrounded by the medieval walls. It is also worthwhile strolling through the side streets of the inner town off the main steets. Here Lagos is not particularly colourful or picturesque, but a plain residential town. A small area in the centre around the Praça Gil Eanes and the Praça da República has been made into a pedestrian zone. There are numerous shops as well as restaurants and cafés where visitors can sit outside and watch the world go by. With all that, however, Lagos has not over-exaggerated the tourist side. Locals sit here together with visitors and live their lives as they have always done. The coast road between the harbour channel and the inner town was opened in 1961 and is known as the Avenida dos Descobrimentos (Avenue of Discoveries).

★Townscape

Sights

Sights in Lagos are limited to a few buildings in the town centre. The setting-out point can be the central Praça Gil Eanes. The Igreja de São Sebastião just north of the square is worth visiting. Then proceed south and down the pedestrian street to the Praça da República, followed by a detour to the sea and along the shore to the Ponta da Bandeira fortress. Finally, visit the well-known Igreja de Santo António and the Museu Municipal, and then continue in a westerly direction to the town wall. Pass through the town gate in order to experience the totally different atmosphere outside the walls. Then return through the small, quiet streets of the western inner town to the setting-out point. Alternatively, a tour of Lagos can equally well begin outside the town gate.

Tour

The Praça Gil Eanes is one of the two main squares in the centre of Lagos. In the middle stands a well-known statue of the "longed for" King Sebastiao

Praça Gil Eanes

Santa Maria Church in the Praça da República

(see Famous People). Dom Sebastiao set out from Lagos to conquer North Africa, but never returned. The statue was carved in 1973 by the famous Portuguese sculptor João Cutileiro. On the east side of the square stands the Town Hall, and a little further on the main post office. Those who are here in the morning should not fail to visit the indoor market, built in 1924 on the marine promenade. All kinds of fresh fish are sold here every day.

Igreja de São Sebastião

From the Praça Gil Eanes the street sweeps round via the little Praça Luis de Camóes to the Igreja de São Sebastião somewhat further north. Steps lead up to the attractive church forecourt. A start was made on building the church in the 15th c., but a lot of changes were made later. In 1755 it was badly damaged in the earthquake. Still standing is the 16th c. Renaissance doorway on which can be seen the Portuguese crown, and this is repeated further up on the façade. The three-aisled interior is divided by tall pillars with beautiful capitals. It is said that the crucifix on the left of the altar was taken to Alcácer-Kibar and is one of the few items saved from that fateful battle and brought back to Portugal. The portrait of Nossa Senhora de Glória in one of the side-chapels comes from a wrecked ship. A small garden next to the church leads to a charnel-house built into the side wall.

Praça da Réublica

A second central square is the Praça da République at the southern end of the pedestrian zone. The square opens onto the Avenida dos Descobrimentos and the harbour channel. On a stone base stands a statue of Henry the Navigator – gazing out to sea. This memorial was erected in 1960 on the 500th anniversary of his death (see Baedeker Special, "Henry in the Light of Research").

Igreja de Santa Maria

On the southern side of the square stands the Igreja de Santa Maria, the successor to an older 14th c. church which was rebuilt after the earthquake. In 1460 Henry the Navigator was interred in the older church, but later his coffin was moved to the Capela do Fundador in Batalha.

Behind the church stands the former Governor's Palace, which is partially integrated into the town wall. Until 1756 the province of the Algarve was administered from here.

Palácio dos Governadores

The northern side of the Praça da República is taken up by the narrow building of the Delegação da Alfândega (customs authority). It was here that the first auction of black African slaves was held in 1444. They were manacled under the arcades where potential buyers could inspect them.

Delegação da Alfândega

Continuing south along the Avenida dos Descobrimentos parts of the old town wall can be seen. There is a memorial to Gil Eanes who was born in Lagos and in 1434 set out from here to sail round Cape Bojador. At one place along the wall a Manueline window has been preserved; it formed part of the Governor's Palace and it is said that it was from here that Dom Sebastião heard his last mass before sailing to North Africa.

Avenida dos Descobrimentos/ Ponta da Bandeira

The broad and palm-lined Avenida dos Descobrimentos leads along the bank of the harbour channel as far as the Ponte da Banderia. The fortified Ponta da Bandeira with its four round corner towers was built in the 17th c. to defend the harbour. The narrow drawbridge provides access to the Museu Maritimo in the interior.

Fishing boats lie at anchor in the Ribeira de Bensafrim which is canalised here – only the name of the Avenida remains as a reminder of the former importance of the Lagos harbour exit.

The Igreja de Santo António is one of the most impressive churches in the Algarve. It was built as the regimental church of the troops stationed in Lagos whose patron saint was St Anthony. Exactly when it was founded is not known, but it is thought that it was built during the reign of João V. between 1706 and 1750. After the earthquake it was rebuilt in accordance with the old plans.

Igreja de Santo António

The small interior is in typical Baroque style. It is almost completely clad with *talha dourada*, the gilded carved wood with which church walls and altars throughout Portugal were decorated in the 18th c. after the long-awaited discovery of the gold mines in Brazil. The altar wall is particularly opulent. On the high altar stands a statue of Santo António with an officer's sash, swagger-stick and the child Jesus on his arm. Between the Solomon pillars St Elói can be seen in the niches on the left and St Joseph on the right.

The side walls above the base are also clad in *azulejos* richly embellished with *talha dourada*. The painted panels depict scenes from the life of St Anthony, including the healing of a blind man and the replacing of a severed foot. The many wooden cherubs and figures under small corbels who appear to be bearing the weight of the pilasters warrant closer attention. Surmounting all this gilded magnificence is a barrel-vaulted roof painted with the Portuguese coat-of-arms. Before leaving take another look at the underside of the gallery; the three virtues – faith, hope and charity – look down from all the gilding upon those entering and leaving the church.

Since 1934 the building adjoining the church has housed the very original collection of the Museu Municipal de Lagos (open: Tues.–Sun. 9.30am–12.30pm and 2–5pm). As well as a collection of azulejos and some religious exhibits there is a small archaeological section where finds from the Neolithic, Bronze and Iron Ages are displayed. There are a few Roman finds, including a bust of the Emperor Gallienus from Milreu, together with ceramics, receptacles and oil lamps from the Moorish period. The history of Lagos is also portrayed, including a collection of German inflationary banknotes. Finally, the whole of the Algarve is represented by way of everyday items and craft objects made from agave and coconut threads, wood and ceramics, small dolls and the chimneys typical of the region.

Museu Municipal da Lagos

Those interested in modern art should visit the Culture Centre opened in 1992 (open: daily 10am–midnight, in winter to 8pm only). Theatrical and

Centro Cultural

A Horse for Ten Men

The year 1444, when slaves were first sold in Lagos, was not a very laudable time for Portugal. The Portuguese had just discovered the mouth of the Senegal and had come upon black Africans for the first time. As evidence of the landing and almost as a sort of souvenir from this African region some of the natives were forced to make the degrading voyage back to Portugal. In 1444 the black slaves were exhibited in Lagos just as some profitable trading items might have been.

The slave trade then quickly became a very lucrative business. Together with trade in spices, the selling of slaves was for a time Portugal's main source of income. In the 16th century one third of the cost of its sea voyages and expansion in Africa, Asia and America was financed by this trade in human lives. After the discovery and conquest of Brazil the Portuguese also took African slaves to South America. For a long time the Cape Verde Islands served as a summer camp for Africans and were the centre of the slave trade between Africa, Europe and America.

The former Slave Market in Lagos

The black Africans' misfortune lay in the fact that they were strong and robust. Work of all kinds – in the house and in the fields – fell on them. The sparsely populated Algarve in particular needed an additional work-force. At the time of Portuguese expansion many Portuguese left their homeland to trade or seek employment in the newly discovered countries, which they knew because as sea-farers they had seen them on voyages or had been shipwrecked there. Those in need of workers made their way to the Praça da République in Lagos. Here slaves could be obtained by barter; in exchange for a horse, for example, one could obtain ten men, although bartering values varied according to requirements and "quality". As a rule slaves baptised into the Christian faith were worth more than heathens.

Before the black Africans came to Lagos to be sold they would have endured terrible voyages. After being captured and torn from the bosom of their families at night, they were transported across the sea in overladen ships under inhuman conditions. Because of the unhygienic conditions and lack of medical care one in every four died on the voyage.

English Quakers were the first publicly to denounce the brutality of this enterprise. Many Jesuits in Portugal followed their example, but it was not until the 18th century that trade in human beings was finally prohibited. In the Cape Verde Islands, which then still belonged to Portugal, such trade was still going on as recently as 1878.

dance performances are arranged as well as exhibitions. A cafeteria adjoins the centre.

Surroundings

The beaches near Lagos provide extremely charming scenery, but are usually crowded in the summer. North-east of Lagos the Meia Praia curves gently for several kilometres around the Baia de Lagos. It offers plenty in the way of water sports. Access to the beach is by bus or a small boat from Lagos, or alternatively on foot past Lagos railway station.

Meia Praia

In the south of the town are the little Praia do Camiló and the well-known Praia de Dona Ana with small rocky islands lying offshore. The latter is the most beautiful of the bays around Lagos, although it too gets very crowded in the high season. Steps lead down to the Praia de Dona Ana which is divided into two small bays by a rocky promontory. At high tide it is not possible to get from one bay to the other without getting wet feet. Above the Praia de Dona Ana are various large hotels, as well as some food stalls and restaurants.

Praia do Camiló, ★Praia de Dona Ana

From the Praia de Dona Ana visitors can drive or walk – there is a path here and there at the top of the cliffs – the 2km to Ponta da Piedade in the south. Here are what are probably the most beautiful rock formations anywhere in the Algarve. They can be seen from the shore but better still from the sea. Boats to Ponta da Piedade sail from Lagos (from where there are also boat trips to various caves nearby). The Ponta da Piedade is an impressive section of foothills falling steeply away into the sea at the southern end of the Baia de Lagos. The rocks are 20m high at their highest point. Rocky overhangs, crags and towers form a beautiful yet bizarre fantasy landscape. Marking the entry and exit to the Bay of Lagos is a lighthouse with steps down into the sea.

★★Ponta da Piedade

To the west of the Ponte da Piedade stretches the Praia do Porto de Mós with bars and beach cafés, a wide sheltered bay with few breakers but good conditions for water sports. Also there are small bays everywhere which can be reached only by boat and are therefore usually quiet.

Praia do Porto de Mós

Luz is a former small fishing village about 5km west of Lagos which has now developed into a tourist centre. It boasts the beautiful Praia de Luz where there are good conditions for water sports – surfing, water-skiing, diving or pedaloes. Above the beach is a pretty restaurant housed in a former fortress and from where there is a fine view of the sea.

Luz

The village of Odiáxere lies 6km from Lagos. It has suffered badly from the N125 which passes straight through it. Once having left the main road, however, there is a sense of how rural and peaceful it must once have been here. Odiáxere has a charming village church which was rebuilt after the earthquake. The Manueline doorway of the old church has been preserved. Immediately behind the church sees the beginning of some fertile countryside with gardens and smallholdings.

Odiáxere

In Odiáxere a road branches off the N125 northwards to Barragem da Bravura or Barragem de Odiáxere. For about 10km the road winds through some superb countryside, first through meadows and orange-groves and then over a plateau and a sea of white and yellow roses. Towards the end of the journey the landscape becomes somewhat more hilly and suddenly the road comes to an artificial lake surrounded by forests of eucalyptus trees. The Barragem da Bravura forms part of a row of such reservoirs which Salazar had built in the late 1950s and which are popular with the Portuguese for a day out but not so attractive to tourists. There is a beautiful viewing-point with a view over the lake, and a small restaurant. Barragem da Bravura is not suitable for bathing or water sports.

Barragem da Bravura

Bizarre rock formations on the Algarve coast

Loulé   C 12

Capital of the administrative district of Loulé
Population: 9000

Situation and importance

Loulé, lying 15km north-west of Faro in the Barrocal, the foothills of the Algarve mountains, is surrounded by hilly countryside with many fig, almond, olive and fruit trees; in spring the fields are full of poppies. The region's beauty has persuaded many Portuguese and foreigners to build week-end retreats or holiday homes here. As a result this region which for a long time remained unspoiled has become increasingly populated in recent years.

Loulé is a busy centre in the middle of which is the colourful and bustling Saturday market which attracts people from far and wide. A characteristic feature is the large number of individual craftsmen still working here. Blacksmiths, silversmiths, potters and saddlers producing artistic or every-day objects have their workshops in Loulé, particularly in Rua 9 de Abril and Rua da Barbaça.

History

From archaeological finds that have been made it is assumed that the Loulé region was inhabited in Celtic times. There are also traces of Romans, Visigoths and Moors. How Loulé was actually founded is not clear. Some researchers believe it was founded by the Carthaginians in 404 B.C., while others hold the view that it dates from Roman times. Under the Moors it was named "Al-Ulyá", which probably became Laulé and then later Loulé. One legend has it that the town's name is derived from a laurel tree, *laurus* in Latin, which is said to have stood near the castle. In 1294 Loulé was taken by Portuguese troops under Dom Paio Peres Correia. The latest important event in its history was being granted its town charter in 1988.

★Townscape

Loulé is a very attractive little town with some magnificent, almost city-like avenues and squares and a pretty Old Town centre full of interesting nooks and crannies. The little whitewashed houses in the Old Town make parts of this quarter seem almost like theatrical backdrops. More vibrant, on the other hand, are the neighbouring streets round the Praça da República, Largo Gago Coutinho and Avenida José da Costa Mealha. There are numerous shops in Rua 5 de Outubro. a pedestrian zone.

Carnival, Almond-blossom Festival

At carnival time Loulé becomes a scene of colourful confusion – the little town is famous throughout Portugal for its lavish carnival celebrations which include the Almond Blosssom Festival. The carnival floats are literally covered in almond blossoms made of paper.

Sights

Tour

A short tour of Loulé could begin at the Largo Bernando Lopes near the tourist information office, continuing past the old castle walls and further south through the narrow streets of the Old Town to the Igreja Matriz de São Clemente. From there go via Rua Engenheiro Duarte Pacheco and Avenida Marçal Pacheco to the Igreja da Misericórdia and – after making a detour to see the remains of the Convento da Graça – to the indoor market. Visitors should then visit the pilgrimage chapel of Nossa Senhora da Piedade outside Loulé to the west.

Castelo

A few remnants of the walls which once marked the boundary of the Old Town are all that remain of the ancient castle. Near the tourist information office some stone steps lead up to the castle walls, from where there is a beautiful view of Loulé and the surrounding countryside as far as the sea.

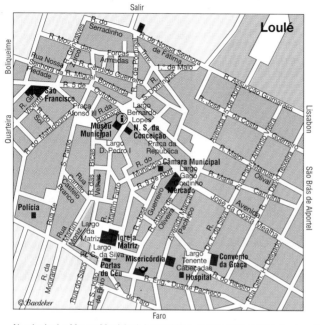

Nearby is the Museu Municipal, housed in a section of the tastefully re-stored Convento do Espirito Santo (open: Mon.–Fri. 9am–12.30pm and 2–5pm). The convent was founded in the late 17th c., partly destroyed in the 1755 earthquake and dissolved in 1836.

The Museu Municipal consists mainly of one room in which are dis-played traditional Algarve kitchen fittings and utensils. Other rooms, which originally would have been the convent kitchen and refectory, now house the municipal art gallery.

Convento do Espirito Santo/ Museu Municipal

Opposite the convent can be seen the simple façade of the Ermida de Nossa Senhora da Conceição. The chapel was built in the middle of the 17th c. in gratitude for the regaining of independence from Spain. The striking altar, decorated with *talha dourada*, was carved by a sculptor from Faro in the middle of the 18th c. The cladding of the interior walls with tile-paintings depicting scenes from the life of Mary dates from the same period.

Ermida de Nossa Senhora da Conceição

Loulé's main church lies in the Old Town between Largo da Silva and Largo da Matriz. It can trace its origins back to the second half of the 13th c., and was probably commissioned by the archbishop of Braga in north Portugal. Parts of it were destroyed in the 1755 earthquake and it suffered further earthquake damage in 1856 and 1969. First to catch the eye in the three-aisled church are the capitals on the columns. Some of the side chapels were built in the 16th c., including the one with a Manueline pointed arch and dedicated to São Brás and that with Manueline ribbed vaulting dedi-cated to Nossa Senhora da Consolação.

Igreja Matriz de São Clemente

The gardens in front of the church invite a rest. Tall palm-trees provide welcome shade and there are beautiful flowers to admire, as well as a good view of the newer part of the town.

Loulé

Portas do Céu and . . .   *. . . archway of the Convento da Graça*

Portas do Céu

South of the church leave the Old Town through one of the old town gates, the Portas do Céu (Gate of Heaven). A small chapel, the Portas do Céu Chapel, is built into the archway of the gate.

Igreja da Misericórdia

From here, access to the Igreja da Misericórdia is by way of Rua Engenheiro Duarte Pacheco and Avenida Marçal Pacheco. The Manueline doorway, which is reached by steps with a granite crucifix, stands out clearly against the façade. Thick ropes carved in stone surround the finely-worked frame of the doorway.

Convento da Graça

Although little remains of the former Convento da Graça, what is left is impressive. Between new houses a relatively well-preserved Gothic arched doorway still stands.

★ Mercado

Loulé's interesting indoor market, built in the Neo-Moorish style, stands on the busy Largo Gago Coutinho. A daily market is held here, with fruit, vegetables, fish and poultry offered for sale, and the neighbouring streets are full of hustle and bustle.

Igreja de São Francisco

The Igreja da São Francisco outside the Old Town is known for its pelican-shaped tabernacle.

Surroundings

★ Capela de Nossa Senhora da Piedade

2km west of Loulé. on the Boliqueime road, stands the Capela de Nossa Senhora da Piedade. A pilgrim's way leads up the hill, on the top of which stands the old Renaissance chapel housing the statue of the Senhora da Piedade which is carried in procession every year two weeks after Easter. The chapel has a wooden vaulted ceiling, and above the altar hangs a small lantern. It is always open, and during the week people from Loulé often visit their patron saint. On the walls are scenes of Christ's agony. A large, gleaming white domed church has been built near the old chapel where mass is celebrated for the pilgrims. From the church forecourt there is a superb view of the hilly Algarve landscape to the north and of the sea far away to the south.

10km to the north-east of Loulé, in a sparsely populated region, lies the village of Querença. The countryside here is less attractive, the fertile Algarve gardens being further to the south. Surrounding Querença is woodland, and the road is lined with expanses of cistus shrubs, while on some hill-tops only macchia grows. The road leads up to the Old Town on a hill and then appears to end at the church forecourt. Actually the little parish church stands at the highest point, and all the village roads lead down from it. With luck the 16th c. church may be open. It has an attractive font and several statues of saints carved by Algarve sculptors. On the broad courtyard in front of the church there are two small restaurants with country cuisine which are popular at weekends. On weekdays they are the only place where the people of Querença can meet in their leisure time. Near Querença, it is worth making a trip to the cave at Salustreira and the spring at Benémola.

Querença

Monchique

A 6

Capital of the administrative district of Monchique
Population: 8000

Monchique is the capital of the Serra da Monchique, the mountain range which marks the boundary between the western Algarve and the Alentejo. The town is 458m above sea-level and nestles in the midst of some pretty wooded countryside. The vegetation includes spruce, eucalyptus, mimosa and strawberry trees.
  The volcanic Serra de Monchique contains several hot springs which are used for healing purposes in the Caldas de Monchique thermal baths. Monchique is a traditional centre for arts and crafts such as textiles, basket-work, wood-carvings and ceramics. This region is also known for the production of "Medronho" brandy made from the fruit of the strawberry tree. However, a large proportion of the population is now employed in service industries along the coast.

Situation and importance

Monchique is picturesquely situated on a hillside. Through the Old Town wind steep streets and narrow lanes, and from everywhere there are superb views of the surrounding mountains. The town itself caters for day visitors and there are plenty of cafés and restaurants most of which do well. Pleasant accommodation can be found in small establishments in the surrounding countryside.

Townscape

Sights

The Largo 5 de Outubro is Monchique's central square, though it is somewhat lacking in atmosphere. There are cafés and an attractive gallery; a modern fountain splashing in the middle of the square represents a *nora*, which formed a part of the irrigation system introduced in the Algarve by the Moors.

Largo 5 de Outubro

The Igreja Matriz, Monchique's small parish church, is worth a visit. Its most striking feature is the 16th c. Manueline entrance door with a five-sectioned fanlight. The three-aisled interior is relatively broad and flat. The tiled frieze is of new *aluzejos*, but depicts a traditional *ponta da diamente* pattern which was very popular in Portugal in the 17th c., while the pillars carry unusual capitals of turned stone bands. On the high altar stands a statue of Nossa Senhora da Conceicão attributed to the famous Portuguese Baroque sculptor Machado de Castro.

Igreja Matriz

Monchique

Igreja de São Sebastião

A little way up from the parish church stands the Igreja de São Sebastião, in which the Senhora do Desterro, the Madonna of Banishment, is revered.

Convento de Nossa Senhora do Desterro

The short walk to the ruins of the Convento de Nossa Senhora do Desterro will be found more rewarding than the neglected ruins themselves. In the town, follow the trail symbols showing a camera and telescope, then once outside the town take the stony woodland path through tall trees. The ruins of the convent, which are reached after a fifteen minute climb from the town centre, are surrounded by old cork-oaks. There is a wonderful view of Monchique from up here.

Surroundings

★Caldas de Monchique

Monchique is famous for its warm springs, the Caldas de Monchique, which are of volcanic origin and lie 6km to the south (see Practical Information, Spas). The Romans knew of the healing properties of the waters and built a thermal bath here named Mons Cicus. The most famous patient who sought a cure here was King João II, but he died shortly after taking the cure (which means nothing, of course!). Dom Sebastião is also said to have visited the Caldas de Monchique.

Bottles of the healing waters of Monchique are on sale all over Portugal. Small though it may be, the Caldas de Monchique is one of the most idyllic and inspiring little places in the Algarve. It has retained a turn-of-the century charm which one would not believe possible a few kilometres away on the coast. The tiny village centre lies in a narrow valley under tall, shady trees, while a quiet square with a café and restaurant invites visitors to rest awhile. The few little houses dotted around, boarding and guest houses, have a cosy and friendly feel about them. Behind the village the hillsides are covered in lush grass and flora which can be enjoyed on a walk from the central square and out alongside the babbling brook; first one will pass a picnic area, then it becomes more isolated.

Caldas de Monchique – a fashionable spa in the early 1920s

Capital of the administrative district of Olhão
Population: 25,000

The town of Olhão lies in the south-east of the Algarve, on the edge of the   **Situation and**
Ria Formosa lagoon region. Between the town and the sea the sand-dune   **importance**
islands of Farol and Culatra extend west almost as far as Faro, while in the
east the island of Armona stretches to the village of Fuzeta.
　　To date tourism has not reached Olhão and the town lives mainly from
fishing. The fishing port on the eastern edge of the town is the largest in the
region; only Portimão in the Faro district can boast comparable catches.
Ships also embark from here on deep-sea fishing expeditions along the
coasts of Africa and Newfoundland.

Compared with other Algarve towns, Olhão is relatively young, and it was   **History**
not until the 14th c. that a fishing village first grew up here. At that time
there were numerous freshwater springs in the Olhão region which were
known as *olhos* (eyes), from which the place gets its name. Numbers of
sea-farers and fishermen used to stop off in the village in order to replenish
their freshwater supplies from the springs. The job of *aquadeiro*, or water-
carrier, was a typical occupation in Olhão for many years.

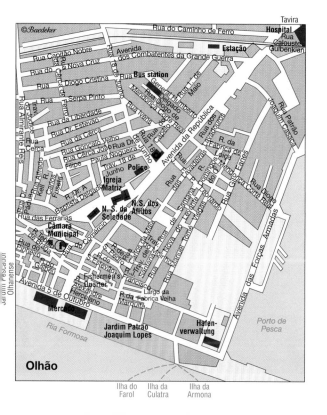

A certain spectacular action on the part of some fishermen has gone down in Portuguese history. In the early 19th c. the people of Olhão took up the fight against the Napoleonic forces in an attempt to regain their independence. After the French had finally been driven out a group of Olhão fishermen set out in a small fishing boat, the "O Bom Sucesso", and crossed the Atlantic to Brazil to bring the good tidings to the exiled royal family. João VI thereupon bestowed on the village the title of "Olhão da Restauração" (Olhão of the Restoration).

The middle of the 19th c. saw an upturn in the town's fortunes as a result of the expanding fishing industry, and the port grew increasingly in importance. As Olhão is so dependent on fishing it has suffered badly from the decline in this section of the economy in recent years.

Townscape

Olhão differs from all other Algarve towns both in its townscape and its general atmosphere. It has been described many times as the most North African of the Algarve towns and a strong Arab influence can certainly be detected. This impression results above all from the characteristic cube-shaped houses; the fishing quarter in particular consists of straight rows of such two or three-storey square dwellings. They are all very similar, but none is exactly the same as any other. Common to all are the *açoteias*, the flat roofs used as terraces. Almost all the roofs also have a small tower up to which the women are said to climb to watch for their menfolk returning from the sea. The North African influence on the architecture can be attributed to the close trading links between Olhão and places on the coast of North Africa. Such styles of building were also regarded as suitable because of the similar climatic conditions. Large parts of the town were built in the 19th c., while newer buildings can be seen further inland towards the N125.

In its general atmosphere the town is perhaps the most unusual that the Algarve coast has to offer. Olhão has an daily life all of its own which has nothing whatsoever in common with the tourist-dominated existence

Typical white cube-shaped houses in Olhão

experienced elsewhere in the Algarve. In the early morning the fishermen roar along to the harbour on their mopeds and after doing their work seek refreshment with a coffee or something stronger in one of the small breakfast bars. Behind it all, however, poverty and social deprivation still exist. Perhaps the visitor will not take to Olhão at first sight – but very soon he or she will be fascinated by the genuine and very typical liveliness of the town.

Sights

There are not very many sights and places of interest in Olhão, it being the atmosphere that holds one's interests more than anything. Those who wish to see some buildings here, however, would do well to follow the main street, the Avenida da República, in the direction of the sea – past the parish church, the Capela de Nossa Senhora dos Aflitos and the Capela de Nossa Senhora da Soledade, and then continue through the pedestrian zone to the two indoor markets and the marine promenade.

Tour

Financed by fishermen, a start was made on building the Igreja Matriz at the end of the 17th c., the foundation stone being laid in 1689. The link with fishing and sea-faring in general is clear from the red navigational light in the seaward side which is lit in the evenings. The single-aisled interior with its barrel-vaulted roof is relatively plain, the most striking feature being the Baroque high altar decorated with *talha dourada*.

A climb up the church tower is a must. From the top there is a magnificent view over the rooftops of Olhão and far into the lagoon countryside and the open sea beyond. As a rule the tower is kept locked, but the verger can be asked for the key.

Igreja Matriz de Nossa Senhora do Rosário

At the rear of the Igreja Matriz will be found the Capela de Nossa Senhora dos Aflitos. This chapel consists of a room open on one side but protected by a grille and with an interior clad with tiles where a number of candles are always burning. Flowers are placed here and stacked up are votive gifts such as wax arms, legs, feet and heads. Fishermen's wives visit this popular chapel to pray for their menfolk's safe return during stormy seas and bad weather in winter.

Capela de Nossa Senhora dos Aflitos

The Capela de Nossa Senhora da Soledade is a single-aisled building with an attractive dome. The Nossa Senhora da Soledade hears the prayers of the lonely.

Capela de Nossa Senhora da Soledade

The Rua do Comércio is the main street in a small pedestrian and shopping zone. The shops are simple and some are quite cheap.

Rua do Comércio

Parallel to the shore lies the Avenida 5 de Outubro. From the town centre go direct to the two indoor markets, where fresh fish, meat, vegetables and fruit are sold each morning. Each of the large halls has four corner towers containing small shops and a café. In the wide alley between the two indoor markets a large open-air market is held on Saturdays and here clothing is also sold.

Mercado

To the west of the market lies this garden dedicated to the fishermen of the town. It has small flower-beds and a playground.

Jardim Pescador Olhanense

Much more attractive is the Jardim Patrão Joaquim Lopes on the east side of the indoor market halls, where visitors can sit on one of the benches and enjoy a view of the mud-flats. Ducks and geese swim in a carefully fenced-in pond, and there is a memorial to the man who gave the gardens their name. A little further away from the town lies the landing-stage for boats going to the islands of Farol, Culatra and Armone.

Jardim Patrão Joaquim Lopes

East of the berth sees the beginning of the port of Olhão. Near the landing-stage lie many small fishing boats and a little further is the large harbour basin with fish-processing works.

Porto

Surroundings

★ Quinta de
Marim/
Parque Natural da
Ria Formosa

The Quinta de Marim, about 1km east of Olhão harbour and near the camp site, is worth a visit (open: daily 9am–12.30pm and 2–5pm). This environmental and conservation centre is a part of the Parque Natural da Ria Formosa. A small information kiosk provides details of the lagoon region of the Ria Formosa, its flora and fauna as well as general information on environmental and conservation issues. Temporary exhibitions are held, and there is an auditorium and library as well as a pleasant cafeteria. The Quinta de Marim cultivates a small area of its own biologically representative piece of countryside. One of the major aims of the centre is the maintenance of the Ria Formosa protected lagoon zone which is becoming increasingly endangered by tourist projects.

In the course of a walk across the terrain several traditional agricultural and fishing techniques can be seen which are not likely to be witnessed anywhere else. These include, for example, an old tunny fishing punt (*barca de atum*) and the interesting tide-driven mill (*moinho de maré*). The latter is the last mill of this kind to have been used much after the Middle Ages. The first tide-driven mill was built in France in the 12th c., and they were first introduced into Portugal in 1290. The Quinta de Marim mill was built in 1885 and in use until 1970. The mills usually included living quarters for the miller and his family and a stable for horses. Normally the Quinta de Marim mill is closed, but the rooms can be seen through the windows.

Excavations carried out in the east of this area have unearthed remains of Roman salt-works. There is also a building here where sick and injured birds are cared for. Finally comes the area used for agriculture where a *nora*, a fountain dating back to Moorish times, can be seen. At one time it was driven by animal power and later mainly by electric motors. Nearby is a breeding centre for the *cao de agua*, which comes from this region and is in danger of dying out. This poodle-like dog was at one time a true companion and helper of the fishermen. It is the only species of dog to have webbed paws. It is also said to be an expert diver down to about 4m.

★ Farol, Culatra,
Armona

These three lagoon islands can be reached by boat from Olhão several times daily from June to September and three times daily in winter. Farol and Culatra, the smallest island, in the west are visited on one trip, while another boat goes to Armona in the east. The boarding-stage is near the harbour in Avenida 5 de Outubro.

All three islands are flat dunes with very good sandy beaches. Few people live on the islands, but there are a few simple restaurants and cafés. Farol, recognisable from afar by its lighthouse, is the most remote of the three islands and can boast only a few small houses and two cafés.

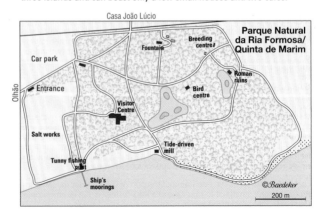
Casa João Lúcio

Parque Natural da Ria Formosa/Quinta de Marim

Fuzeta is a small fishing village about 8km west of Olhão. It lies fairly high and there is a wide view over the mud-flats and the island of Armona. This little village is not strikingly pretty, but on the other hand does give an impression of vibrancy and originality. It has a harbour and an indoor market, and its cubic houses resemble those in Olhão. At the northern end of the village is a typical Portuguese cemetery with graves like small houses laid out in proper little streets.

Fuzeta

North of Olhão lies a beautiful stretch of countryside with fruit plantations, orange groves and small villages. A somewhat larger village typical of this region is Moncarapacho, 8km north-east of Olhão. It boasts two churches, the parish church with a beautiful Renaissance doorway and nearby the Santo Cristo chapel adjoining which is a small open-air museum with an archaeological collection (open by arrangement: tel. 089/9 22 17).

Moncarapacho

North of Moncarapacho stretches the Serra de Monte Figo which rises to a height of 410m at São Miguel. A very narrow little road leads up to the mountain; on a clear day there is a beautiful view from the top over the coastal strip of the eastern Algarve.

Serra de
Monte Figo

Portimão

C 6

Capital of the administrative district of Portimão
Population: 30,000

Portimão lies 60km west of Faro at the mouth of the Rio Arade. To the south, towards the coast, it has expanded so that it almost joins the tourist centre of Praia da Rocha (see entry) with its high-rise hotels. While the whole region south-west and south-east of Portimão is tourist dominated, the northern suburbs are relatively unaffected. This is clearly seen when coming from the Faro direction and crossing the long bridge over the Rio Arade. Looking towards the coast all one can see is a veritable sea of houses, while to the north lie unpopulated hillsides.

Situation and
importance

Apart from the Guadiana, the Rio Arade is the major river in the Algarve. However, over the years the river bottom has become increasingly muddied so that only flat-bottomed boats can navigate it as far as Silves and then only shortly before and after high tide.

In the north of Portimão an iron bridge and an old traffic bridge cross the Arade and lead to the town centre. For many years the latter bridge was the only one across the river and consequently a permanent bottleneck. Eventually the new bridge was built further north and now this takes the N125 expressway.

Together with Faro and Olhão, Portimão is one of the three largest towns in the Algarve. First and foremost it is an industrial and harbour town and a shopping centre only second. For a number of years Portimão was the centre of Portuguese sardine fishing and its highly subsidised processing industry. Until the mid-1970s more than 70 fishing trawlers regularly set sail and fish was processed in a total of 61 factories. After the end of the Salazar regime subsidies were drastically cut. Today there is but one fish-canning factory in Portimão, six trawlers still fish and the river banks are lined with sardine factories which have been forced to close down. In the north of the town are some shipyards.

Tourism also contributes to the economy of Portimão, and there are several hotels and guest houses, numerous restaurants and popular cafés catering mainly for day-trippers coming to Portimão from the nearby tourist centres. The town is a good place for shopping and in the centre north-west of Praça Manuel Teixeira Gomes there is just one shop after another.

Portimão can trace its history back to a Phoenician trading post. Greeks and Carthaginians also settled at the mouth of the Arade, and two names have

History

105

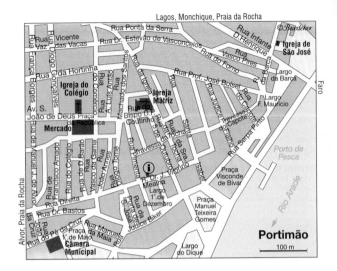

Lagos, Monchique, Praia da Rocha

Portimão

100 m

come down from Roman times, Portus Magnus and Portus Hannibali; which one is correct is in dispute. Under the Moors Portimão was already an important fishing port; the Moors were skilled sailors and set out from Portimão on quite long fishing trips.

In 1242 Portimão, like the neighbouring towns of Silves and Alvor, was captured by Christian knights of the Order of Santiago. In 1476 Afonso V. made a gift of the town to Count Gonçalo Castelo Branco as a reward for for his honourable military service, and at the end of the 15th c. the Count had strong walls built round it. The port of Portimão grew in importance as a result of the voyages of discovery and conquest undertaken in the 15th and 16th c. and ship-building broke all records. Wood for the caravelles was cut from forests on the nearby Monchique mountains. In 1487 Bartolomeu Diaz set out from here on the voyage which was to see the first European sail round the Cape of Good Hope. There was an official embarkation ceremony for him in a sheltered bay on the Rio Arade north of Portimão. After the route to India had been discovered in the early 16th c. ships returned laden with spices and landed in Portimão harbour. Trade flourished.

In the 16th and 17th c. Portimão was attacked by British, Dutch and North African pirates, and for this reason the entrance to the harbour was safeguarded by means of the defensive installations of Fortaleza de São João on the opposite side of the mouth of the Arade, and Fortaleza de Santa Catarina, the remains of which can still be seen near the Praia da Rocha.

The 1755 earthquake caused devastating damage in Portimão as it did in so many other places in the Algarve, and the town took a long time to recover from the disaster. A rapid economic upswing began with the growth of the fishing industry in the middle of the 19th c.

Townscape

Portimão is a vibrant town with an authentic everyday life which is not devoted solely to tourism although foreign visitors do play a part, and one can detect something of the atmosphere of a harbour town around the approach to the old traffic bridge. Here there are many simple cafés and restaurants, small family businesses offering superb fresh fish, especially sardines of course. Further to the south lies an attractively laid out area on the river bank with lovely squares where tourists can while away the time in cafés, and gardens where the children can enjoy rides on the mini-railway.

Azulejos decoration on houses in Portimão

In the busy town centre the buildings are somewhat taller than in other Algarve towns, and in the afternoons the streets are choked with traffic.

Sights

Portimão can boast only a limited number of really interesting places to see. Nevertheless, a stroll through the town is well worthwhile. It is best to begin at the riverside promenade where there are several very different squares, including the Praça Manuel Teixeira Gomes and the Praça Visconde de Bivar. From here pause for a time near Largo 1° de Dezembro to look around the shopping zone, view the Igreja Matriz and perhaps make a detour to the Praça da Republica. Those interested in the harbour area can then return to the river bank and continue north.

Tour

The Praça Visconde de Bivar on the banks of the river is attractively laid out as a small park. From here there is a beautiful view across the Arade to the opposite bank and the town of Ferragudo. The best thing to do is spend a while sitting on a bench or in a café. There is a children's railway which goes through the park and round the statue of the Visconde de Bivar.

Praça Visconde de Bivar

Next to the Praça Visconde de Bivar lies the comparatively plain Praça Manuel Teixeira Gomes, the centre of tourist Portimão. From here there are trips through the grotto and river excursions along the Arade to Silves. Organised walks can be booked here, and there are a number of cafés, including the popular Casa Inglesa which has become the regular haunt of many locals and tourists alike. There is a fountain in the centre of the square with a statue of Teixeira Gomes, a diplomat who was born in Portimão and who was also an author. In 1924 he was elected President of the Republic.

Praça Manuel Teixeira Gomes

The Largo 1° de Dezembro has a completely different atmosphere. Almost rectangular in shape, it is laid out as a small park and has a comfortable feel.

Largo 1° de Dezembro

Portimão

There is a fountain surrounded with beautiful flower-beds. Quite striking are the ten benches with *azulejo* pictures portraying important events in Portuguese history, including the capture of Ceuta on August 21st 1415, the discovery of Brazil by Pedro Álvares Cabral on April 24th 1500, the regaining of independence from Spain in 1640 and the proclamation of the Republic in 1910.

Igreja Matriz

North of the Largo 1° de Dezenbro towers the Igreja Matriz. Before the 1755 earthquake a 14th c. church stood on this site, and its Gothic doorway has been preserved and stands out clearly against the new façade. Note the now weathered capitals portraying various heads. The interior is three-aisled, and there are statues of saints some of which were saved from the old damaged church. Above the main altar can be seen a beautifully painted vaulted ceiling.

The church is used from time to time as a concert centre, and events forming part of the international Algarve music festival are held here.

Praça da República

Portimão's indoor market stands on the busy Praça da República. Opposite is the single-aisled Igreja do Colégio which once belonged to a Jesuit college. It dates originally from the 17th c. and was rebuilt following the earthquake. Nearby stands an old people's day centre together with the Museu Diogo Gonçalves, an art gallery.

Surroundings

Praia da Rocha

The neighbouring town to the south of Portimão is the tourist centre known as Praça da Rocha.

★★Ferragudo

On the opposite side of the Rio Arade to Portimão lies the fishing village of Ferragudo, a popular subject for picture postcards. As well as its very

Ferragudo: a charming fishing village with narrow winding streets

attractive church standing on a hill it boasts the Fortaleza de São João, built in 1622 to protect the river entrance; the castle is now in private ownership. A villa nearby belongs to the Portuguese "Rei sem Reino" (king without a kingdom), a descendant of the Bragança family who represented the last king.

Ferragudo is like an oasis preserved from olden times – little narrow streets with fishermen's houses, a few simple guest houses and inns, and a pleasant atmosphere. But even here many houses have been sold recently and it is feared that in the near future Ferragudo too will fall into the hands of non-Portuguese. One annoyance is the Praia da Rocha opposite, with its skyline which, seen from Ferragudo, is a clear reminder of the popular Portuguese tourist resorts.

South of Ferragudo lies the Praia Grande which, as the name suggests, is an extensive beach. A breakwater makes bathing safe here, and it is very popular with surfers. It also has restaurants and cafés.

Praia da Rocha   C 6

Administrative district: Portimão
Population: 2000

The tourist centre of Praia da Rocha is a suburb coming under the administration of Portimão (see entry). Its skyline and atmosphere are similar to those of Quarteira and Armação de Pêra. No longer does it possess the aura of the stylish seaside resort which it must have been in the first half of the 20th c. Today it has a good tourist infrastructure with plenty of facilities for sport and amusement as well as numerous restaurants, cafés and bars. The reason for this escalation in building is the magnificent beach which extends to the mouth of the Rio Arade.

Situation and importance

It has to be said that with its faceless apartment buildings and hotels Praia da Rocha is one of the real eyesores in the Algarve. Above the main beach, which is nearly 2km long and almost 100m wide, runs the Avenida Tomás Cabreira, lined with hotels, restaurants, cafés, boutiques and shops. At the eastern end of the Avenida the Fortaleza de Santa Catarina, a 17th c. defensive installation, watches over the mouth of the Rio Arade. Today it houses a restaurant and café with a terrace. From here there is a fine view towards Ferragudo on the other side of the river and the Fortaleza de São João opposite.

Townscape

A splendid view of the steep coastline of Praia de Rocha, on the other hand, can be obtained from the western end of Avenida Tomás Cabreira.

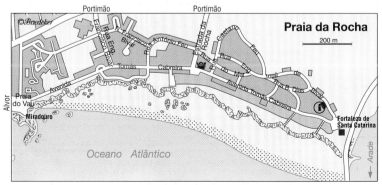

Praia da Rocha

The lovely wide sandy beach at Praia da Rocha

★Beaches

Praia da Rocha's main beach is quite picturesque and accordingly gets crowded. To the west lie a row of idyllic sandy bays most of which are divided from one another by rocky reefs and arches. Here too, however, it is difficult to find a quiet spot.

Boat trips

A boat trip from Praia da Rocha along the steep coast with its bizarre rock formations as far as the Praia dos Três Irmãos (Beach of the Three Brothers; see Alvor) is of particular interest.

Surroundings

Praia do Vau

The beach neighbouring Praia da Rocha to the west is the Praia de Vau. Although the hinterland here is also heavily populated it is nevertheless quite tranquil compared to Praia da Rocha.

Quarteira   D 11/12

Administrative district: Loué
Population: 9000

Situation and importance

The tourist centre of Quarteira lies on the coast about 15km west of Faro. The long, sandy beaches, the short distance from the airport and the wide range of amusement and leisure facilities appear to make holidays in Quarteira attractive. At any rate, the town is completely dominated by tourism, the hinterland back as far as the N125 is heavily built-up with tourist accommodation and there are also many holiday houses further north.

Townscape

Quarteira is one of those places which have given the Algarve its bad reputation. It is a town of high-rise buildings and with an unattractive appearance similar to that of Armação de Pêra or Praia da Rocha. The only compensation is the beach; accommodation on the coast road, the Avenida Infante de Sagres, with a view of the open sea might possibly offer some charm of its own. But for those whose accommodation lies "in the second row", so to speak, there is little to commend it. All the streets to the left and right of Avenida Dr. Sá Carneiro, the main street – named after a candidate for the presidency in 1980 who died in an air crash shortly before the elections – are lined with multi-storey concrete apartment blocks. The part around the Largo do Mercado in the west still has a few little old houses but they are completely unable to hold their own against the competition. There are still a few nice beach cafés along the coast road on the edge of the beach.

Near Quarteira there are two aquatic sports and leisure parks, the Atlântico Park on the N125 and the Aqua Show on the N396 which leads north-east from Quarteira.

Aquaparks

Sagres   D 1

Administrative district: Vila do Bispo
Population: 2000

From Sagres it is only 5km to the Cabo de São Vicente, the most south-westerly point of the mainland continent of Europe. Both Sagres and the Cabo de São Vicente lie on a rocky plateau which terminates abruptly at the coast to form steep cliffs up to 150m high. The plateau is divided into two constituent parts, one ending at the Ponta de Sagres south of the town of the same name and the other somewhat further north-west where the Cabo de São Vicente falls away into the sea. Between the two headlands lies the Bay of Beliche, a relatively sheltered anchorage. Further east, on the other side of the Ponta de Sagres, Sagres Bay offers excellent shelter especially when the wind is in the north. Like the climate, the countryside around Sagres is harsh and barren with only a few low-growing macchia bushes.
  Sagres is known largely through its history. The town played an impor-

Situation and importance

tant role when the Portuguese adventurers sailed the seas in the 15th and 16th c., and to a large extent the region is still trying to live off that reputation and tour-ism has gained only a small foot-hold. There are admittedly some hotels and some private accom-modation in and around Sagres, but the tourist infrastructure is not comparable with that in the holiday centres further east. However, those who just want a quiet holiday in natural surround-ings with some isolated beaches may well find what they are seek-ing here.

History
Archaeological investigations have shown that this most south-westerly region of Europe must have attracted settlers back in the Stone Age. Traces have been found of grave-sites dating from the 3rd c. B.C. which are of Celtic or Iberian origin. An early written reference to the Cabo de São

© Baedeker

Vila do Bispo,
Raposeira, Lagos

Cabo de São Vicente

Rua S. Pedro
Rua da Praça
Rua Nova
Estrada Nacional
Rua Comandante Matoso
Rua Mestre
Rua S. Vicente
Rua Infante Dom Henrique
Rua da Fortaleza

Praia do Martinhal
Praia da Baleeira
Porto da Baleeira
Ponta da Baleeira
Praia do Tonel
Praia da Mareta
N.S. da Graça
Rosa dos Ventos
Ponta da Atalaia
Oceano Atlântico
Fortaleza de Sagres
Ponta de Sagres

Sagres

Henry in the Light of Research

Dom Henrique O Navegador is back in the limelight. This time, however, under different circumstances. Although his memory was fêted and honoured on the 500th anniversary of his death in 1960, Portuguese historical researchers have for some time been engaged in studying him more closely as a person. Who was Henry in actual fact? Is the picture that the 19th century – when men loved to glorify historical figures so much – painted of him the right one, or in retrospect was he then built up into a false ideal?

Possibly the much vaunted and still quoted school for seafarers near Sagres where the latest techniques of navigation were said to have been taught to young sea captains from the 15th century onwards was in fact simply a figment of the Portuguese imagination. That was the first unpalatable suggestion put forward by the researchers. Then came the realisation that in fact personal interests had been allowed to play a prime role in what for a long time had been thought of as purely unselfish and altruistic researches on the part of the Infante Dom Henrique. He was apparently involved with a trading company in Lagos which at that time had a monopoly of all the new wares coming to Portugal from Africa. He himself had held a monopoly of tuna fishing for some time already. Finally it also became obvious that Henry was financing his researches not only with money from the Order of Christ but also to a considerable degree from taxes imposed on the simple people of the Algarve. Last but not least, research has now shown that the Infante pursued his aims with such rigour that he would not even bother to save his own brother when the latter was taken prisoner by the Moors and could have been freed in exchange for Ceuta. Henry refused to get involved and his brother Fernando died in a Moor gaol.

So, what remains of the romantic picture we have of the Infante? What nobody can or will dispute is that Henry the Navigator was one of the most important figures of the early Portuguese period of discovery and had a great thirst for knowledge – there is still no doubt whatsoever about that. Born in Oporto on March 4th 1394, Henry was just 21 years old when, following the capture of Ceuta, he listened eagerly to tales and reports by Arab traders who had sailed along the coasts of Africa or had undertaken trade journeys on the African mainland. He wanted to know exactly what this distant country looked like. Gradually it dawned on him that south of the Cabo Bojador in the *mar tenebroso*, the Sea of Darkness, there were in fact no lurking monsters which could do harm to seafarers. The sea there was apparently not always saltier, more viscuous, glutinous or hotter, as people in Portugal had said it was. And the idea that ships on the far side of the cape of southern Morocco would be sucked into a whirlpool and would fall off the end of the earth now appeared comical to him. At the end of the day the reports by the Arabs appeared far more believable than the medieval fantasies of his own countrymen.

The Portuguese rulers supported Henry's seafaring ambitions. In October 1443 he was granted sole rights to arrange all voyages south of the Cape of Bojador. A few days later the region of Sagres was assigned to him. Between 1443 and 1447 Henry frequently stayed in the Algarve, and from 1452 onwards preferred it to any other place of residence and from 1457 he lived mainly in Sagres.

At that time, apart from the fortified walls, there were just a few houses there. Various contemporary reports indicate that the Infante intended to realise an ambitious port project here. However, there are no documents to support this; it is merely assumed that in Sagres, on the south-western tip of Portugal, Henry assembled seafarers, geographers, navigators, astronomers and cartographers around him in order to put all their knowledge together and make use of it for practical seafaring purposes. At that time the Algarve was without doubt the centre of Portuguese seafaring. His researches must have been well organised and very effective. The caravel, a new type of ship incorporating both Arab and North European ideas, was developed. It proved in practice to be extremely stable, nimble and manoeuvrable.

The wind-rose in the Fortaleza of Sagres

With his ideas which were so unconventional at the time Henry the Navigator, who is known to have made only one sea voyage himself to Ceuta, distanced himself from the medieval beliefs of his age – and this is a contribution to history which nobody would question. Henry did not live to experience the results of his efforts. Probably he did not even foresee that after him the world would change irretrievably. He died in 1460 – before the Portuguese had even crossed the equator.

Vicente was by the Greek geographer and historian Strabo, who wrote of the "holy mountain range". From Pliny the Elder, too, we read that this region was known to the Romans as "Promontorium Sacrum" (Holy Foothills). The Romans believed that this isolated place must have been the home of the gods. The contemporary concept that this was "the most westerly point not only of Europe but of the whole of mankind", as Strabo described it, explains the fearful and sacred respect with which it was regarded. This exposed region was also occupied by the Moors who built a shrine here. The Portuguese finally made it an important centre in European history (see Baedeker Special "Henry in the Light of Research").

Townscape

The modest houses of this port and fishing town are spread over a barren and windy plateau. A town centre in the normal sense of the word does not exist, and the main street ends at the busy harbour.

Beaches

The beaches around Sagres are suitable for bathing and sun-bathing only to a limited degree. The best protection from the wind is offered on the Praia do Martinhal 4km to the north-east, but it is not favoured by windsurfers. Scenically more attractive is the Praia de Beliche to the west. Here, however, there is little protection from the mainly strong west winds.

Surroundings

★ Fortaleza de Sagres

2km along a road running south from Sagres is Ponta de Sagres with the Fortaleza de Sagres, the very hub of the history of Portuguese exploration and conquest in the 15th and 16th c. It is thought that there was an academic centre here in the time of Henry the Navigator (see Famous People) which taught the theoretical principles employed in sailing the oceans of the world. Only scanty remains of the early fortifications still exist, and at present these are gradually being restored as part of a lengthy building project. Visitors can see the renovated walls with the massive gateway providing entrance to the fort. The walls in their present form date from 1793 and number among the most impressive fortifications in the whole of Portugal.

In the paving to the left will be found a large circle of stones, measuring 43m in diameter, and known locally as the *rosa dos ventos* (wind rose). For centuries it lay concealed and overgrown and it was between 1918 and 1959 before it was uncovered. It is thought to date from the 15th c. but its original function is uncertain. For a long time it was thought to be a wind rose or compass face, but if it was it is unusual in being divided up into more than 40 irregular segments whereas other wind roses have a maximum of 32. On the other side can be seen the 16th c. Igreja de Nossa Senhora de Graça. It is believed that previously a church dedicated to the Virgin Mary stood on this site. A memorial nearby was erected in 1960 to mark the 500th anniversary of the death of Henry the Navigator.

There are plans to convert the former stables and neighbouring buildings into an information and exhibition centre and to equip it for conferences, but when and whether this project will materialise is uncertain.

Fortaleza de Baleeira

Above Sagres harbour can be seen the remains of the walls of a former fort which guarded Baleeira harbour. They must date from before 1587 but were badly damaged by Sir Francis Drake and rebuilt in the early 17th c., only to be destroyed yet again in the 1755 earthquake.

Fortaleza de Beliche

The Cabo de São Vicente lies about 6km west of Sagres. The road crosses the inhospitable rocky plateau with scarcely a tree or bush to be seen on either side – which gives the feeling of being at the end of the world. About halfway to the cape lies the Fortaleza de Beliche. It is not known when this little fort was originally built, it is only known that it was almost completely destroyed during an attack by Sir Francis Drake and an inscription indicates that the present building dates from 1632. On the site a small chapel dedicated to St Catharine stands high above the sea. The fort now houses a restaurant and a few hotel rooms belonging to the Pousada de Infante.

Earthenware vessels used by fishermen of Sagres for catching squid

The 24m-high lighthouse on Cabo de São Vicente

★★Cabo de São Vicente

The Cabo de São Vicente is the south-westernmost point of the Iberian Peninsula and thus of the continent of Europe. The Portuguese dedicated the cape to St Vincent, because according to legend the body of this Christian martyr was washed ashore here in an empty boat in the year 304.

The road to the cape ends at a lighthouse which stands 60m above the foaming sea crashing against the rocks below. The present-day lighthouse was built in 1846 on the instructions of Maria II. The fortifications dotted round about date from the 16th c. when the Bishop of Silves had the first lighthouse, defensive walls and a convent built here. The convent was run by Hieronymites until 1516 and was then taken over by the Order of Santa Maria de Piedade. Accommodation was also provided for pilgrims who came to this remote spot. In 1587 a large part of the building was destroyed during an attack by Drake's fleet.

São Bartolomeu de Messines   A 9

Administrative district: Silves
Population: 8500

Situation and importance

São Bartolomeu de Messines is a friendly little town in the Algarve hinterland, at least 20km north of Albufeira. Although lying very close to the motorway which leads north from the Algarve, São Bartolomeu de Messines nevertheless appears quite secluded and gives the impression of an authentic Portuguese town with no trace of the tourism found on the coast. It is attractively situated in a broad valley at the foot of the Penedo Grande, part of the Serra do Caldeirão, and is surrounded by hilly countryside with fig, olive and carob trees. A few kilometres further north flows the Rio Arade which rises in the Serra do Caldeirão and enters the Atlantic near Portimão.

João de Deus, a well-known 19th c. writer (see Famous People), was born in São Bartolomeu de Messines and there is a memorial to him in the town.

Another famous son of the little town was José Joaquim de Sousa Reis, known as "Remixido" (see Famous People). He came to the fore during the civil wars in the 19th c. as leader of an Algarve guerilla group which fought on the side of the absolutist Miguelists and caused havoc in southern Portugal. He faced a firing squad in 1838.

History

In the Moorish era São Bartolomeu de Messines was known as Masîna or Musssiene. In the 19th c. the theory was put forward that emigrants from the Sicilian port of Messina landed here and named the town Messines. After capturing it the Portuguese dedicated the town to St Bartholomew who has been its patron saint ever since.

Townscape

São Bartolomeu de Messines is a typical little country town with a not particularly attractive centre. Those who like to experience something of Portuguese everyday life, however, should make a detour here. It is particularly vibrant on market days (with an animal market, on the last Monday in each month).

Sights

Igreja Matriz

The Igreja Matriz, which can trace its origins back to an earlier 14th c. church, is worth a visit. The present church is 16th c., with marked changes made in the 18th c. The Baroque main front in red sandstone and dating from 1716 is striking. The entrance is framed by two turned columns – a rarity in the Algarve. The three-aisled interior is worth seeing for its pillars which are reminiscent of Early Manueline stone-rope pillars. Manueline ceilings have been preserved in some of the side-chapels. There is an attractive small marble pulpit the surrounds of which are being dismantled.

A short way outside the town to the north-west stands the little Ermida de São Pedro which is normally closed. Architecturally nothing out of the ordinary, it is pleasantly situated on a small hill.

Ermida de São Pedro

Surroundings

15km north-west of São Bartolomeu de Messines lies the village of São Marcos da Serra, with a small church at its highest point. Near the village the motorway and the railway line run north from the Algarve and are the main arteries linking the south with Lisbon. On a hill to the east of São Marcos da Serra is where the Miguelist guerilla Remexido (see above) is said to have been captured.

São Marcos da Serra

São Brás de Alportel   C 14

Capital of the administrative district of São Brás de Alportel
Population: 8000

São Brás de Alportel nestles in gently undulating countryside in the mountain foothills some 17km north of Faro at the junction of the N2 and the N270. A short distance to the north the hills of the Serra do Caldeirão rise to a height of 500m above sea-level. Surrounding São Brás de Alportel is some lovely garden country, and the region is particularly worth a visit when the almond trees are in blossom in February and March. As well as almonds, fig, carob and olive trees grow here together with small lemon and orange groves. São Brás de Alportel depends mainly on agriculture, while tourism plays a minor role in a more quiet and rural manner. 2km north there is a *pousada* from which there are fine views of the foothills. In the first half of the 20th c. São Brás de Alportel was a popular holiday spot because of its dry and mild mountain climate.

Situation and importance

Archaeologists have found traces of Roman remains in the region. It is also believed that there was an Moorish settlement called Xanabus or Xanabras on the site of the present town. The first recorded mention was in 1517; this related to the small chapel dedicated to St Blasius around which a few houses were built. The earthquake in the middle of the 18th c. caused great damage in the town, so that most of the buildings now date from post 1755.

History

São Brás de Alportel is a typical little Algarve town with small buildings. Its centre is the Largo de São Sebastião which forms the junction between the N270 and the N2 and is accordingly very busy. The Avenida da Liberdade is also quite lively, with shops, cafés, a provincial cinema and a gallery. Lying south-east of the Largo de São Sebastião in the direction of the church is a quiet and pleasant residential quarter.

Townscape

Sights

From the Largo de São Sebastião the Rua Gago Coutinho leads directly to the Igreja Matriz on the edge of São Brás de Alportel. From the attractive church forecourt there is a fine view of the garden countryside around. In the 15th c. there was a small chapel here dedicated to São Brás. It was extended and altered several times, and in 1725 a start was made on extensive restoration work which took over 26 years to complete. During that time the choir and roof were replaced and other detailed interior work carried out. Sadly, a few years after work was completed large parts of the church were destroyed in the 1755 earthquake. In 1792 the then Bishop of the Algarve, Francisco Gomes do Avelar, initiated further rebuilding. The church is three-aisled and has three barrel-vaulted ceilings, while slender columns divide the interior. On the left in the choir is a mid-20th c. copy of

Igreja Matriz

an early 18th c. painting of the Trinity. The copy was done in Rome and presented as a gift to the church community of São Brás de Alportel in 1991. At the front of the left aisle is a striking neo-classical side-altar in marble, a rarity in both form and material in this region. It was probably done until the Italian architect Francisco Xavier Fabri who undertook much work in the Algarve after the earthquake.

Palácio Episcopal

After the episcopal see had been transferred from Silves to Faro in the 16th c. São Brás de Alportel was considered as the site for a summer residence for the bishops. However, nothing was actually done until the initiative was taken first by Simão de Gama and then by António Pereira da Silva, two bishops who held office in the late 17th and early 18th c. Today all that can be seen is a reconstruction of those parts of the former Episcopal Palace which were rebuilt in the first decades of this century. One section of the building houses a school. The palace once had a small garden, and visitors can still see the pretty, domed pavilion, the former Fonte Episcopal (Episcopal Fountain).

Museu Etnográfico do Trajo Algarvio

Somewhat set back on the left-hand side of Rua Dr. José Dias Sancho going in the Tavira direction is the Museu Etnográfico do Trajo Algarvio (open: 10am–noon and 2–6pm, Sat. and Sun. 2–6pm only). In this small museum, so typical of Portugal, temporary exhibitions of clothing, items of furniture, household objects and Algarve customs and traditions are lovingly arranged. For those who wish to learn something about rural Algarve in days gone by this museum should not be missed. A permanent exhibition covers old agricultural implements such as cork presses and cork-boiling pans, blacksmiths' tools, carriages and donkey-carts.

Surroundings

Barranco Velho/ Ameixial

Further north the little used (but very winding) N2 passes through some lonely and largely unspoiled countryside. Only occasionaly is a village to be seen – Barrancoa Velho, a typical small village, after 10km and the secluded hamlet of Ameixial after 30km.

Serra de Monchique   A 5/6

Situation and geology

The Serra de Monchique ridge of mountains stretches across from east to west, forming a protective wall in the north of the coastal plateau of the western Algarve. It forms an effective barrier against cold weather from the Atlantic and thus helps to maintain the coastal region's North African climate. Geologically, the massif presents itself as a boldly structured eruptive mass deposited on the uneven subsoil and bisected by the Ribeira de Odelouca to form a western and an eastern block. Thanks to the more or less impermeable nature of the ground rainfall collects in streams and rivulets and finds its way to the coastal plain. As the mountains are volcanic there are a number of warm springs.

★★Landscape

The chief town in the Serra de Monchique is Monchique (see entry); just below it in a wooded valley lies the spa of Caldas de Monchique.

★★Fóia

A ride up to the Fóia peak, at 902m the highest mountain in the Serra de Monchique, is well worthwhile. From Monchique a very scenic and winding road first leads up the south side of the mountain. Here the road is lined with houses, some very neat in appearance, and several tourist cafés. A brief stop at a *miradouro* with a small fountain will be rewarded with a panoramic view of the whole of the Algarve coast. Directly below lies Portimão and to the west the Cabo de São Vicente and the west coast, while

Beautiful scenery in the Serra de Monchique ▶

to the east Faro can be seen on a clear day. Higher up the mountain the vegetation becomes more and more sparse, with some cistus shrubs and rhodendrons, while herds of sheep and goats roam the valleys. After a further bend in the road there is a view northwards to the Alentejo.

Having arrived at the peak it will be found rather inhospitable. Portuguese Telecom, the RDP broadcasting station and the air force are stationed under a forest of antennae. There is also a café and a souvenir shop.

Silves   B 7

Capital of the administrative district of Silves
Population: 12,000

Situation and importance	Silves, the old Moorish capital of the Algarve, lies in the hinterland about 8km north-east of Portimão. The little town extends along the right bank of the Rio Arade and is visible from a long way off. It is surrounded by gently undulating countryside, the southern foothills of the Serra de Monchique (see entry). Here the hinterland is no longer as delightful and garden-like as that in the east of the Algarve, although there are orange and lemon groves, fig and almond trees, as well as eucalyptus, cork-oaks and cistus shrubs. Little remains of the town's former greatness. Silves has the appearance of a rather sleepy little town although it can still boast a few historically significant buildings and it therefore attracts considerable numbers of day visitors. However, there are not many restaurants and cafés.
History	It seems likely that Celtiberian tribes settled in this region. It is known that Silves was of interest to the Phoenicians as a river port. They established an important trading-post here which provided good links between the interior and the Mediterranean. The Carthaginians and the Romans also valued the site and named it Silbis.

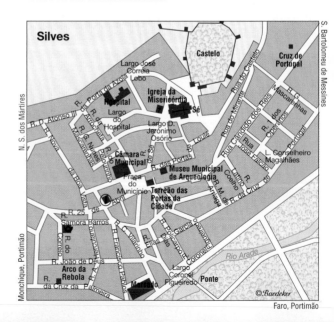

©Baedeker

Faro, Portimão

Imposing castle ruins at Silves

In the 8th c. Moors, assumed to have originated from the Yemen and Egypt, ruled Silves which they called Xelb. During the Moorish era Xelb was known far beyond the Iberian peninsula; its importance resulted primarily from its situation – a sheltered harbour near the sea and within easy reach of North Africa. Lively trade between the climatically favourable south-west of the Iberian peninsula and Mediterranean countries ensured a strong economy. The Moors introduced their tried and tested methods of irrigation and were thus able to farm the land very efficiently. Xelb is believed to have had a population of some 40,000 at that time and became the capital of the province of Al-Gharb, which was under the control of the emirate and later caliphate of Córdoba. Historians, jurists, philosophers, writers and musicians all helped the town to gain a good reputation far beyond its borders; it became famous in song and verse and is said to have been a finer town than Granada. Its prosperity attracted the attention of enemies as well as that of friendly admirers, and in 922 Vikings sailed up the Rio Arade and tried to take Xelb, but were cut off.

Troops of the Portuguese King Sancho I conquered Xelb in 1189. Taking part in the campaign were large numbers of knights, including Frederick I (known as Barbarossa, or Redbeard) and Richard the Lionheart, who had entered into an alliance with Portugal. Immediately after the town had been captured a Flemish priest was appointed bishop. Two years later the Moors won Xelb back again but the Portuguese, who had already conquered the greater part of present-day Portugal with the help of the Knights of the Crusade, were determined to advance all the way to the south coast. A few years later they moved down from the north and encircled the Silves region for two decades. In 1242, under the leadership of the Master of the Order of the Knights of Santiago. Dom Paio Peres Correia, the Portuguese finally succeeded in capturing Xelb and they renamed it Silva. The last Moorish ruler of Xelb was Aben Afan.

The withdrawal of the Moors saw the beginning of the region's economic decline. The little town again enjoyed a short-lived flowering in the early

16th c. at the time of the Portuguese voyages of discovery and conquest, when ships laden with pepper and other wares sailed up the Rio Arade to Silves. However, the Arade became increasingly silted up and this spelt the end for the port.

In 1577 the episcopal see was transferred from Silves to Faro. Lagos became the capital of the Algarve. In 1755 Silves was badly ravaged by the earthquake, and many of the buildings and other treasures which could have borne witness to the town's earlier cultural and economic standing were destroyed. Silves then drifted into comparative insignificance.

★Townscape

The central Praça do Municipio is still magnificent, and the Cathedral and the Castle with its battlements still bear witness to the town's former greatness. Between the town hall and the castle small streets with old whitewashed houses line the side of the hill.

Sights

Tour

A tour of Silves can commence at the Praça do Municipio. From there continue up the hill to the Cathedral and the Igreja da Misericórdia opposite, and then on to the Castle. After visiting the interesting Archaeological Museum refreshments can be taken at a café at the point where the tour began. A short visit to the famous Cruz de Portugal on the north-eastern edge of town is worthwhile. A little out of the way in the north-west of the town centre lies the small Ermida de Nossa Senhora dos Mártires. End the tour with a walk down to the Rio Arade.

Praça do
Município

The Town Hall (Câmara Municipal) of Silves is more the type of building one would expect to find in a city, and it stands out against the rest of the townscape. An impressive arcaded walk is surmounted by two storeys. Impressive, too, is the Torreão das Portas da Cidade in the eastern corner of the square, a former watch-tower which once formed part of the town wall

The inner courtyard of the Castelo dos Mouros

and was also the town gate. More of the route taken by the old town wall can be detected on the other, western, side of the Town Hall. Near the former town gate stands a *pelourinho*, the pillory which, like the tower, is built of the red sandstone so typical of the region.

The Cathedral was built in the 13th c. in the Gothic style after the town had been captured by the Portuguese, and stands on the site of an earlier mosque. Many changes were made in the centuries which followed. From 1242 to 1577 Silves was an episcopal see and so the cathedral was then the major church in the Algarve. ★ Sé

Most of the nave was destroyed in the 1755 earthquake, but the crossing and choir were saved, and this can clearly be seen particularly from the inside, although from the outside too it is not difficult to recognise the Gothic features which the earthquake left undamaged or which could be restored. The massive pointed doorway of yellow sandstone from the coast stands out clearly against the entrance façade. Note the heads of animals and humans above the arch. The Gothic pinnacles in the upper section of the Baroque façade are also of interest. Walking round the church, note the long Gothic windows in the south transept and the choir. The choir is built of red sandstone from the Monchique mountains.

The differing styles can clearly be seen in the interior. Much of the nave was repaired after the earthquake with red sandstone in such a way that it blends in very well with the undamaged parts. The sandstone pillars are very plain as are the capitals, but their basic forms and the simple plant motifs used in the decoration relate well to those Gothic capitals which remained undamaged. The pure Gothic decoration and the choir with its ribbed-vaulted ceiling are unique in the Algarve, since all the other Gothic buildings were more seriously damaged than this one. Moreover, apart from Silves cathedral only the Sé in Faro was of comparable size. One of the keystones in the choir bears the Portuguese coat-of-arms. On the plain altar stands a statue of the Senhora de Conceição. In the floor of the choir can be seen the tombstone of João II, who died in Alvor to the south-west of Silves after having taken the cure in Monchique. In 1499 his body was moved to the Capela do Fundador in the convent church of Batalha. Tombs of crusaders and bishops can be seen in the left transept and the main choir.

The Igreja da Misericórdia dates from the 16th c., and on the rather plain side facing the cathedral can be seen some Manueline decoration from that date. The main doorway is in Classical style. Inside can be seen some 17th c. paintings; that by the high altar was the work of a well-known 19th c. lay artist from the Algarve. Igreja da Misericórdia

The dominant feature of the townscape and visible from afar is the Castle (open: daily 9am–5pm, to 6pm in summer) with its walls of red sandstone and its turrets. There are believed to have been fortifications on this site during the Phoenician, Celtiberian and Roman eras. ★★ Castelo

The present castle dates back to the Moors, but its present appearance is the result of work done in 1940. Archaeological digs in the inner courtyard have revealed parts of the Moorish castle. Other remains include the wells and underground storage chambers. Because they had these good facilities for food storage and access to freshwater the Moors could withstand long sieges. A number of legends have been woven around the two wells, the Cisterna da Moura Encantada (Well of the Enchanted Moorish Maiden) and the Cisterna dos Cães (Well of Dogs), which was probably built by the Romans. In the Cisterna da Moura Encantada a beautiful Moorish girl is said to cross a subterranean lake in a silver sailing-boat, but she is visible only when the moon is full. There was thought to have been access to the banks of the Arade river from the Cisterna dos Cães. On the castle site there is also the shaft of a former mine from which the Romans and the Moors obtained copper.

The broad inner courtyard is attractively planted with trees and bushes which the Portuguese introduced from abroad; jacaranda trees with their trumpet-shaped blue flowers and pepper trees from Brazil, cedars from

Bolivia, Japanese medlars with their yellow fruits and date-palms from the Canaries. In the courtyard stands a memorial to Sancho I, who in 1189 set out from Xelb on the first successful voyage of conquest.

Visitors can walk round the red walls of the whole complex and climb the little turrets, from where there are fine views of the countryside around Silves. In the north can be seen fruit plantations, and to the north-east lies modern Silves. To the east a former British cork factory, which operated until 1901, can be easily picked out. Corks for port-wine bottles were made here, but today the premises are used only for the storage of cork. From the castle walls it is also possible to see into a second inner courtyard with a fountain in its centre. From time to time concerts are held in the castle precincts, and once a year the "Festival da Cerveja", or Beer Festival, is celebrated here.

Museu Municipal de Arqueologia

The Museu Municipal de Arqueologia in Rua das Portas de Loulé was opened in 1990 (open: Tues.–Sun. 10am–5pm). Before the earthquake a large private house stood on this site, and in the course of excavations below the remains of the old walls a large number of utensils and everyday items were uncovered. The museum's exhibits are mainly finds from around the house and from the castle precincts as well as some from Loulé and São Bartolomeu de Messines. A Moorish well has been incorporated into the exhibition room. On a tour of the museum – the labels and captions are in Portuguese – visitors are taken in chronological order through an archaeological collection of exhibits from the Palaeolithic, Neolithic, Bronze and Iron Ages; as well as Roman finds a lot of items from the Moorish period and finally objects from post-1189/1242, namely, those relating to Portuguese culture, are on display.

A particulary beautiful exhibit is seen at the start of the tour, a red sandstone *menhir* (upright monumental stone) from the 4th or 3rd c. B.C. Examples of Iron Age culture include several fragnments of burial pillars from the period between the 8th and 6th c. B.C. Roman remains include coins and vessels and the base of a statue of Jupiter. There is an interesting small collection of surgical instruments dating from between the 5th and 7th c. Mementoes of the Moorish era include ceramics and two 10th c. capitals as well as a 12th c. well with a shaft 10m deep. On the lower floor are exhibited finds from 1189 onwards – coins, vessels, belt-buckles, small thimbles and other sewing utensils.

★Cruz de Portugal

The well-known Cruz de Portugal, worked in white limestone in the 16th c., stands at the town exit leading to São Bartolomeu de Messines. This work of religious sculpture is an example of a Manueline Way of the Cross which is unique in the Algarve. On the front is a portrayal of Jesus on the Cross and on the back of His Descent from the Cross. The year 1025 on the base of the cross has given historians something of a puzzle; it is assumed that this means that the lower section dates from the Moorish period.

Ermida de Nossa Senhora dos Mártires

The Ermida de Nossa Senhora dos Mártires, to the north-west of the Praça do Município, dates back to a 12th c. building, from the time when Silves was first taken by the Knights of the Cross led by Sancho I. At that time those who died in the battles near the town were buried here. A second building dating from the Manueline epoch fell victim to the 1755 earthquake, after which it was rebuilt. The tomb inside is probably that of a 13th or 14th c. bishop.

Arco da Rebola

Near a building in Rua da Cruz da Palmeira remains of an original Moorish gateway have been preserved. Apparently it was also the entrance to the town in the Portuguese period.

Ponte/ Mercado

The bridge over the Rio Arade can be traced back to a river crossing of Roman times. The present bridge dates from the Middle Ages and was strengthened in later centuries. Here the Rio Arade is quite idyllic, and visitors may occasionally see a turtle basking on its banks.

The indoor market near the bridge sees much coming and going all through the week.

Surroundings

The Rio Arade is dammed a few kilometres north-east of Silves to form the Barragem de Arade. The intention was to create a water reservoir for the Silves region and a recreation area with facilities for water sports, restaurants and cafés. Although a start has been made the water shortage in the Algarve has now unfortunately become so serious that very little of the original project is likely to materialise. The catastrophic drought situation can clearly be witnessed here at the Barragem de Arade where the water level has dropped so much that already a large, arid and ravaged stretch of the river bank is visible.

Barragem de Arade

Tavira   C 17

Capital of the administrative district of Tavira
Population: 10,000

The little town of Tavira lies in the south-east of the Algarve a good 20km from the Spanish frontier and along both banks of the Rio Gilão (or Rio Séqua) which here flows into the Atlantic. Tavira lies not by the open sea but in the lagoon region of the Ria Formosa; offshore to the south-west is the Ilha de Tavira, a lagoon island of sand-dunes. The wide-ranging fruit plantations – mainly orange and lemon groves – in the hinterland of Tavira exude a delightful aromatic scent when in bloom in the spring.

Situation and importance

Fishing is of some importance in Tavira – for a period it was the centre of the tuna-fishing industry on the Algarve coast – and so is salt production, as evidenced by the salt-works at the mouth of the Rio Gilão. In spite of the beautiful sandy beaches nearby tourism has so far not really gained a foothold in Tavira and there are no hotels of any size; this makes it all the more attractive for a day trip.

It is not wholly clear when Tavira was founded. It probably dates back to an Iberian settlement in the 2nd c. B.C. and the Phoenicians are also thought to have established a trading post here. The Romans found a settlement named Balsa at the mouth of the Rio Gilão and kept the name. The present name is derived from Tabira, as it was known under the Moors, under whom and until well into the Middle Ages Tavira was a major port. In 1242 the town was captured by the Portuguese led by Dom Paio Peres Correia — according to legend the treacherous murder of seven Portuguese knights by the Moors in spite of a cease-fire resulted in the town being taken by force by the Portuguese. In the colonial period the Portuguese army of occupation in North Africa received support and assistance from Tavira because it was so near to the Moroccan coast. The port lost its importance when the North African colonies were given up; the gradual silting-up of the harbour basin added to its problems, and Spanish subjugation of Portugal between 1580 and 1640 followed by plague in 1645/46 were the final blows to its prosperity. In 1755 the earthquake destroyed large areas of the town and since then Tavira has remained of relatively minor importance.

History

Tavira is one of the prettiest little towns in the Algarve. As it had to be rebuilt following the earthquake few of the buildings are more than 250 years old. Nevertheless, the uniform style of building employed lends Tavira a strong air of harmony. It is particularly picturesque along the banks of the Rio Gilão, which area is sometimes compared with Venice (although perhaps an exaggeration). Typical of Tavira are the characteristic hipped roofs seen on many old houses; similar roofs are now sometimes used on modern buildings. It is interesting to contrast the architecture with that of neighbouring Olhão, where building styles are basically quite different.

★ Townscape

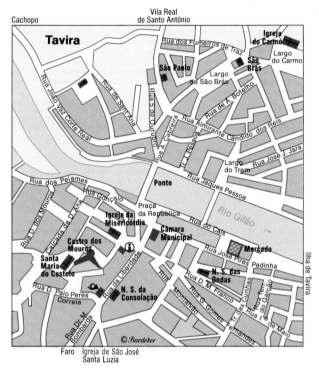

Sights

Tour

Tavira is the sort of town where visitors can enjoy a quiet, relaxed stroll and just soak up the atmosphere. Those wishing to view a few of the sights could start at the Praça da República and see the south-west part of the town centre first. The Igreja da Misericórdia, the Castle, the Igreja de Santa Maria do Castelo and finally the Capela de Nossa Senhora da Consolação are all worth a visit. Then cross the river and stroll through the pretty residential streets of the more peaceful quarter on the other side. Here will be found the Igreja de São Paulo, the Capela de São Brás and the Igreja do Carmo, although these are often closed. The view across the river from Rua Jaques Pessoa, the riverside road, is not to be missed. There are several restaurants along the river bank.

On the south-west side of the river, a little way out from the town centre, the Igreja de São José and the Igreja de Nossa Senhora das Ordas are worth a visit.

Praça da República

The Praça da República, on the right bank of the river, forms the centre of Tavira. On the eastern side of the square lies a municipal park tastefully laid out with flower-beds and trees. At the south-east end of the square will be found Tavira's indoor market with some enticing cafés nearby. Rua da Liberdade, one of the main streets in the town centre, enters the Praça da República in its western corner. From the square there is a fine view of the Rio Gilão and that part of the town which lies opposite.

18th century houses in Tavira

In recent years several bridges have been built over the Rio Gilhão and this has changed the character of the town centre. For centuries previously there had only been the one seven-arched bridge north of the Praça da República. This bridge is of Roman origin and all the traffic using the Roman road linking Faro and Mértola passed over it. The present bridge is a 17th c. reconstruction. In the winter of 1989/90 it was badly damaged by floods and had to be closed; now reopened to pedestrians only.

Ponte

The narrow Rua da Galeria branches off Rua da Liberdade and leads to the Igreja da Misericórdia. The Arco da Misericórdia next to the church is a part of the old town gate dating to the time of the Moors.

★Igreja da Misericórdia

In spite of the rebuilding work undertaken after the 1755 earthquake the church, originally dating from 1541, is still one of the finest examples of Renaissance religious architecture in the Algarve. Details of the façade are of interest; under a projecting canopy, or baldachin, in the centre of the door can be seen the Senhora da Misericórdia, the Madonna of Mercy, supported by angels. To the left are crowns and the Portuguese coat-of-arms, to the right the coat-of-arms of Tavira with the seven-arched bridge, a Portuguese king with his crown and a Moorish king wearing a turban. Various figures can be discerned in the door frame, including some little musicians. The two saints are St Peter on the left and St Paul on the right.

Spanning the triple-aisled interior are three barrel-vaulted wooden ceilings. The blue-and-white *azulejo* pictures with expensive frames and the gilded high altar are very striking. Again the Portuguese crown and the coat-of-arms can be seen below the canopy. A closer examination of the capitals will reveal some masks. The little organ in the gallery is attractive – organs are something of a rarity in Algarve churches.

A little way up from the town centre the Travessa da Fonte leads to the site of the former Castle (open: daily 9.30am–5.30pm). A few fragments of the

★Castro dos Mouros

Tavira – the Birthplace of the Man who Never Was

Although he never was, he was born on October 15th 1890 in Tavira. Álvaro de Campos came from a Jewish family. After attending grammar school he became apprenticed to a shipbuilding engineer in Glasgow. A long voyage took him to the Orient. In 1914 he returned to Portugal and lived in Lisbon, where he devoted a large proportion of his time to doing nothing, and the remainder to writing. He was a follower of a "non-Aristotelic aesthetic" and produced poems based on this doctrine. He published numerous odes. He wore a monocle, was tall in stature, thin and with a slight stoop. He was described as irascible and even devoid of feeling. But – as we have already said – he never actually existed.

Álvaro de Campos was no pseudonym, no character in a novel, not even a fabricated person – Álvaro de Campos was a heteronym, one of several in whose existence the poet and writer Fernando Pessoa wrapped himself or divided or multiplied himself. Much has been ruminated about the heteronym of the best-known Portuguese writer of the 20th century. Pessoa spent his childhood in South Africa, grew up bilingual there and even wrote English poems under another name. Perhaps his heteronym stems from this time. It has also been suggested that the rather lonely Pessoa used this means to create a circle of friends and people to whom he could closely relate.

Portrait of Pessoa by Almada Negreiros

His main heteronyms other than Álvaro de Campos were Alberto Caeiro, described as a bucolic poet, and Ricardo Reis, a doctor from Oporto who wrote Neo-Classical poetry. Bernando Soares was a semi-heteronym, who always appeared when Fernando Pessoa was tired and sleepy. Each of them had a well-defined character, an unmistakable appearance, a date of birth, a birthplace and much more; Pessoa even produced horoscopes for them. The heteronyms could be readily interchanged, and they also held lively discussions with Pessoa.

Of Álvaro de Campos it is known that he moved in Lisbon avant-garde circles which caused considerable disquiet among the citizens of the city. He is said to have got on well with Alberto Caeiro, even to have dedicated a book to him and to have regarded him as the one man in the country who lived in the timeless present of children and animals and had opened his eyes to the truth. He felt himself linked even more strongly with the poet Fernando Pessoa. This "spiritual relationship" must have been so close that in 1935, the year when Pessoa died, Álvaro de Campos also departed this life.

Typical of many houses in Tavira is the fine exterior decoration

defensive walls are all that remain of the originally Roman and later Moorish castle which was rebuilt after the Portuguese under Dom Dinis I had captured the town. Today a pretty garden has been laid out in part of the walls; it is privately owned but is open to visitors. From the gardens and from the top of the walls and the tower there are fine views over Tavira and the Rio Gilão.

Near the castle garden towers the Igreja de Santa Maria do Castelo. It was built by the Portuguese on the site of a former Moorish mosque. Originally a 13th c. edifice, it was rebuilt after the earthquake in accordance with the old plans. Remains of the Gothic church include the entrance door and, inside, the interiors of some of the side-chapels and the arch above the side-altars.

   In the choir can be seen the tombs of Dom Paiao Peres Correia and the seven Portuguese knights who are said to have been murdered by the Moors during a period of truce, whereupon the town was attacked and taken by Christian troops. Note also the three side-chapels on the left decorated with attractive blue-and-white tiles. The second side-chapel still has some Manueline ceiling adornment and is clad in 18th c. *azulejos*.

★Igreja de Santa Maria do Castelo

The interior of the plain Capela de Nossa Senhora da Consolação in Rua da Liberdade boasts some 17th c. *azulejo* decoration and an altarpiece from the Flemish school (16th c.).

Capela de Nossa Senhora da Consolação

This trapezium-shaped church dedicated to the "Madonna of the Waves" stands on an acutely-angled street corner near the Praça da República. Its 16th c. predecessor was destroyed in the earthquake, and the church of today dates from the second half of the 18th c.

Igreja de Nossa Senhora das Ondes

An equally unusual design is that of the Igreja de São José on the Praça Zacarias Guerreiro, south-east of the town centre, which is octagonal in

Igreja de São José

plan with unequal sides. The high altar is adorned with *trompe l'oeil* paintings. Two side-chapels are of Gothic/Manueline origin.

Praça 5 de Outubro/Igreja de São Paulo
After crossing the Rio Gilão by the old bridge, Rua 5 de Outubro then leads to the Praça 5 de Outubro, a square which is attractively laid out with flower-beds and trees. At its northern end stands the Igreja de São Paulo, originally a 17th c. Renaissance church with some beautiful 15th and 16th c. paintings.

Largo de São Brás/Capela de São Brás
The long Largo de São Brás with its small judas-trees is another square with a lot of atmosphere. The sparingly decorated façade of the small Capelo de São Brás at the north-east end of the square is quite pleasing.

Igreja do Carmo
A little way to the north-east of the Largo de São Brás can be found the unpretentious Largo do Carmo on which stands the former Carmelite monastery with the Igreja do Carmo. Built in the 18th c., the church is notable for some important interior carvings and the magnificently decorated 18th c. choir-stalls.

Surroundings

★ Ilha de Tavira
The Ilha de Tavira, lying off the coast to the south-west, can be reached by boat during the holiday season. The ferry sails from the end of the riverside road which runs along the right bank of the Rio Gilão behind the indoor market. There is also a footbridge to the island further west near Santa Luzia. The Ilha de Tavira has a sandy beach which is about one kilometre long with flat dunes. The sea is not too rough and is suitable even for children to bathe.

Santa Luzia
Santa Luzia, 2km west of Tavira, is a fishing village which has been somewhat spoiled by modern development. The local inhabitants specialised in

The wide sandy beach at Ilha de Tavira

fishing for squid. They would let earthenware jugs attached to a length of string down into the water; the squid, attracted by the absolute darkness they offered, swam into the jugs and were trapped. Colourful fishing boats lie in the mud-flats, and on the far side lies the Ilha de Tavira. Near the holiday resort of Pedras d'el Rei on the western edge of Santa Luiz is a bridge leading to the island. Visitors can go on foot or direct to Barril beach by a little island railway.

Luz de Tavira lies 5km west of Tavira near the busy N125. The Igreja Matriz on the through road dates from the 16th c.; it is one of the few churches which survived the 1755 earthquake and is an impressive example of Algarve Renaissance architecture. A number of Manueline features have been preserved, such as the attractive side door and the font. Mention should also be made of the *azulejo* decoration made in Sevilla in the 15th c. and found in the main chapel.

Luz de Tavira

Near the coast, 2km south-west of Luz de Tavira, some scanty remains of a medieval watch-tower have survived. However, it is the journey here which is more rewarding than the place itself; a small group of typical little Algarve houses will be seen en route.

Torre de Ares

The rather unspectacular village of Conceição lies 7km east of Tavira. Close to the railway line between Lagos and Vila Real de Santo António stands an interesting parish church which was originally Gothic.

Conceição

Cabanas, lying about 2km south of Conceição, is enjoying a tourist boom. The broad and mainly empty beach on a sandbank offshore is highly regarded by the holidaymakers staying in the large bungalow village. The beach can be reached by fishing boat or even on foot in some places at low tide. On the coast road there are several small restaurants and cafés designed for tourists.

Cabanas

Vilamoura   C/D 11

Administrative district: Loulé. Population: 50,000

In the 1970s and 1980s the holiday resort of Vilamoura developed near a highly modern marina a few kilometres west of Quarteira and 10km east of Albufeira. In contrast to its neighbour Quarteira, this "Moorish village" has the air of an exclusive resort with ample luxurious accommodation and a wide spectrum of leisure facilities. There are several golf-courses quite near the town, numerous tennis courts, riding schools and, of course, many opportunities to indulge in watersports of all kinds. A number of bars and night-clubs and a casino provide evening entertainment.

Situation and importance

The houses in Vilamoura are spread over a wide landscaped area which clearly originated on the drawing-board; there is nothing in the way of natural vegetation. Blocks of similar looking apartments and high-rise buildings are not all grouped together, but stand in indivudual settings. There are wide streets laid out in semi-circular or horseshoe shapes with the result that it is very easy to get lost. Fortunately there are town plans everywhere to help in finding the way.

Townscape

Sights

The marina at Vilamoura is famous for its "international set". It was built in the 1970s and is one of the largest, most luxurious and well appointed of its kind in Europe, with almost 1000 berths for luxury yachts and small pleasure boats. Restaurants and cafés line the promenade.

Porto

It is possible that even the Phoenicians discovered a good anchorage and harbour on this section of the coast; remains of a Roman patrician's house have been unearthed a few hundred metres from the harbour, proving that

Cerro da Vila Estação Arqueológica

there was a Roman settlement here between the 1st and 5th c. A.D. As well as some rather unimpressive foundations there are some interesting 3rd c. A.D. mosaics. All the items that have been unearthed to date are on display in the little museum adjoining th site (open: daily 8.30am–5pm). Traces of later cultures have also been discovered, including those of the Visigoths from the 5th to the 8th c. and of the Moors from the 8th to the 13th c.

Excellent bathing can be enjoyed on the Praia da Falésia (see Albufeira) to the west of Vilamoura.

Beach

Vila do Bispo   C 1/2

Capital of the administrative district of Vila do Bispo
Population: 1400

Although the village of Vila do Bispo in the extreme south-west of the Algarve is actually an uninspiring little place it nevertheless now acts as the region's administrative headquarters, a function once undertaken by, among others, Sagres when it was more important than it is now. Far from the tourist hurly-burly on the Algarve coast, Vila do Bispo could perhaps be described by some as being "at the end of the world", although the N125 provides a good link with Lagos 26km away.

Situation and importance

In the Middle Ages the village was known as Santa Maria do Cabo and was often confused with Cabo de São Vicente 10km away. Later it was gifted to the Bishop of Faro and thus got its name of Vila do Bispo (Town of the Bishop). Vila do Bispo is a quiet rural village without any particular features. The pretty village church, built at the end of the 18th c. after the earthquake. The interior is rich in 18th c. *azulejos* and gilded wood-carving.

Surroundings

A number of places in the immediate and more distant surroundings include in particular Sagres (see entry) and the Cabo de São Vicente.

Sagres

The beaches west of Vila do Bispo, some rather remote, are very beautiful. They can be reached only by car along a small road from Vila do Bispo leading to the Praia do Castelejo which is often almost deserted during the week, while at weekends it is visited mainly by local people when the weather is good. A beach bar provides food and drink. From the little road to the Praia do Castelejo tracks (no signposts) lead to the Praia da Cordama and Praia da Barriga further north. There are also some scenically very beautiful bays with flat sandy beaches surrounded by high cliffs. The breakers of the Atlantic crash upon the shore; it is rather colder here than further east along the Algarve coast and there is little protection from the westerly winds.

Praia do Castelejo, Praia da Cordama, Praia da Barriga

Although a popular destination for walkers the Torre de Aspa can also be reached by car (tracks lead southwards to it from Vila do Bispo). The Torre de Aspa is an obelisk standing in the middle of the barren plateau and marking the highest point (156m above sea-level) on the south-western coast of the Algarve. A little further west steep cliffs drop down to the Atlantic from a height of at least 150m.

Torre de Aspa

From Vila do Bispo the N125 continues northwards through thinly populated countryside, with numerous small side-roads branching off westwards down to lonely bays. On some of them the final stretch has to be negotiated on foot. 14km along the N125 lies the fishing village of Carrapateira where individual tourists can find simple accommodation.

Carrapateira

The village of Raposeira, 2km east of Vila do Bispo, has become quite famous because Henry the Navigator is said to have lived here in the Casa do Infante. There is a little village church with a Manueline doorway.

Raposeira

◄ *Remains of the original Roman settlement Cerro da Vila at Vilamoura*

Vila do Bispo Church

Praia do Castelejo; one of the beautiful beaches on the west coast

Outside Raposeira to the east and north of the N125, from where it can be seen, stands the chapel in which Henry the Navigator is said to have worshipped. The oldest church in the Algarve, it was built in the 13th c. and has an Early Gothic door and a simple rosette above the entrance. Particularly attractive are the capitals in the interior which are decorated with human and animal heads. In spite of the proximity of the busy N125 this place still has a special atmosphere all of its own.

★Ermida de Nossa Senhora de Guadalupe

4km to the south of Raposeira will be found the Ingrina and Zavial beaches. They are small sandy bays as yet almost undiscovered by tourists.

Praia de Ingrina, Praia do Zavial

Salema, 8km east of Vila do Bispo, on the other hand, is gradually falling prey to tourism. In recent years some sizeable hotels and apartment blocks have been built around the village with its picturesque centre. However, a number of houses still offer individual accommodation. There is a small municipal beach, but it is more peaceful on the Praia da Figueira to the west (approached via the little hamlet of Figueira).

Salema

Burgau, a little fishing village on the cliffs above a relatively narrow bay 12km east of Vila do Bispo, has been more successsful than Salema in retaining its originality. It is frequented mainly by individual tourists who are quite happy with more basic accommodation. The village square near the beach can get a bit crowded during the high season mainly because of the many parked cars. Near Barão de São João to the north of Burgau are some woods which are ideal for walks.

Burgau

Vila Real de Santo António   B 19

Capital of the administrative district of Vila Real de Santo António
Population: 14,000

Vila Real de Santo António lies in the extreme south-east of the Algarve on the right bank of the Guadiana, which forms the border between Portugal and Spain. The little border town is linked to the Spanish town of Ayamonte on the opposite bank by a regular ferry service. The latter has declined in importance since a motorway bridge was built over the Guadiana a few kilometres to the north, but river trips from Vila Real de Santo António are still charming and popular. The town is also the terminus of the railway line from Lagos which serves the Algarve coast. As Vila Real de Santo António lies a little way inland it is not unduly affected by tourism. Nevertheless it is a vibrant little place with plenty of shops in the town centre. Most visitors are day trippers, both Algarve holidaymakers and Spaniards who find shopping cheaper here. Until the 1960s the town had several fish-canning factories processing mainly sardines and tuna; today only two remain.

Situation and importance

The town of Vila Real de Santo António is relatively new, having been built in 1774 in place of Santo António da Arenilha which had been destroyed in a catastrophic flood in the early 17th c. Santo António da Arenilha had been a little fishing community which also helped to defend the region against invaders from North Africa, and some of the towers which formed part of its fortifications survived until the 19th c. Vila Real de Santo António, however, was a completely new town built under the supervision of the Marquês de Pombal (see Famous People), minister to José I, and not just a reconstruction of its predecessor. Some of its inhabitants were fishermen from Aveiro on the west coast of Portugal who had been forced to give up fishing there after the town had been cut off from the sea following a storm. Other new residents came from various regions of the Algarve, including the nearby village of Monto Gordo, many as a result of strong government pressure to move. Within a short time official subsidies produced an upturn in fishing, shipbuilding, commerce and agriculture, and by 1777 Vila Real de Santo António had some 5000 inhabitants.

History

Vila Real de Santo António

The Praça do Marquês de Pombal in the centre of Vila Real de Santo António

Townscape

The town centre by the river is marked by a rather uniform style of architecture. This well-ordered lay-out is the work of the Marquês de Pombal who had previously overseen the rebuilding of Lisbon after it had been largely laid to waste in the 1755 earthquake. Like Lisbon, the centre of Vila Real de Santo António is laid out in a chessboard fashion, a principle used in Greece back in the 5th c. B.C. As the town had to be completely rebuilt this concept could readily be employed throughout. It was in accord with the philosophy of the Marquis who was the major advocate of absolutism in Portugal; clean lines and functional practicality were the basic principles. The historic town centre is also known as the Pombaline Centre, in memory of the Marquis. The major planners and architects involved were Reinaldo dos Santos, Ramão de Sousa and Carlos Mardel, the latter having also been concerned with the Lisbon rebuilding.

Sights

★ Praça do Marquês de Pombal

The Praça do Marquês de Pombal forms the centre of Vila Real de Santo António. This magnificent square was paved with a radial mosaic design in 1879; the rays spread out from the obelisk in the centre the top of which is adorned with a crown and an armillary sphere or skeleton globe. It was erected in 1775 for José I during whose reign many reforms in education and agriculture were carried out. Surrounding the square are some low-built and relatively uniform houses. The severity of the square is softened by the beautiful orange trees – which exude a delightful scent across the square in spring – and a few street cafés. A building on the eastern side houses the Municipal Library and the Manuel Cabanas Museum in which are displayed some wood-carvings of regional scenes.

Igreja Paroquial

The fronts of the houses on the north side of the square is broken by the Igreja Paroquial. This church has no side-aisles; built in the 18th c. but extensively restored in 1949. The tiled baptistry is very attractive.

View of the coast from the church forecourt at Cacela Velha

The Avenida da República extends along the bank of the Guadiana in the centre of Vila Real de Santo António. Parts of the avenue are lined with pleasant parks where visitors can sit on the benches and enjoy the view across the river with Ayamonte in the distance.

Avenida da República

Surroundings

Monte Gordo, the town neighbouring Vila Real de Santo António to the west, is the only really unappealing tourist centre east of Faro. Like so many places in the central part of the Algarve, huge hotel and apartment blocks have been built right by the seashore in this former fishing village. Near the town and for some kilometres either side there are some very fine sandy beaches, and the tourist infrastructure is good, with plenty of shops, restaurants, pubs, discothèques and a casino.

Monte Gordo

Manta Rota is a small village rather lacking in infrastructure lying about 10km west of Vila Real de Santo António. The lagoon system of the Rio Formosa ends here, with the result that Manta Rota lies directly by the open sea. It boasts superb, long beaches reaching as far as Monte Gordo in the east; the best-known section of beach is the Praia Verde which is lined with small pine woods.

Manta Rota

Charmingly situated above the coastal strip a further 2km to the west is the tiny hamlet of Cacela Velha which was once a more important village. Today it has only a few houses but blends in very well with its surroundings. It probably dates back to a Phoenician settlement. The church forecourt is extraordinarily beautiful and offers a view of the mud-flats, the offshore islands and the open sea beyond. The 16th c. church has a Renaissance main door and a Gothic side-door. Tourism is not as yet really catered for and the village can boast only one restaurant.

★Cacela Velha

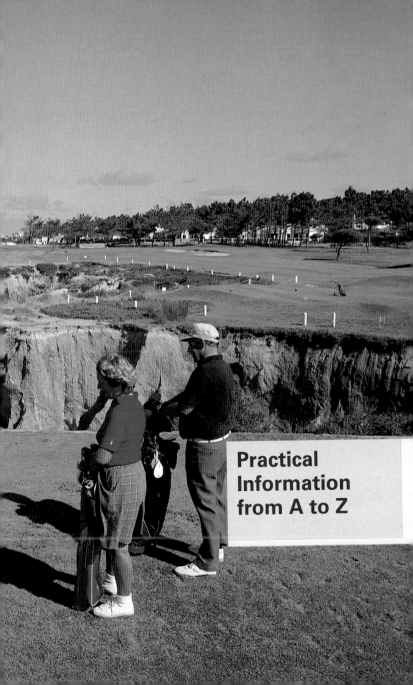

**Practical
Information
from A to Z**

Practical Information from A to Z

Accommodation

Camping	See entry
Hotels	See entry
Pousadas	See entry

Turismo de Habitação

Portugal's "turismo de habitação" is a special kind of accommodation provided for visitors by the owners of some stately homes. Their spacious guest rooms are almost invariably tastefully furnished, often with antiques, and there are usually other leisure facilities in the vicinity. The historic homes in this scheme receive government subsidy, are registered with the National Tourist Office, and must have the appropriate sign at the entrance. Other similar schemes include "turismo rural", rural accommodation in country houses and wineries, and "agroturismo" where it is possible to stay on farms and in farmhouses.

Information is available from travel agents and from TURIHAB (Associação de Turismo de Habitação), Praça da República, 4990 Ponte de Lima; tel. 058/94 27 29, fax 058/74 14 44.

Faro region

Quinta de Benatrite, Santa Bárbara de Nexe, 8000 Faro; tel. 089/9 04 50, 3 rooms

Lagoa region

Casa Bela Moura, Alporchinhos, Porches, 8365 Armação de Pêra; tel. 082/31 34 22, fax 082/31 30 25, 8 rooms

Lagos region

Casa do Pinhão, Praia do Pinhão, 8600 Lagos; tel. 082/6 23 71 and tel. 01/848 40 59, 3 rooms
Quinta da Alfarrobeira, Estrada de Palmares – Odeáxere, 8600 Lagos; tel. 082/79 84 24, 2 rooms

Loulé region

Casa de Alte, Largo da Igreja, Alte, 8100 Loulé; tel. 089/6 84 26
Casa Belaventura, Alfontes, 8100 Loulé; tel. 089/36 06 33, 4 rooms
Quinta das Rochas, Fonte Coberta, Almansil, 8100 Loulé; tel. 089/39 31 65, fax 089/39 91 98, 6 rooms
Quinta da Várzea, Várzeas de Querença, 8100 Loulé; tel. 089/41 44 43, 9 rooms

Portimão region

Casa Três Palmeiras, João d'Arens, Praia do Vau, 8500 Portimão; tel. 082/40 12 75, fax 082/40 10 29, 5 rooms
Vila Rosa de Lima, Estrada da Torre, 8500 Portimão; tel. 082/41 10 97, 4 rooms

Silves region

Quinta da Figueirinha, Figueirinha, 8300 Silves; tel. 082/44 26 77, 3 apartments
Quinta do Rio, Santo Estevão, 8300 Silves; tel./fax 082/44 55 28, 6 rooms

Tavira region

Quinta do Caracol, S. Tiago, 8000 Tavira; tel. 081/2 24 75, 7 apartments
Quinta da Fonte do Bispo, EN 270, Sítio da Fonte do Bispo, 8000 Tavira; tel. 081/97 14 84 and 01/54 29 94, 6 rooms

Youth hostels

See entry

◀ *One of the most beautiful golf courses in the Algarve: Vale do Lobo*

Air Travel

Air Portugal (TAP), Rua D. Francisco Gomes 8   Airlines
8000 Faro; tel. 089/80 02 00
This is now only a ticket office. Reservations have moved to Lisbon.
Faro airport: tel. 089/80 07 31/2. Open weekends and holiday periods.

British Airways; Faro airport: tel. 089/21 21 25

Portugália; Faro airport: tel. 089/81 59 62

Aeroporto Faro, the Algarve's international airport, is about 6km east of the   Faro airport
town. It mainly takes charter flights and scheduled flights from the rest of
Europe. TAP (Air Portugal) and Portugália also operate domestic flights to
Lisbon and Oporto.
     Information: tel. 089/81 82 81, 81 89 46
     Lost property: tel. 089/81 83 02

Buses run from the airport into Faro town centre, with stops at the railway   Airport buses
station and central bus station, but they are relatively infrequent and not   and taxis
very reliable. Bus No. 18 runs to town centre until approximately 8pm.
     A taxi to the centre of Faro costs about 1100 Esc., plus extra for luggage.

Aero Clube de Lagos; tel. 082/76 29 06, 76 76 12, fax 76 76 12   Sightseeing
         flights

Aero Clube de Faro; tel. 089/82 38 46

Aeródromo de Portimão; tel. 082/49 59 42, fax 41 67 84

Water fun at an aquapark near Monte Gordo

Aquaparks

The Algarve has a number of aquaparks with giant flumes, high-diving shows and various other attractions.

Slide & Splash. East of Portimão at Lagoa on the N125; tel. 082/34 16 85

The Big One. East of Portimão at Porches on the N125; tel. 082/32 28 27

Pinguim. Monte Gordo, close to the campsite

Atlântico Park. At Quarteira on the N125; tel. 089/32 28 27

Aqua Show. At Quarteira on the N396; tel. 089/30 11 45

Zoomarine. On the N125 at Guia/Albufeira; tel. 089/56 11 04
See A to Z, Albufeira

Beaches

The coast of the Algarve is famous for the beauty and variety of its beaches. In the rocky Algarve to the west they mostly take the form of small and sometimes very scenic sandy coves at the foot of tall cliffs. Here the Atlantic is still a force to be reckoned with, especially on stormy days in spring, autumn and winter. This western section of the coast is generally speaking very good for diving. In the east, roughly from Quarteira onwards, there are lovely flat sandy beaches stretching for miles along the coast and often completely empty. The beaches listed below, running from west to east, are all good, long sandy beaches, or the larger beaches in rocky coves. There are places to eat on all the tourist beaches; the empty bays on the west coast usually only have temporary eating places that are put up specially for the holiday season.

Beach signs and warning flags
Some beaches have signs indicating whether they have life-guards or not. "Area Concessionada" means there are life-guards on duty, while "Praia não vigilida" means the beach is unsupervised. Supervised beaches use flags to show when it is safe to go in the water. A red flag means it is forbidden to enter the sea, even close to the coast for paddling; a yellow flag means no swimming, and a green flag indicates that paddling and swimming are safe. A blue/white chequered flag means the beach is temporarily unsupervised.

The best beaches from west to east

Aljezur
Several breathtakingly scenic, empty beaches at the foot of the cliffs south-west of Aljezur. These are often difficult to get to, and the Atlantic still pounds this coast with its full force, but sections of the Praia de Monte Clérigo are relatively safe.

Vila do Bispo
A few miles west of Vila do Bispo signs point the way down little roads and sandy tracks to the beaches of Castelejo, Cordama and Barriga; beautiful sandy coves in the as yet relatively unspoilt rocky Costa Vicentina.

Sagres
Beliche, 5km north-west of Sagres, has a 500m stretch of beach reached by a path; relatively windy, so suitable for the expert surfer. Martinhal beach, east of Sagres, has 750m of white sand and dunes, and is in the shelter of the harbour, making it a good beach for children. The beach at Zadival is much smaller, is of fine sand and free of rocks.

Evening light on the beach at Portimão

Salema has a pleasant sandy beach 750m long surrounded by cliffs; good for surfing. There are rocky and sandy coves east and west of the town.

Salema

Holidaymakers in Burgau have to content themselves with a relatively small beach 300m long.

Burgau

200m of sandy beach with rocks, very good for children; various watersports including scuba-diving.

Luz

Lagos itself only has quite small beaches but the nearby beaches range from the vast flat expanse of sand at Meia Praia a mile to the east to those in the photogenic rocky coves to the west at Praia Dona Ana, Praia Porto de Mós, etc.; good diving and surfing.

Lagos

Very long flat sandy beach, with watersports; another good beach for watersports is the smaller Praia de Três Irmãos.

Alvor

Broad beach with picturesque rocks; high-rise apartments line the clifftop road directly overlooking the beach; very popular in the holiday season.

Praia da Rocha

Well-kept beach at the mouth of the Rio Arade, with a number of smaller rocky coves within walking distance, but rather spoilt by the skyline of Praia da Rocha on the other side.

Ferragudo

Small cove with rocks on both sides; packed in summer.

Carvoeiro

Very long beach of golden sand stretching along the coast to the east, with a few fishing boats, and room to spare even in the peak holiday season, plus rocky coves to the west, including the extremely scenic Praia da Senhora da Rocha.

Armação de Pêra

143

Beaches

A sandy bay near Armação

Albufeira	Albufeira's lovely town beach gets packed in the holiday season, but there is more chance of finding some space further east at Oura; there are also some very pretty coves west of the town such as Praia de São Rafael, Praia da Coelha and Praia do Castelo.
Olhos de Água	Long beach of fine sand with rocks and cliffs; good surfing.
Vilamoura	Long child-friendly sandy beach; tourist infrastructure, good watersports, ideal for surfers.
Quarteira	Good sandy beach, with safe swimming for children; high-rise apartments line the road overlooking the beach – very much a tourist resort, with plenty of sports facilities.
Vale do Lobo	Flat beach of fine sand with rocks and cliffs; watersports, good surfing conditions.
Quinta do Lago	Long idyllic beach with dunes out in the lagoon; good surfing.
Faro	Praia de Faro beach, over half a mile long, is on the sandspit which forms the lagoon and is accessible by car from near the airport. There are several other good beaches on the islands in the lagoon such as Ilha da Barreta, accessible by boat.
Olhão	Boats run regularly from Olhão to the islands of Farol, Culatra and Armona out in the lagoon which have long flat sandy beaches with dunes and are ideal for children.
Tavira	Ilha de Tavira, which can be reached by boat from Tavira, or by road from Santa Luzia further west, has miles of sandy beaches, dunes and a small wood.
Cabanas/Cacela	Very good long, deserted beach on a spit which can be reached by fishing boat or on foot at low tide. It is possible also to walk there from Manta Rota.

Miles of golden sandy beaches and dunes extend along the coast either side of Monte Gordo.

Monte Gordo

Bullfighting

Bullfighting in Portugal is different from its Spanish counterpart in that the bull leaves the arena alive, although it still gets slaughtered later just the same (see Baedeker Special, "Of Touros and Cavaleiros"). As a rule the bullfighting you see in the Algarve is aimed at the tourist trade and is therefore likely to be of a different quality from elsewhere in Portugal.

Buses

See Public Transport

Business Hours

See Opening Times

Camping

Portugal's public and private campsites are graded according to one to four stars. Besides passport or identity card campers may also need to produce a "camping carnet" – issued by the International Federation of Camping and Caravanning – if they want to use sites owned by clubs or the Portuguese Camping and Caravanning Federation.

Campsites

Camping is usually not permitted by the roadside, in laybys or anywhere else that is not an official campsite.

Unofficial camping

★★★★Parque de Campismo de Albufeira, 8200 Albufeira; tel. 089/58 76 30: 3km from station

Albufeira

★★★Parque de Campismo do Serrão (at Aldeia Velha), 8670 Aljezur; tel. 082/9 86 12: 800m from bus stop
★★★Parque de Campismo Municipal de Aljezur (at Vale da Telha), 8670 Aljezur; tel. 082/9 84 44, 5km from bus stop

Aljezur

★★★Parque de Campismo de Canelas (at Armação de Pêra), 8300 Silves; tel. 082/31 47 18
★★Parque de Campismo da Praia de Armação de Pêra, 8300 Silves; tel. 082/31 22 60: 20m from bus stop, 4km from station

Armação de Pêra

★★★Parque de Campismo de Lagos (at Porto de Mós), 8600 Lagos; tel. 082/76 20 89: 50m from bus stop, 1.5km from station
★★★Parque de Campismo de Valverde (at Luz), 8600 Lagos; tel. 082/78 92 11: 50m from bus stop, 5km from station
★★Parque de Campismo de Espiche, 8600 Lagos; tel. 082/78 94 31: 5km from station
★Parque de Campismo da Trindade (at Praia de Dona Ana), 8600 Lagos; tel. 082/76 38 93: 800m from bus stop, 1km from station

Lagos

★★★Parque de Campismo e Caravanismo do Sindicato dos Bancários do Sul e Ilhas, 8700 Olhão; tel. 089/70 54 02: 400m from bus stop, 1.5km from station

Olhão

Of Touros and Cavaleiros

Visitors to the Algarve may perhaps share the reservations voiced by the writer Felix Krull when invited to a Portuguese bullfight: "I'm rather squeamish, I said, and if I know me, not one for butchery in the guise of folklore. Take the horses for instance – I'd heard that the bulls often slice them open so that their guts spill out; I wouldn't want to see that, let alone what happens to the bull, which I'd just feel sorry for. You could say that I ought to be able to put up with, if not exactly enjoy, a spectacle that even ladies can tolerate. But these ladies, these Iberians, are born and raised in this tough tradition, while I'm just a rather delicate foreigner . . ."

And don't believe it if you are told that Portuguese bullfighting is bloodless compared with the Spanish version. The bull may not actually be killed in the ring, but death still awaits it in the wings.

Portugal's top "touradas", as bullfights are called, take place in the Lisbon arena in front of around 8000 spectators, and in the arenas of Santarém and Vila Franca de Xira, north-east of the capital. And everywhere throughout the country you will come across small local bull rings, or "corridas", often no more than a few wooden slats nailed together. In the villages touradas are often simply put on in the market place or on the playing field on the edge of the village.

On the coast of the Algarve, however, it is not the true classical bullfighting of the great Portuguese arenas. The heroism and costumes of the bullfighters often leave a lot to be desired, the events are only half as long as elsewhere in Portugal, and all in all it is basically bullfighting for tourists.

The typical tourada always begins with a contest between the "touro", the bull, and the "cavaleiro", an elegantly costumed bullfighter on horseback. The cavaleiro first limbers up against a "tourinha", an artificial bull consisting of horns mounted on a chassis. But then the whole affair gets going in deadly earnest. The bull, which has been moving rather aimlessly round the perimeter, catches sight of the cavaleiro and his horse and gallops wildly at them, repeatedly charging them head on, diagonally and from the side. Horse and rider dexterously avoid it in a series of skilful manoeuvres or "sortes". While these are going on the cavaleiro tries to plant a "farpa" or the shorter "ferros" in the snorting beast's neck. The onlookers howl their appreciation depending on how the cavaleiro performs – clearly the bolder he is the better. Really daring cavaleiros hold their ground till the very last minute or, equally death-defying, ride straight at the charging bull. Luckily for them, the horns of the Portuguese bulls are rendered virtually harmless by leather padding.

A Portuguese bullfight in Albufeira

Once all the farpas and ferros have been planted in the bull the referee, "O Intelligente", decides whether touro and cavaleiro have had enough. Then follows the second part of the action, the "pega", a no less tense encounter between man and beast. The cavaleiro withdraws and eight intrepid "forcados", unarmed and on foot, advance one behind the other in teams of four to bring down the bull. The first hurls himself valiantly at the bull's horns and tries to hold onto its neck. The next grabs the bull's head, the third its shoulders or whatever comes to hand, and the last seizes it by the tail so that, using all their might and main, they bring it to a stop. This procedure is as dangerous as it looks and was banned in the 19th c. because of the number of forcados who were being killed. Accidents can still happen, and many of them end up in hospital. It is hard to believe that, as unpaid amateurs, their heroic deeds go unrewarded except for what the spectators care to give them. The cavaleiros, on the other hand, are professionals and earn large fees for their appearances.

The bullfighting season is from Easter to October. They are usually held on Thursdays and Sundays, and last for about three hours. During this time six bulls will follow one another into the ring. As has been said, they are not killed until after the fight is over when, depending on how badly injured they are, they will either be despatched immediately or slaughtered the next day. The supposedly "bloodless" Portuguese tourada may actually appear to be easier on the bulls, but when the touro dies at the height of the bullfight it is at least spared several more hours of suffering.

Car Hire

Portimão	★★Parque de Campismo da Dourada (at Alvor), 8500 Portimão; tel. 082/45 80 02: 4km from station
	★★Parque de Campismo de Ferragudo, 8400 Lagoa; tel. 082/46 11 21: 100m from bus stop, 2.6km from station
Quarteira	★★★Parque de Campismo de Quarteira/Obitur, 8100 Loulé; tel. 089/30 28 21: 30m from bus stop, 6km from station
Tavira	★★Parque de Campismo Municipal da Ilha de Tavira, 8300 Tavira; tel. 081/2 35 05: 400m from bus stop, 2km from station
Vila do Bispo	★★Parque de Campismo Quinta dos Carriços, 8650 Vila do Bispo; tel. 082/6 52 01: 100m from bus stop
Vila Real de Santo António	★Parque de Campismo O Caliço (at Vila Nova de Cacela), 8900 Vila Real de Santo António; tel. 081/95 11 95: 500m from bus stop, 1.5km from station
	★Parque de Campismo Municipal de Monte Gordo, 8900 Vila Real de Santo António; tel. 081/4 39 60: 200m from bus stop, 1.3km from station
Camping guides	The Direcção-Geral do Turismo in Lisbon publishes an up-to-date and multi-lingual official guide to campsites (Parques de Campismo, Guia oficial), obtainable from: Direcção-Geral do Turismo, Av. António Augusto de Aguiar 86, 1000 Lisbon; tel. 01/57 50 86, fax 01/3 52 58 06.

Car Hire

See Motoring

Casinos

The Algarve has casinos in Alvor, Vilamoura and Monte Gordo. Here in the gaming room French and American roulette, blackjack and baccarat are available plus the usual one-armed bandits. The casinos are normally open daily from 3pm to 3am, and there is usually an international floor show in the casino restaurant.

Chemists

See Health Care

Children

The Algarve coast is a great place for family holidays with both younger and older children. Fine weather means that they can play on the beach even in spring and autumn, although remember that the Atlantic in the east of the Algarve is less rough and a bit warmer than in the west, and that the east has long sandy beaches. The best beaches for children are at Martinhal, Luz, Vilamoura (Praia da Falésia, Praia da Marinha), Farol, Culatra, Armono, Monte Gordo and on Ilha de Tavor, plus the tourist resorts of Armação de Pêra and Quarteira (see Beaches). Many hotels and apartment blocks have their own swimming pool and children's paddling pool, and some have special child care facilities. There are also plenty of sports on offer and organised programmes for older children and young people.

Excursions suitable for children are boat trips to the caves and coves of the west coast, from Portimão to Silves on the Rio Arade, along the Spanish border on the Guadiana, or by a little ferry to the islands in the lagoon on the east coast. Another option is to go on an organised ride and explore the hinterland on the back of a donkey (see Excursions).

There are several big aquaparks to delight young and old alike (see Aquaparks). You could happily spend a whole day at Zoomarine, for example, where the attractions include performing dolphins and a parrot show. Other interesting excursions include a trip to Europe's most south-westerly point (see A to Z, Sagres), a visit to the wildlife centre at Quinta de Marim (see A to Z, Olhão) or to the Costa Vicentina nature park (see Aljezur).

Excursions

Consulates

See Diplomatic Representation

Currency

The Portuguese unit of currency is the escudo (Esc.) which is sub-divided into 100 centavos, and its symbol – the dollar sign $ – is written between the escudos and the centavos. There are banknotes for 500, 1000, 2000, 5000 and 10,000 Esc. and coins in denominations of 1, 2½, 5, 10, 20, 50 100 and 200 Esc. and 50 and 10 centavos.

Currency

The escudo is subject to considerable fluctuations and, as is usually the case with countries that have a weak currency, it pays to change money before going to Portugal. When changing back Portuguese banknotes you usually lose from 11 to 30% on the deal.

Exchange rates

Membership of the European Union means there are no restrictions on how much foreign currency a private individual can take into Portugal, although amounts in excess of one million escudos should be declared on entry.

Currency import and export

Eurocheques can be issued up to an amount of 35,000 Esc. It is possible to withdraw cash up to that amount from banks' automatic cash dispensers (these often take credit cards as well). If your Eurocheque card is lost report this straightaway to the relevant number in the country of issue so that it can be cancelled immediately.

Eurocheques

Banks, the larger hotels, top restaurants, car hire firms and some shops accept most international credit cards. Visa and Eurocard are widely recognised but the same does not always apply to American Express and Diner's Club. If a credit card is lost it should be reported immediately.

Credit cards

Customs Regulations

In theory there is now no limit to the amount of goods that can be taken from one EU country to another provided they have been purchased tax paid in an EU country, are for personal use and not intended for resale. However, customs authorities have issued guide lines to the maximum amounts considered reasonable for persons over 17 years of age. These are: 10 litres of spirits or strong liqueurs, 20 litres fortified wine (port, sherry, etc.) 90 litres of table wine (of which not more than 60 litres may be sparkling wine), 110 litres of beer, 800 cigarettes or 400 cigarillos or 200 cigars. There is no limit on perfume or toilet water.

Allowances between EU countries

Cycling

Entry from Non-EU countries	For those coming from a country outside the EU or who have arrived from an EU country without having passed through custom control with all their baggage, the allowances for goods obtained anywhere outside the EU for persons over the age of 17 are: 1 litre spirits or 2 litres of fortified wine and 2 litres table wine; 60cc perfume, 250cc toilet water; 200 cigarettes or 100 cigarillos or 50 cigars or 250 grammes tobacco
Duty-free goods	The allowances for goods purchased "duty-free" from airports, on aircraft and ferries are the same as for entry from non-EU countries above. Duty-free allowances are scheduled to be phased out by January 1st 1999.

Cycling

The only really good routes for cycling are the smaller country roads away from the coast. These go through some lovely scenery, but remember that it can be relatively hilly. Near the coast the main roads are very busy, there are virtually no cycle lanes and cyclists are given little or no consideration. Cycles – and scooters – can be hired in Albufeira, Armação de Pêra, Carvoeiro, Lagos, Praia da Rocha, Tavira, Vilamoura, Quarteira and Monte Gordo.

Organised cycling tours	To join a small group on an organised cycling tour contact: Bahia Biketours, Rua Prof. Luíz de Azevedo 53, 8600 Lagos; tel. 082/76 77 19. Details of cycling tours are also available from some travel agents.

Diplomatic Representation

Australia	Embassy: Avenida da Liberdade 244 1200 Lisbon; tel. 01/52 30 66
Canada	Embassy: Avenida da Liberdade 144–156 1200 Lisbon; tel. 01/347 48 92
Eire	Embassy: Rua da Imprensa a Estrela 1 Lisbon; tel. 01/66 15 69
South Africa	Embassy: Avenida Luís Bivar 10/10a Lisbon; tel. 01/53 50 41
United Kingdom	Consulate: 7.1 Lg Francisco A Maurício 8500 Portimão; tel. 082/41 78 00
	Embassy: Rua S. Domingos â Lapa 37 Lisbon; tel. 01/396 11 91
United States of America	Embassy: Avenida das Forças Armadas 16 Lisbon; tel. 01/726 66 00

Electricity

The electricity supply is 220 AC, with continental two-pin plugs. Most standard European plugs can be used in the big hotels, but American flat-pin plugs require a transformer and an adaptor.

Embassies

See Diplomatic Representation

Emergency Calls

Throughout Portugal the free-phone number for police, fire, medical and rescue services is 115.

Call 115

There are free-standing orange emergency phones alongside the motorways.

On motorways

Breakdown assistance can be requested from the Portuguese Automobile Club: tel. 01/942 50 95.

Breakdown assistance

Events

Like the rest of Portugal the Algarve has a full calendar of festivals and ceremonial events, especially where its local saints are concerned. Every town and almost every village has its own patron saint and an annual festival in their honour which goes beyond purely religious observance to a day of free fun for the whole community. The festival usually begins with a packed church for a full high mass in the saint's honour. This is often followed by a "romaria" when everyone processes through the streets behind the image of their saint. Eventually the whole place is given over to all the fun of the fair, with music and folk-dancing. There are also a number of traditional seasonal events such as the almond blossom festival.

During the summer the Algarve also stages its share of concert series, film, folklore and dance festivals.

During the first twelve days of January strolling musicians, or "charolas", tour all round the villages performing "janeiras", songs to mark the new year, an age-old tradition in southern Portugal.

January

Vilamoura: celebration of the almond blossom festival in late January or early February.

Carnival, especially in Loulé, Moncarapacho and Portimão

February/March

Loulé: Loulé is famous throughout Portugal for its carnival parade; it also celebrates the almond blossom festival at the same time.

Salir: Festa das Espigas, an Alpine-style festival as befits a pretty mountain village.

Alte: in neighbouring Alte, Festa dos Chouriços, sausage festival in honour of São Luís.

Good Friday and Easter Day processions in a number of places.

Easter

Loulé: Festa da Mãe Soberana, a famous romaria on the second Sunday after Easter when the Virgin is carried in procession up the rugged hillside to the chapel of Nossa Senhora da Piedade. This is followed by general festivities.

General: celebrations, with rallies, song and dance, to mark Liberation Day, the public holiday commemorating the Carnation Revolution and an end to years of dictatorship on April 25th 1974.

April

General: celebrations, similar to April 25th, with rallies and fairs, to mark May 1st.

May

Alte: Festa da Grande Fonte, early in May, when a grand picnic is held around the village spring; parades, music and dancing.

General: many places show amateur films as part of the Algarve's international festival of low-budget films.

151

Excursions

General: during the international music festival between April and June many places in the Algarve stage concerts and ballets starring prominent artistes.

June   General: Festas dos Santos Populares take place throughout Portugal. These popular saints are obviously particularly fêted in the places where they are the patron saints.

Faro: the feast of Santo António, patron saint of Faro, is celebrated on June 13th with a procession and a public festival. Saint Anthony is also the patron saint of the forgetful, lovers and children.

Silves: Festival da Carveja, beer festival with music, folklore and dance.

July   Faro: Feira do Carmo, grand public festival in mid-July.

Fuzeta: Festa do Carmo is celebrated in Fuzeta, near Olhão, with a water-borne procession.

August   Olhão: Festival of the Sardines

Castro Marim: São Bartolomeu is honoured on August 15th with a festival inside the castle walls.

September   General: Algarve folklore festivals in various place with dance perform-ances and competition for the Algarve prize; finals in Praia da Rocha.

Albufeira: Festa do Beato São Vicente

Vila Real de Santo António: Festa de Nossa Senhora da Encarnação

October   Faro: people flock from miles around to Faro's famous fair, the Feira de Santa Iria.

Monchique: October fair.

December   General: various concerts in the run-up to Christmas, the most important family festival of the year for the Portuguese.

Excursions

There are plenty of opportunities to get around and explore the Algarve on excursions. The big hotels normally offer trips to various Algarve destina-tions, and in all the main tourist centres trips by boat along the rocky coastline or sightseeing tours by coach can be booked.

Individual outings by car, train or bus can be made. Trains only go to the main towns and smaller places close to the coast however. Some of the inland villages are accessible by bus, but there are very few bus services in the more isolated parts (see Public Transport). For more than one day's outing it is better to go by car (see Suggested Routes). Another option is to tour the hinterland by cycle (see Cycling), but remember it can be quite hilly.

If you are holidaying in the east of the Algarve it is posisible to get to Seville relatively quickly by motorway. And Mértola, in the south-east of the Alentejo, is another possibility for an excursion from this part of the Algarve.

Portimão and surroundings   Tempo Passa, a tour operator in Portimão, has some highly individual excursions in its programme. These include boat trips to the caves along the coast, a cruise up the Arade River from Portimão to Silves, and a "mule safari" through the foothills of the Serra de Monchique. Also on offer is trekking in the Serra de Monchique and walking the cliffs at Ferragudo: Tempo Passa, Kiosk Praça Teixeira Gomes; tel. 082/41 71 10, 47 12 41.

In the Sandy Algarve there are some lovely day-trips by boat from Faro, Olhão and Tavira out to the islands in the lagoon. You can also see something of the beautiful hinterland of the eastern Algarve by taking a river trip along the frontier up the River Guadiana. These are operated by Transguadiana from Vila Real de Santo António (tel. 081/51 29 97); information is available from the tourist office in Monte Gordo.

Eastern Algarve

Turinfo in Sagres organises walks in the Costa Vicentina national park, as well as jeep, donkey and cycle safaris and boat trips around Cabo de São Vicente and along the Costa Vicentina (Turinfo, tourist information centre; tel. 082/6 45 20, 6 45 51).

Western Algarve

Ferries

See Public Transport

Fado

Fado, Portugal's own distinct form of folk music, is said to have originated in the backstreets of Lisbon and is essentially a ballad of the cities. Nowadays you may be lucky enough to hear authentic fado live in the bars of Lisbon or Coimbra, but you are unlikely to find a really good "fadista" in the Algarve. Here it is mostly fado for tourists but to get some idea of what this typically Portuguese music is like there are a few places which occasionally stage fado nights (noites de fado).

Lagoa:
Casa Velha, Rua Mouzinho de Albuquerque 60
Tel. 082/34 26 00 (noites de fado from time to time)

Fado nights

Porches:
Porches Velho
Tel. 082/38 16 92 (Fridays and Saturdays)

Alvor:
Alvila, 1km east of Alvor on the road to Praia da Rocha
Tel. 082/45 87 75 (usually on Tuesdays)

There are some very good fado recordings on CD, tape, etc. which are available in Portuguese record stores (see Shopping).

Recordings

Food and Drink

Eating out plays a relatively important part in the life of the Portuguese. Many of them get their lunch (almoço) at a regular place close to where they work, and meet their friends in restaurants for dinner (jantar) in the evening. They like going out to eat on family occasions such as birthdays too, when they really enjoy celebrating with a leisurely meal in their favourite little restaurant.

Eating out in Portugal

The Algarve has many restaurants catering solely for tourists and these do have the advantage of providing menus in English, but they rarely provide genuine Portuguese cuisine. Usually the best place to find the very good local dishes is somewhere quite unpretentious. Generally speaking Portuguese food is quite simple and most palatable, if eventually somewhat lacking in variety. Lovers of fish and seafood will be in their element but the

Local cuisine

Food and Drink

Grilled sardines – a traditional Portuguese dish

same cannot be said for those who want vegetables and salads; these often have to be ordered separately. Sauces are few and far between – with fish, for example, you often just get potatoes and melted butter.

Meal times	Lunch-time is usually between 12.30 and 2pm and dinner between 8 and 10pm in the evening.
Breakfast	Breakfast (pequeno almoço) is comparatively unimportant where the Portuguese are concerned, and they usually just have something on the way to work. Hotels and pensions normally provide a continental-style breakfast of tea or coffee, and rolls plus jam, cheese or ham, etc. while the larger hotels have self-service buffets. To get breakfast in a bar order a roll or a sandwich (sanuíche) with cheese (com queijo) or ham (com fiambre), buttered toast (torrada) or a ham and cheese toastie (tosta mista).
Midday and evening meals	Lunch and dinner normally consist of three courses – starter, main course and dessert. A starter (entrada) is usually one of the excellent Portuguese soups. The main course will be a fish or meat dish with chips, potatoes or rice and occasionally vegetables and salad. Dessert (sobremesa) will be a delicious, often home-made sweet (doce), ice-cream or fruit. There is always bread on the table and sometimes, before the starter, you will also get cheese and olives with it, or small saucers of seafood. Just remember that every little extra probably costs extra, whether you ask for it or not. The Portuguese like to round off the meal with a small black coffee (bica) and a brandy (auardente) or marc (bagaço).

Soups (sopas)		
	sopa do dia	soup of the day
	caldo verde	cabbage and potato soup with a slice of sausage
	sopa de legumes	vegetable soup
	sopa de feijão	bean soup

sope de peixe	fish soup	
creme de marisco	seafood bisque	
canja	chicken broth	
açorda à Alentejana	clear bread soup with a poached egg, seasoned with lots of garlic and coriander, from Alentejo	
caldeirada	fish stew (Portuguese bouillabaise)	
feijoada	bean stew	
cozida à portuguesa	vegetable soup with pieces of meat	
bacalhau	dried cod (Portugal's national dish, once a poorman's food, now quite expensive, but still an ingredient in many dishes)	Fish (peixe)
bacalhau cozido	boiled bacalhau	
bacalhau na brasa	grilled bacalhau	
bacalhau à brás	bacalhau fried with egg, potatoes and onions	
sardinhas assadas	grilled sardines	
cherne, robalo	perch	
lulas grelhadas	grilled baby octopus	
polvo	octopus	
peixa espada	swordfish	
atum	tuna	
truta	trout	
salmão	salmon	
linguado	sole	
enguia	eel	
camarães	shrimp	Seafood (mariscos)
gambas	scampi	
sapateira	crab	
lagosta	spiny lobster	
amêijoas	clams	
arroz de marisco	seafood risotto	
bife (com ovo)	steak (with fried egg)	Meat (carne)
costeleta	cutlet	
carne de porco	pork	
carne de porco à Alentejana	pork with clams	
leitão assado	roast suckling pig	
lombo de porco	roast leg of pork	
carne de vaca	beef	
borrego	lamb	
cabrito assado	roast kid	
espetada de carne	meat kebab	
frango assado	spit-roast chicken	
frango com piri-piri	barbecued chicken with hot little Angolan peppers (Algarve speciality)	
peru	turkey	
ovos mexidos	scrambled egg	Eggs (ovos)
ovos estrelados	fried egg	
omeleta	omelette	
cogumelos	mushrooms	Vegetables (legumes)
cenouras	carrots	
alho francês	leeks	
pimentos	peppers	
feijães	beans	
ervilhas	peas	
cebola	onions	
alface	lettuce	

Food and Drink

	salada de tomate	tomato salad
	salada mista	mixed salad
Fruit (frutas)	salada de fruta	fruit salad
	maçã	apple
	pêra	pear
	melão	melon
	melancia	water melon
	morangos	strawberries
	pêssego	peach
	uvas	grapes
	laranja	orange
Desserts (sobremesa)	gelado, sorvete	ice cream
	arroz doce	rice pudding
	pudim molotov	egg-white floating islands
	pudim flan	crême caramel
	leite creme	baked custard
	toucinho do céu	sweet of sugar, eggs and ground almonds
	tarte de amêndoa	almond tart
	bolo de chocolate	chocolate cake
Snacks (salgados)	pastéis de bacalhau	little potato, parsley and dried cod fish-cakes
	rissois de camarão	little shrimp patties
	chamuça	little spicey minced meat patties
	prego no pão	hamburger

Drink (bebidas)

Soft drinks
All the usual international soft drinks, plus mineral water (água mineral), both still (sem gás) and carbonated (com gás), and good fruit juices (usually bottled rather than freshly pressed) are available.

Beer
Beer (cerveja) is very popular with the Portuguese. The best known brand is "Sagres", brewed near Lisbon; "Superbock" is somewhat sweeter. If you ask for "cerveja" you get a bottled beer. "Imperial" will get you a small draught beer, "caneca" a large one.

Wine
Wine served with food is normally either a "vinho da mesa" (table wine) or a "vinho da casa" (house wine). "Vinho tinto" is red wine and "vinho branco" is white wine. The most popular wines are those from the Dão, Douro, and Ribatejo regions, from Colares, north-west of Lisbon, and, more recently, from Alentejo. "Vinho verde" is a mildly sparkling youthful wine from northern Portugal which accounts for about 20% of the nation's wine output. Its name "green wine" refers to its method of production: the grapes are harvested early and only fermented for a short time.

Portugal's most famous wine is undoubtedly port, which gets its name from the northern town of Oporto. The grapes are chiefly grown on the upper slopes of the Douro on the slatey soils which give it a flavour that is all its own. The partly fermented red wine is fortified with brandy then stored for a number of years in casks or bottles. Dry port is mostly drunk as an aperitif, while sweet port is traditionally served at the end of a meal.

Spirits
A favourite fruit brandy in the Algarve is "medronho", a fiery spirit distilled from the fruit of the arbutus or strawberry tree which grows particularly well in southern Portugal. Other popular spirits include "bagaço", made from grape residue like a French marc, and "aguardente velha", a form of old brandy. "Ginjinha" is a cherry liqueur which can be ordered with (com) or without (sem) cherries.

Coffee
Coffee comes as "café" or "bica", a small cup of espresso, or you can order "galão", white coffee in a glass. If you ask for "café com leite" you normally

get white coffee in a cup. "Meia de leite" means a cup of coffee too, but with less milk, while "meia de leite à máquina" is a cappucino.

Golf

Golf has been played in Portugal since 1890, and the Algarve is legendary among golfers for the quality of its golf courses and a climate where it is possible to play golf all year round on sixteen golf-courses, most of them 18-hole, in beautiful settings; Vilamoura has the largest golf-complex in Europe.

Pine Cliffs Golf   Albufeira
Praia da Falésia, 9 holes
Tel. 089/50 17 67, fax 089/50 17 95
one of Portugal's finest golf-courses

Salgado Golf
Praia da Galé, 18 holes
Tel. 089/59 19 64, fax 089/59 19 66

Carvoeiro Golf Club   Carvoeiro
2 18-hole courses
Tel. 082/35 72 68, fax 082/35 77 25

Vale do Milho Club
2 9-hole courses
Tel. 082/35 85 02, fax 082/35 84 97

Palmares Golf Club   Lagos
Meia Praia, 18 holes
Tel. 082/76 28 53, fax 082/76 25 34

Parque da Floresta Golf Club
Vale do Poço, 16km west of Lagos, 18 holes
Tel. 082/6 53 33, fax 082/6 51 57

Vila Sol Club   Loulé
Alto do Semino, 18 holes
Tel. 089/30 12 99, fax 089/30 12 99

Quinta do Lago Golf Club
Almansil, 4 9-hole courses
Tel. 089/39 45 29, fax 089/39 40 13

Vale do Lôbo Golf Club
Vale do Lobo, 3 9-hole courses
Tel. 089/39 44 44, fax 089/39 47 13
hilly terrain, lovely greens; illus. pp 138–39

São Lourenço Golf Club
Quinta do Lago, Almansil, 18 holes
Tel. 089/39 65 22, fax 089/39 69 08

Pinheiros Altos Club
Quinta do Lago, Almansil, 18 holes
Tel. 089/39 43 40, fax 089/39 43 92

Vilamoura I Golf Club
Vilamoura, 18 holes
Tel. 089/38 99 08, fax 089/31 22 62

Vilamoura II Golf Club
Vilamoura, 18 holes
Tel. 089/31 55 62/3, fax 089/38 07 26

Vilamoura III Golf Club
Vilamoura, 27 holes
Tel. 089/38 07 24, fax 089/38 07 26

Portimão   Alto Club
Quinta do Alto do Poço, Alvor, 18 holes
Tel. 082/45 91 19, fax 082/45 95 58

Penina Golf Club
Penina, 18 holes
Tel. 082/41 54 15, fax 082/41 50 00
one of Portugal's most difficult courses

Getting to the Algarve

By air

There are scheduled flights to the Algarve's international airport at Faro from Britain by Air Portugal (TAP) and British Airways, and from the United States by Transworld Airlines (TWA) and TAP, mostly via Lisbon. There are also charter flights to Faro from Britain and elsewhere in Europe. These are often particularly cheap off-season, and there are some very good package deals to be had, with flight and accommodation in one of the main holiday resorts included.

Faro airport is about 9km from the town centre. International and local car hire firms have desks in the arrival hall (see Motoring). There are buses and taxis from there into town (see Air Travel), and there are bus and train links from Faro serving the rest of the Algarve coast (see Public Transport).

By car

Travelling from Britain to the Algarve by car there is a choice of cross-Channel car ferries to France, or the Channel Tunnel. Faro is approximately 2170km from the French Channel ports. The recommended western route is Paris to Bordeaux–Biarritz–Burgos–Madrid then Badajoz–Setúbal–Algarve, or Mérida–Seville–Algarve. The eastern route is Paris to Lyons–Perpignan–Le Perthus/La Junquera–Barcelona–Madrid, etc. When calculating the cost remember to include a substantial amount for motorway tolls. Another option is motorail from Paris to Lisbon: information from French Railways, 179 Piccadilly, London W1V 0BA; tel. 0990 300 003.

Another alternative from Britain is to take the car ferry from Plymouth to Santander in Spain – this takes 24 hours – and pick up the route via Burgos from there; from Santander to Faro is about 1300km. Information from Brittany Ferries, Millbay Docks, Plymouth PL1 3EW (reservations: tel. 0990 360 360).

By coach

There are regular coach services between London and Lisbon, Oporto, Coimbra, Lagos and Faro. Tickets and information are available from any National Express or Eurolines agent.

By rail

A daily service runs between London (Victoria) and Lisbon via Paris and Irún/Hendaye or Madrid. From Paris this takes 23 or 26 hours respectively. Information from British Rail Travel Centres. In Lisbon you have to change from Santa Apolónia station to Estação Sul e Sueste on the Praça do Comércio. The train from there to Faro takes between 4½ and 7 hours. For anyone with an Interrail pass this is a relatively cheap way to travel and can cost as little as a bargain charter flight.

Health Care

Emergency

Throughout Portugal the number to call for any emergency service, including medical assistance, is 119.

Most hospitals (hospital) have a 24-hour emergency service. In urgent cases visitors can go straight to the casualty department (urgência) of the nearest hospital. Many of the smaller places have health centres (centro de saúde) which are open during the day. Telephone numbers of hospitals and health centres can be found on the first page of the local telephone directory.

Emergency medical care

The central call numbers for hospital emergency services are:
Faro: tel. 089/80 34 11
Portimão: tel. 082/41 51 15
Lagos: tel. 082/76 30 34

Names and addresses of doctors and dentists who speak English are available from tourist offices.

English-speaking doctors/dentists

Members of EU countries are entitled to obtain medical care under the Portuguese health service, but it is necessary to have obtained an E111 before leaving home.

Treatment costs

It is however advisable, even for EU nationals, to take out some form of additional short-term health insurance. Nationals of non-EU countries should certainly have insurance cover.

The sign for a chemist (farmácia) is a green cross. Chemists are usually open Mon.–Fri. 9am–1pm and 3–7pm, Sat. 9am–1pm.

Chemists

Besides medicines manufactured in Portugal they also carry well-known brands from elsewhere and these can often be cheaper here than in their country of origin.

The addresses of chemists on duty at night and on Sundays (farmácias de serviço) are posted up in chemist's shops, listed in the local press, and obtainable by calling 118.

Hotels

Hotels are officially graded from five star (de luxe) to one star, but the quality within a single category can vary considerably. The grading of motels and aparthotels is more or less equivalent to that of hotels.

Grading system

Pensions are similar to guest houses and are found almost everywhere in Portugal. They are graded from one to four stars. Those in the lower categories can be cheaper but just as well-equipped as hotels of an equivalent grade. A "residencial" is a small pension or hotel which is comparable with a pension in terms of comfort and price and is usually family-run. "Albergarias" correspond to top-ranking pensions.

Pensions (pensão)

Pousadas (see entry) are top of the range state-run hotels which are usually located in historic buildings or at particularly historic or scenic sites.

Pousadas

Turismo de habitação is a similar kind of special accommodation. In this case it takes the form of stately homes, ranging from castles and palaces to country houses, which are still privately owned but part of a state-controlled scheme (see Accommodation).

Turismo de habitação

The cheapest option is probably bed and (usually) breakfast on a private basis, and this is easy to find in the main tourist resorts along the Algarve coast. The rooms are clean but modest and breakfast is mostly included.

Private rooms (quartos)

Prices for hotels and pensions can vary considerably according to the season. A double room in a pension will cost between 3000 and 15,000 Esc. The rates given below are guidelines for a night in a well-appointed hotel room for two people. The price of single room, both in pensions and hotels, is about 30% less than a double room.

Prices

Hotels

Grade	Double room	Grade	Double room
★★★★★	25,000–40,000 Esc.	★★	5000–10,000 Esc.
★★★★	20,000–35,000 Esc.	★	3000–6000 Esc.
★★★	10,000–20,000 Esc.		

Albufeira

★★★★★Sheraton Algarve (215 rooms)
Praia da Falésia, 8200 Albufeira; tel. 089/50 19 99, fax 089/50 19 50
This clifftop Sheraton is one of the Algarve's finest hotels. All the rooms
and suites in this luxurious low-rise hotel complex are very spacious; there
is a lift down to the beach.

★★★★Alfa Mar Resort (264 rooms)
Praia da Falésia, 8200 Albufeira; tel. 089/50 13 51, fax 089/50 14 04
Resort with hotel, apartments and bungalows, between Albufeira and
Quarteira on Falésia beach. The bungalows are particularly well suited for
family holidays; a wide range of sports facilities cost extra.

★★★★Hotel Boa Vista (93 rooms)
Rua Samora Barros 20, 8200 Albufeira; tel. 089/58 91 75, fax 089/58 91 80
Built into the cliff with a wonderful view of the sea, although this is not
exactly on the doorstep; charming stylish interior, swimming pool but no
sports facilities or organised activities.

★★★Aparthotel Auramar (287 rooms)
Praia dos Aveiros, 8200 Albufeira; tel. 089/51 33 37, fax 089/51 33 27
Very good value; friendly atmosphere, solid comfort without lots of extras.

★★★Hotel da Galé (62 rooms)
Cerro da Piedade, 8200 Albufeira; tel. 089/58 69 66, fax 089/58 67 83
Relatively inexpensive hotel in the centre of Albufeira, no frills but no
extras; its roof terrace is already famous for the view over the old town.
Closed in winter.

Hotel Almansor near Carvoeiro

★★★★★Hotel Alvor Praia (217 rooms)   Alvor
Praia de Três Irmãos, 8500 Portimão; tel. 082/45 89 00, fax 082/45 89 99
Situated on a lovely beach between Alvor and Portimão. High-rise luxury
hotel with wide range of organised activities and entertainment. Extremely
well-appointed rooms.

★★Hotel Vale da Telha (26 rooms)   Aljezur
Vale da Telha – Apartado 101, 8670 Aljezur; tel. 082/9 81 80, fax 082/9 81 76
Out of town and not too far from the beach, this is one of the few places to
stay in these parts, and is worth it if only for the lovely, lonely beaches.

★★★★★Vila Vita Parc resort (194 rooms)   Armação de Pêra
Alporchinhos, 8365 Armação de Pêra; tel. 082/31 53 10, fax 082/31 53 33
Luxurious resort outside Armação de Pêra with plenty to offer; a good
place to get away from it all – an entire holiday could be spent in the
complex.

★★★★Albergaria do Lageado (21 rooms)   Caldas de
Caldas de Monchique, 8550 Fóia; tel. 082/9 26 16, 9 38 69   Monchique
Comfortable old-established pension in idyllic village centre.

★★Pensão Central
Caldas de Monchique, 8550 Fóia; tel. 082/9 22 03
Simple little pension with fin-de-siècle charm.

★★★★Apartamentos Rocha Brava (375 rooms)   Carvoeiro
Alfazina, Carvoeiro, 8400 Lagoa; tel. 082/35 87 75, fax 082/35 85 42
Very large and imposing resort high above the rocky coast, with very
well-furnished apartments and its own good infrastructure. Because of its
location it is convenient to have the use of a car.

★★★★Hotel Almansor (293 rooms)
Praia do Carvoeiro, 8400 Lagoa; tel. 082/35 80 26, fax 082/35 87 70
Almost every room in this comfortable hotel has a sea view. Several
restaurants and bars, swimming pool, sauna, two tennis courts and other
sports facilities form part of the amenities. Suitable for conferences of up to
900 people.

★★★★Estalagem Monte do Casal (12 rooms)   Estói
Cerro do Lobo, 8000 Faro; tel. 089/9 15 03, fax 089/9 13 41
Small elegant country house with rooms and suites, between Estói and
Moncarapacho; has its own famous restaurant.

★★★Hotel Eva (146 rooms)   Faro
Avenida da República 1, 8000 Faro; tel. 089/80 33 54, fax 089/80 23 04
Large modern hotel with attractive rooms right on the harbour; central
location and easy to get to.

★★Pensão São Filipe (10 rooms)
Rua Infante D. Henrique 53, 8000 Faro; tel. 089/2 41 82
Simple and inexpensive pension, central but quiet location.

★★★★Hotel Casabela (53 rooms)   Ferragudo
Vale de Areia, 8400 Lagoa; tel. 082/46 15 80, fax 082/46 15 81
Grand villa-like hotel outside the town close to the beach; little in the way of
organised activities, sport etc., good for anyone in search of peace and
quiet.

★★★Meia Praia Beach Club (77 apartments)   Lagos
Meia Praia, 8600 Lagos; tel./fax 082/76 99 80
Outside Lagos on a beach with dunes, relatively inexpensive; good standard of service and fittings, will suit families with children (but no child
care).

Hotels

★★★Hotel São Cristovão (77 rooms)
Praça de D. João II, 8600 Lagos; tel. 082/76 30 51, fax 082/45 91 71
Modern, well-run, on the edge of town.

★★★★Pensão Residência Sol e Mar (103 rooms)
Praia de D. Ana, 8600 Lagos; tel. 082/76 20 26, fax 082/76 02 47
Quiet pension on the beach which gets crowded in summer.

Loulé   ★★★Hotel Loulé Jardim (52 rooms)
Praça Manuel de Arriaga, 8100 Loulé; tel. 089/41 30 94–5, fax 089/6 31 77
In an old mansion by a little park.

★★★Pensão Dom Payo (26 rooms)
Rua Antero de Quental; tel. 089/41 44 22, fax 089/41 64 53
Pleasant pension with modern facilities.

Monchique   ★★★★Estalagem Abrigo da Montanha (6 rooms)
Estrada de Fóia/Corte Pereira, 8550 Fóia; tel. 082/9 21 31,
fax 082/9 36 60
Very civilised, just outside Monchique on the road up to the highest point in
the Serra de Monchique.

Monte Gordo   ★★★★Hotel Casablanca (42 rooms)
Rua Sete, 8900 Monte Gordo; tel. 081/51 14 44, fax 081/51 19 99
Stylish little hotel in the centre of Monte Gordo away from the promenade,
few rooms with sea views, surrounded by a terrace, very pleasant service
and decor, no organised activities, no sport – peaceful relaxation
guaranteed.

Olhão   ★★Hotel Ria Sol (52 rooms)
Rua Genéral Humberto Delgado 37, 8700 Olhão; tel. 089/70 52 67,
fax 089/70 52 68
Relatively central but quiet little hotel, the only one in the town.

★★Pensão Bela Vista (9 rooms)
Rua Teófilo Braga 65, 8700 Olhão; tel. 089/70 25 38
Very simple pension in the old centre.

Portimão   ★★★Hotel Globo (68 rooms)
Rua 5 de Outubro 26, 8500 Portimão; tel. 082/41 63 50, fax 082/8 31 42
Solid hotel with good, unobtrusive service, central location so rather noisy.

★★★Pensão do Rio (11 rooms)
Largo do Dique 20, 8500 Portimão; tel. 082/2 30 41, fax 082/41 18 95
In a busy square on the riverbank in the centre of Portimão.

Praia da Rocha   ★★★★★Hotel Algarve (220 rooms)
Av. Tomás Cabreira, 8500 Portimão; tel. 082/41 50 01, fax 082/41 59 99
Established luxury hotel facing the beach, well appointed, excellent ser-
vice, children's pool and supervised play area.

★★★★Hotel Bela Vista (14 rooms)
Av. Tomás Cabreira, 8500 Portimão; tel. 082/2 40 55, fax 082/41 53 69
A hotel with one of the richest traditions in the Algarve. The beautifully
restored old house radiates an extremely pleasant atmosphere; needless
to say, high standard of service and comfort: on the promenade.

★★★★Hotel Apartamento Oriental (200 rooms)
Av. Tomás Cabreira, 8500 Portimão; tel. 082/41 30 00, fax 082/41 34 13
Popular Moorish-style modern hotel, in a garden setting. Nearly every
room has a sea view, with air-conditioning, phone, radio and satellite TV.

Quarteira   ★★★Hotel Beira Mar (51 rooms)
Rua Infante de Sagres 49, 8125 Loulé; tel. 089/30 25 30, fax 089/30 25 32
Solid hotel on the coast road.

Built in Moorish style: the Hotel Oriental in Praia da Rocha

★★★★★Hotel Quinta do Lago (141 rooms)
8135 Almansil; tel. 089/39 66 66, fax 089/39 63 93
The smartest place on the Algarve coast, out and out luxury, very attractive
with lots of lawns and greenery, quiet but with plenty of sports facilities.

Quinta do Lago

★★★Hotel da Baleeira (118 rooms)
8650 Sagres; tel. 082/6 42 12–13, fax 082/6 44 25
Relatively central, functional decor, few extras.

Sagres

★★★★★La Réserve (20 apartments)
Estrada de Esteval, 8000 Faro; tel. 089/9 04 74, fax 089/9 04 02
Exclusive little luxury hotel in lovely scenery and – although away from the
crowds – quite good location.

Santa Bárbara
de Nexe

★★Pensão Santo António de Poço dos Ferreiros (6 rooms)
Poço dos Ferreiros, 8150 São Brás de Alportel; tel. 089/84 21 75,
fax 089/84 39 96
Small, very simple pension.

São Brás de
Alportel

★★★★Albergaria Solar da Moura (22 rooms)
Horta do Pocinho Santo, 8300 Silves; tel. 082/44 31 06–7,
fax 082/44 31 08
Very well-run little hotel with garden and children's play area.

Silves

★★Aldeamento Turístico Pedras d'el Rei (239 apartments, 127 houses)
Santa Luzia, 8800 Tavira; tel. 081/32 53 52, fax 081/32 40 20
Pleasant green holiday complex particularly suitable for children; simple
decor, no extras; a bridge to Tavira Island can be crossed on foot or by train
to get to the long sandy beach.

Tavira

Hotels

★★★Pensão Horizonte Mar (20 rooms)
Av. Almirante Cândido dos Reis, 8800 Tavira; tel. 081/32 50 35,
fax. 081/32 50 37
Small pension in the eastern part of town.

Vale do Lobo

★★★★★Hotel Dona Filipa (136 rooms)
Vale do Lobo, 8135 Almancil; tel. 089/39 41 41, fax 089/39 42 88
Luxury hotel on a grand scale in large grounds, very good infrastructure
including various sports facilities.

Vilamoura

★★★★Hotel Dom Pedro Marina (151 rooms)
Vilamoura, Rua Tivoli, 8125 Quarteira; tel. 089/38 98 02, fax 089/31 32 70
Particularly popular with the Portuguese, a comparatively authentic
atmosphere in the synthetic glitz of Vilamoura; relatively inexpensive,
pleasantly furnished rooms, close to beach, short on child care and organised activities.

Vila Real de Santo
António

★★Hotel Apolo (42 rooms)
Av. dos Bombeiros Portugueses, 8900 Vila Real de Santo António; tel.
081/51 24 48, fax 081/51 24 50
The only hotel in the pretty little border town, clean and unassuming.

Information

Portuguese National Tourist Offices abroad:

Canada

Suite 1005, 60 Bloor Street West
Toronto, Ontario M4W 3BO; tel. (416) 921 73 76

Ireland

Portuguese Embassy
Knocksinna House, Knocksinna
Fox Rock, Dublin 18; tel. (01) 289 35 69

United Kingdom

22/25a Sackville Street
London W1X 1DE; tel. (0171) 494 14 41

United States

4th Floor, 590 Fifth Avenue
New York NY 10036; tel. (212) 354 44 03

Algarve

There are tourist information offices (turismo) in every place of any size in
the Algarve. Here the English-speaking staff will help you with information
on the locality and the region.
   There are no standard opening hours but turismos are usually open
Mon.–Fri. 10am–1pm and 3–5pm. In tourist resorts some stay open longer
and open for a couple of hours at the weekend.

Albufeira: Rua 5 de Outubro; tel. 089/51 21 44
Alcoutim: Praça da República; tel. 081/4 61 79
Aljezur: Largo do Mercado; tel. 082/9 82 29
Armação de Pêra: Avenida Marginal; tel. 082/31 21 45
Carvoeiro: Largo da Praia do Carvoeiro; tel. 082/3 57 78
Castro Marim: Praça 1° de Maio 2–4; tel. 081/53 12 32
Faro: Rua da Misericórdia 8–12; tel. 089/80 36 04
   (airport): tel. 089/81 85 82
Lagos: Largo Marquês de Pombal; tel. 082/76 30 31
Loulé: Edifício do Castelo; tel. 089/46 39 00
Monte Gordo: Avenida Marginal; tel. 081/4 44 95
Olhão: Largo da Lagoa; tel. 089/71 39 36
Portimão: Largo 1° de Dezembro; tel. 082/2 36 95
Praia da Rocha: Rua Tomás Cabreira; tel. 082/2 22 90
Quarteira: Av. Infante de Sagres; tel. 089/31 22 17
Sagres: Turinfo, Praça da República; tel. 082/6 45 20, 6 45 51

São Brás de Alportel: Rua Dr. Evaristo Gago 1; tel. 089/84 22 11
Silves: Rua 25 de Abril; tel. 082/44 22 55
Tavira: Rua da Galeria 9; tel. 081/2 25 11

Language

The foreign languages most commonly spoken in Portugal are Spanish, English and French, and there are now also numbers of returned "guest workers" who have learnt some German while working in Germany. In any event, however, it is well worth having at least a smattering of Portuguese.

Knowledge of foreign languages

On first hearing Portuguese spoken a visitor may not quite know what to make of it because it can sound rather like a Slav language (e.g. Polish). The written form of the language, however, can at once be recognised as a Romance language, and some knowledge of Latin or Spanish will be a great help in understanding it.

Portuguese

Portuguese grammer is notable for the rich tense system of the verbs, in particular for the preservation of the Latin pluperfect (e.g. fora, "I had been"). A further peculiarity is the inflected personal infinitive: "entramos na loja para comprarmos pão" = "we go into the shop to buy bread".
  The plural is formed by the addition of "s", in some cases with the modification of the preceding vowel or consonant:

Grammar

Singular	Plural
o animal	os animais
o hotel	os hotéis
a região	as regiões

The definite article is "o" (masculine) or "a" (feminine) in the singular, "os" or "as" in the plural. The declension of nouns and adjectives is simple. The nominative and accusative are the same; the genitive is indicated by "de" (of), the dative by "a" (to). The prepositions "de" and "a" combine with the definite article as follows:

de + o = do	de + a = da
de + os = dos	de + as = das

a + o = ao	a + os = aos
a + a = à	a + as = às

The Portuguese spoken in Portugal seems lacking in resonance, but is soft and melodious, without the hard accumulations of consonants and the rough gutturals of Castilian Spanish. It is notable for its frequent sibilants and for the nasalisation of vowels, diphthongs and triphthongs. Unstressed vowels and intervocalic consonants are much attenuated or disappear altogether. The stressed syllable of a word so dominates the rest that the vowels of the other syllables are radically altered in tone quality and not infrequently are reduced to a mere whisper. In the spoken language the boundaries between words are so blurred (in the phenomenon know as "sandhi") that the individual word within a group largely loses its independence: thus the phrase "os outros amigos" ("the other friends") is run together into a single phonetic unit and pronounced something like "usótrushamígush".
  The nine vocalic phonemes used in Portuguese are represented by the five vowels a, e, i, o and u together with three diacritic signs or accents (í ì î), two of which (í and î) also indicate the stress. Nasalisation is indicated by the tilde (Portuguese "o til": ī) or by the consonant "m" or "n".
  The stress is normally on the penultimate syllable of a word ending in a vowel or in "m" or "s" and on the last syllable of a word ending in a consonant other than "m" or "s". Exceptions to this rule are marked by the

use of an accent. It should be noted that "ia", "io" and "iu" are not treated as diphthongs as in Spanish but as combinations of separate vowels. Thus the word "agrário", for example, with the stress on the second "a", requires an accent to indicate this in Portuguese but not in Spanish where it is "agrario" without an accent.

Some peculiarities of Portuguese pronunciation

a	unstressed, like a whispered e
à	long "ah"
c	k before a, o and u; s before e and i
ç	s
ch	sh
e	unstressed, like a whispered i; in initial position before s, practically disappears ("escudo" pronounced "shkúdo"; Estoril pronounced "Shturíl")
ê	closed e
é	open e
g	hard g (as in "go") before a, o and u; zh (like s in "pleasure") before e and i
gu	hard g
h	mute
i	nasalised after u ("muito" pronounced "muínto")
j	zh
l	in final position as in English or, in Brazil, like a weak u ("animal" pronounced "animáu")
lh ly	(with consonantal y): cf. Spanish ll
m, n	in final position nasalise the preceding vowel
nh ny	(with consonantal y): cf. Spanish ñ
o	unstressed, like u
ô	closed o
ó	open o
qu	k
r	trilled
rr	strongly rolled
s	s before vowels; z between vowels; sh before hard consonants and in final position; zh before soft consonants
v	v
x	sh
z	in final position sh; otherwise z

The Brazilian pronunciation of Portuguese is markedly different from the Portuguese mainland. In particular final "s" and "z" are pronounced "s" and not "sh", and initial "r" sounds almost like "h".

Numbers

Cardinals

0	zero	16	dezasseis
1	um, uma	17	dezassete
2	dois, duas	18	dezoito
3	três	19	dezanove
4	quatro	20	vinte
5	cinco	21	vinte-e-um
6	seis	22	vinte-e-dois (duas)
7	sete	30	trinta
8	oito	31	trinta-e-um (uma)
9	nove	40	quarenta
10	dez	50	cinquenta
11	onze	60	sessenta
12	doze	70	setenta
13	treze	80	oitenta
14	catorze	90	noventa
15	quinze	100	cem, cento

101	cento-e-um (uma)	700	setecentos, -as	
200	duzentos, -as	800	oitocentos, -as	
300	trezentos, -as	900	novecentos, -as	
400	quatrocentos, -as	1000	mil	
500	quinhentos, -as	2000	dois (duas) mil	
600	seiscentos, -as	1 million	um milhão de	

1st	primeiro, -a	11th	undécimo, -a; décimo primeiro	Ordinals
2nd	segundo, -a	12th	duodécimo, -a; décimo segundo	
3rd	terceiro, -a	13th	décimo terceiro	
4th	quarto, -a	20th	vigésimo, -a	
5th	quinto, -a	21st	vigésimo primeiro, -a	
6th	sexto, -a	30th	trigésimo, -a	
7th	sétimo, -a	40th	quadragésimo, -a	
8th	oitavo, -a	50th	quinquagésimo, -a	
9th	nono, -a	60th	sexuagésimo, -a	
10th	décimo, -a	100th	centésimo, -a	

½ meio, meia	¼ um quarto	Fractions
⅓ um terço, uma terça parte	¾ três quartos, três quartas partes	

Idioms and Vocabulary

Men are usually addressed as "Senhor", women as "minha Senhora". If you know a man's name you should address him by his name with the prefix "Senhor"; ladies are addressed by "Senhora Dona" and their Christian name, if this is known. "You" in direct address is "o Senhor", "a Senhora" or "Você", in the plural "os Senhores", "as Senhoras" or "Vocês".

Forms of address

In Portuguese names, which are frequently very long, the maternal surname usually comes first.

Good morning, good day	Bom dia	Idioms
Good afternoon	Boa tarde	
Good evening, good night	Boa noite	
Goodbye	Adeus, Até à vista	
Yes, no (Sir)	Sim, não (Senhor)	
Excuse me (apologising)	Desculpe, Perdão	
Excuse me (e.g. when passing in front of someone)	Com licença	
After you (e.g. offering something)	A vontade!	
Please (asking for something)	Faz favor	
Thank you (very much)	(Muito) obrigado	
Not at all (You're welcome)	De nada, Não tem de quê	
Do you speak English?	O senhor fala inglês?	
A little, not much	Um pouco, não muito	
I do not understand	Não compreendo (nada)	
What is the Portuguese for . . .?	Como se diz em português . . .?	
What is the name of this church?	Como chama-se esta igreja?	
Have you any rooms?	Tem um quarto livre?	
I should like . . .	Queria . . .	
A room with private bath	Um quarto com banho	
With full board	Com pensão completa	
What does it cost?	Quanto custa?	
Everything included	Tudo incluído	
That is very dear	É muito caro	
Bill, please!	Faz favor, a conta!	
Where is . . . Street?	Onde fica a rua . . .?	
the road to?	a estrada para . . .?	
a doctor?	um médico?	
a dentist?	um dentista?	

Language

Right, left	À direita, esquerda
Straight ahead	Sempre a direito
Above, below	Em cima, em baixo
When is it open?	A que horas está aberto?
How far?	Que distância?
Wake me at six	Chamé-me às seis

Road signs

Alfândega	Customs
Alto!	Stop
Atenção!	Caution
Auto-estrada	Highway
Bifurcação	Road fork
Cuidado!	Caution
Curva perigosa	Dangerous curve
Dê passagem!	Give way/yield
Desvio	Diversion
Devagar!	Slow
Direcção única; Sentido único	One-way street
Estacionamento proibido	Parking prohibited
Ir a passo!	Dead slow
Ir pela direita, esquerda	Keep right, left
Nevoeiro	Mist, fog
Obras na estrada	Road works
Parque de estacionamento	Car park, parking place
Passagem proibida	No entry
Peões	Pedestrians
Perigo!	Danger!
Portagem	Toll
Praia	Beach
Proibido ultrapassar	No overtaking
Rebanhos	Beware of livestock
Serviço de reboque	Towing service

Vehicle terms

accelerator	o acelerador
automobile	o auto, o carro
axle	o eixo
battery	a bateria
bearing	a chumaceira
bolt	o parafuso
bonnet/hood	o capot
brake	o travão
breakdown	a avaria
bulb	a lâmpada eléctrica
bumper	o pára-choque
bus	a camioneta (de passageiros)
car	o auto, o carro
carburettor/carburetor	o carburador
change (oil, tyre/tire, etc.)	mudar
charge (battery)	carregar
check	verificar
clutch	a embraiagem
contact	o contacto
cylinder	o cilindro
damaged	avariado, avariada
diesel engine	o motor Diesel
direction indicator	o indicador de direcção
distributor	o distribuidor
driver	o motorista, o condutor
driving licence	a carta de condutor
dynamo	o dínamo
engine	o motor
exhaust	o escape

fan belt	a correia da ventoinha
fault	a avaria
float	o flutuador
fuse	o fusível
garage	a garage, a garagem
gas/petrol	a gasolina
gas/petrol pump	a bomba de gasolina
gas/petrol station	o posto de gasolina
gas/petrol tank	o depósito de gasolina
gasket	o empanque
gear	a velocidade, a mudança
gearbox	o câmbio de velocidades
grease (verb)	lubrificar
headlamp	o farol
hood/bonnet	o capot
horn	a buzina
ignition	a ignição
inflate	dar à bomba
inner tube	a câmara-de-ar
jack	o macaco
jet	o gicleur
lorry/truck	o camião
magneto	o magneto
make (of car)	a marca
map	o mapa das estradas
maximum speed	a velocidade máxima
mixture	a mistura
motorcycle	a motocicleta
number-plate	a placa, a matrícula
nut	a porca
oil	o óleo
oil-pump	a bomba de óleo
park (verb)	estacionar
parking place, car park	o estacionamento
petrol/gas	a gasolina
petrol/gas pump	a bomba de gasolina
petrol/gas station	o posto de gasolina
petrol/gas tank	o depósito de gasolina
piston	o postão
piston ring	o segmento de pistão
pump	a bomba
radiator	o radiador
rear light	a luz traseira
repair	reparar
repair garage	a oficina de reparação
road map	o mapa das estradas
scooter	o scooter
shock absorber	o amortecedor
snow chain	a cadeia antideslizante
spanner	a chave inglesa
spare part	a peça de sobresselente
sparking plug	a vela
speedometer	o velocímetro
spring	a mola
starter	o arranque
steering	a direcção
steering wheel	o volante
tow away	levar a reboque
transmission	a condução
truck/lorry	o camião
two-stroke engine	o motor do dois tempos
tyre/tire	o pneu

Language

	tyre/tire pressure	a pressão dos pneus
	valve	a válvula
	wash	lavar
	water-pump	a bomba de água
	wheel	a roda
	windscreen/windshield	o párabrisas
	windscreen/windshield wiper	o limpa-pára-brisas
	wing	o guarda-lama
Travelling	aircraft	aeroplano, avião
	airport	aeroporto
	all aboard!	partida!
	all change!	mudar!
	arrival	chegada
	baggage	bagagem
	baggage check	guia, senha
	bus	autocarro, camioneta
	conductor (ticket-collector)	revisor
	couchette car	furgoneta
	departure	partida
	fare	preço
	flight	vôo
	information	informação
	line (railway)	via férrea
	luggage	bagagem
	luggage ticket	guia, senha
	no smoking (carriage)	não fumadores
	platform	plataforma, gare
	porter	moço de fretes
	restaurant car	carruagem restaurante
	railway station	estação
	sleeping car	carruagem-cama
	smoking (carriage)	fumadores
	steward	comissário de bordo
	stewardess	hospedeira (do ar)
	stop	paragem
	ticket	bilhete
	ticket-collector (conductor)	revisor
	ticket office	bilheteria, guichet
	timetable	horário
	toilet	lavatório
	train	combóio
	waiting room	sala de espera
Months	January	janeiro
	February	fevereiro
	March	março
	April	abril
	May	maio
	June	junho
	July	julho
	August	agosto
	September	setembro
	October	outubro
	November	novembro
	December	dezembro
	month	mês
	year	ano
Days of the week	Monday	segunda-feira
	Tuesday	terça-feira
	Wednesday	quarta-feira

Thursday	quinta-feira	
Friday	sexta-feira	
Saturday	sábado	
Sunday	domingo	
day	dia	
holiday, feast-day	dia de festa, dia feriado	
New Year's Day	Ano-Novo	Holidays and
Easter	Páscoa	Religious Festivals
Ascension	Ascensão	
Whitsun	Espírito Santo, Pentecostes	
Corpus Christi	Festa do Corpo de Deus	
All Saints	Todos os Santos	
Christmas	Natal	
New Year's Eve	Véspera do Ano-Novo, Noite de São Silvestre	
address	endereço	At the post office
air mail	correio aéreo	
by airmail	por avião	
express letter	carta urgente	
letter	carta	
letter-box, post-box	marco postal	
packet	embrulho	
parcel	pacote	
postage	porte	
postcard	bilhete postal	
poste restante	poste-restante	
postman	carteiro	
post office	correio	
registered letter	carta registrada	
stamp	selo, estampilha	
telegram	telegrama	
telephone	telephone	
telex	telex	
abadia	abbey	Glossary
água	water	
aldeia	small village, hamlet	
altura	hill, eminence	
ancoradouro	anchorage	
anfiteatro	amphitheatre	
aqueduto	aqueduct	
arquipélago	archipelago	
avenida	avenue	
azulejos	glazed tiles	
baía	bay	
bairro	district of town	
balneário	bath(s)	
barco	boat	
barragem	dam, reservoir	
bolsa	purse	
cabo	cape	
caldas	hot springs, spa	
calvário	calvary	
câmara municipal	town hall	
caminho	path, track road	
caminho de ferro	railway	
campo	field, countryside	
capela	chapel	
capela-mór	main chapel with high altar	
casa	house	

casal	farm, hamlet
cascata	waterfall
castelo	castle
cemitério	cemetery, churchyard
cidade	town, city
ciências naturais	natural history
circulação	round trip
citânia	prehistoric fortified settlement
claustro	cloister
colina	hill
convento	convent (in the general sense of religious house)
coro	choir
costa	coast
cova	cave, pit
cumeada	mountain ridge
cúpula	dome
desfiladeiro	pass, defile
doca	dock
encruzamento de ruas	street intersection
ermida	pilgrimage chapel, hermitage
estabelecimento balnear	spa establishment
estrada	road
estreito	straight
farol	lighthouse
floresta	forest
fonte	spring, fountain
fortaleza	fortress, castle
foz	mouth of river
fronteira	frontier
funicular	funicular
garganta	gorge
hospital	hospital
hotel	hotel
igreja	church
ilha	island
janela	window
jardim	garden
lago	lake
lagoa	small lake, lagoon
landa	heath, moor
leste	east
mar	sea
mirador	viewpoint
montanha	mountain (range)
monte	hill
muralha	(town) wall
museu	museum
norte	north
oeste	west
paço	palace
paço de concelho	town hall
padrão	monument
palácio	palace
pântano	marsh, bog
parque	park
parque nacional	national park
pátio	courtyard
pelhourinho	pillory column
península	peninsula
pensão	pension; guest house
pico	peak

pintura	painting
planalto	plateau
planície	plain
poço	well, spring
ponte	bridge
portão	gateway
porto	harbour, port
pousada	(State-run) hotel, inn
povoação	village
praça	square
praça de touros	bullring
praia	beach
quinta	country house
retábulo	retable, reredos
rio	river
roca, rocha	rock, crag
rua	street
sala	hall, room
sé	cathedral
serra	mountain range, range of hills
sul	south
tapeçaria	tapestry
termas	hot springs, spa
tesouro	treasure
torre	tower
vale	valley

a conta	the bill	Portuguese menu
açorda	garlic and bread soup	
água	water	
água mineral	mineral water	
aguardente, brandy	brandy	
alho	garlic	
almoço	lunch	
amêndoa	almond	
antepastos	starter, hors d'oeuvre	
arroz	rice	
assado	grilled	
aves	poultry	
azeite	olive oil	
azeitonas	olives	
batatas	potatoes	
batatas fritas	fried potatoes	
bebidas	drinks	
bife	steak	
bolo	cake	
cabrito	kid (goat)	
caça	game	
café	coffee	
café com leite	coffee with milk	
carne	meat	
carneiro	mutton	
carta (or lista, ementa)	menu	
cebolas	onions	
ceia	late-night snack, supper	
cerveja	beer	
chá	tea	
chávena	cup	
chocolate	chocolate	
coelho	rabbit	
colher	spoon	
colher de chá	teaspoon	

Language

copo	glass
corço	venison
cordeiro	lamb
couve	cabbage
couve-flor	cauliflower
cozido	cooked
doces	sweets
ervilhas	peas
espargos	asparagus
espinafre	spinach
faca	knife
feijões	beans
frango	chicken
fruta	fruit
garfo	fork
gelado	ice cream
guardanapo	napkin
jantar	dinner, evening meal
javalí	boar
laranja	orange
lebre	hare
leitão	sucking pig
leite	milk
legumes (hortaliça)	vegetables
maçã	apple
manteiga	butter
massa(s)	pasta
molho	sauce
mostarda	mustard
óleo	oil
ovo (ovos estrelados)	egg (fried)
pão	bread
pãozinho	roll
pato	duck
peixe	fish
pepinos	cucumber
pequeno almoço	breakfast
pera	pear
perdiz	partridge
perua	turkey
pimenta	pepper
pimento	paprika, green pepper
porco	pork
prato	plate
prato do dia	dish of the day
presunto	ham
queijo	cheese
repolho	white cabbage
sal	salt
salada	salad
salame	salami
sobremesas	dessert
sopa	soup
sumo de fruta	fruit juice
talher	cutlery
tomates	tomatoes
uva	grapes
vaca	beef
vinagre	vinegar
vinho	wine
vitela	veal

Language Schools

A number of tour operators offer special language packages to Portugal. There are also various schools where you can follow language courses. These generally last between two and four weeks, and in some cases include an additional events programme.

Centro de Línguas Intergarb   Albufeira
Travessa das Violas 13
8200 Albufeira; tel. 089/51 22 13

CIAL   Faro
Rua Almeida Garrett 44
8000 Faro; tel. 089/81 32 11, fax 089/80 31 54

Interlínguas   Lagos
Rua Dr. Joaquim Teles
8600 Lagos; tel. 082/76 10 70

English School of Loulé/Europa Algarve   Loulé
Rua José Fernandez Guerreiro 66
8100 Loulé; tel. 089/41 41 28

CLCC–Centro de Língua, Cultura e Comunicação   Portimão
Rua Maria Luísa 12–2
8500 Portimão; tel. 082/41 64 96

Markets

Since almost everywhere in the Algarve has its own regular market only a selection can be given here.

First and third Tuesday in the month. This oriental bazaar of a market has stalls selling household wares and clothing – and souvenirs of course – as well as fresh fruit and vegetables.   Albufeira

A pottery market forms part of the May Day celebrations.   Alcoutim

Second Sunday in the month. Country market selling just about anything, including chickens and sheep.   Estói

First Friday and Saturday in the month. Large colourful market, particularly famous for its many flower stalls.   Faro

Every Saturday. The bus station is the place to find shoes and leather goods at bargain prices, plus some fine ceramics.   Lagos

Every Saturday. Stalls in the covered market and surrounding streets sell ceramics, wickerwork, wooden and leather goods as well as fruit and vegetables.   Loulé

First Sunday in the month. People flock here from throughout the district to stock up with everything from boots and clothes to seeds and even donkeys.   Moncarapacho

October 26th–28th. A typical Algarve market, with people coming from far and near, and wares of all sorts including livestock and crafts.   Monchique

Every Saturday. Cassettes, baskets, wickerwork and household goods are on sale between and around the two covered markets.   Olhão

175

Typical weekly markets held in many small towns in the Algarve

Pereiro	Fourth Sunday in the month. Country market, selling pottery, rugs, shoes and clothes.
Quarteira	Every Wednesday. Food of course, but also just about everything else for the home.
São Brás de Alportel	Every Saturday. Cheap and cheerful domestic wares, clothes, china and woodcarvings.

Media

Radio	Portuguese radio (RDP) broadcasts a short daily programme in the summer for tourists in English, French and German. Times vary, but it is usually transmitted between 8 and 10.30am. Solar Radio puts out English news bulletins at 8.30am on 90.5 FM, and it is possible to get the BBC World Service, Voice of America, and Radio Canada International on short wave.
Television	There are four channels on Portuguese television, the two state-run channels (RTP 1 and 2) and TVI and SIC. Foreign films are usually shown in the original language with sub-titles. Satellite TV is available in hotels and many pensions and cafés.
Newspapers, magazines	English and American newspapers and magazines are on sale in all the main towns and tourist resorts. Local publications in English include a fortnightly newspaper, the Algarve News, a monthly magazine, the Algarve Gazette, and a weekly magazine, the Algarve Resident. Discover, the free monthly what's on magazine, can be obtained from tourist offices.

Motoring

The best way of really getting to know the Algarve is undoubtedly by car, if only because of the poor public transport away from the coast. There is a good road network, mainly well surfaced, but minor roads are sometimes rather rough. Some of the remoter areas have hard-surfaced sand tracks, but driving on them is not a problem. In the Algarve high speed is to be expected, and motorists should beware of drivers overtaking, etc. dangerously, especially on winding mountain roads. At night be on the alert for vehicles with poor lights, or no lights at all – even on main roads.

The main road along the south coast is the N125, which can have very heavy traffic, especially between Lagos and Faro. In the east of the Algarve this is relieved by the N270 further inland which is quieter but narrower and not such a well-made road. The IP1 is a new motorway which runs parallel to the N125 from Albufeira to Ayamonte in Spain. Although toll-free it is little used as yet, making it a very attractive route to take.
Main routes

There are orange emergency phones at regular intervals on the motorways. On other roads telephone the Portuguese Automobile Club (tel. 01/942 50 95) for help.
Breakdowns

The Portuguese Automobile Club (ACP) has its main office in Lisbon: Rua Rosa Araújo 24–26, 1200 Lisbon; tel. 01/356 39 31, fax 01/357 47 32 ACP in Faro: Rua Francisco Barreto 26; tel. 089/80 57 53
Portuguese Automobile Club

Filling stations are concentrated in the larger places and on the N125. It is only in the hinterland that it can be difficult to get fuel. Most filling stations are open between 7am and 8pm, but they stay open longer on the N125. All filling stations have unleaded petrol (gasolina sem chumbo).
Fuel and filling stations

Portugal's traffic rules and regulations are more or less the same as in other European countries: drive on the right, overtake on the left and give way to traffic from the right. Road signs and markings are of the usual international type. Drivers who have held a licence for less than a year may not drive faster than 90kmph and must display a yellow disc with "90" on it. This is obtainable from the Portuguese Automobile Club (ACP). A green (insurance) card must be produced in the event of an accident. Visitors driving a vehicle which is not their own must have authorisation from the owner. Vehicle and speed checks are relatively frequent.
Traffic rules and regulations

The speed limit for cars and motorcycles is 60kmph in built-up areas, 90kmph elsewhere, and 100kmph on dual carriageways and 120kmph on motorways. This speed limit of 60kmph and 90kmph changes in bad weather conditions. For lorries, coaches and cars with trailers speed limits are lower at 70kmph outside built-up areas, and 80kmph on motorways. These also have a minimum speed of 40kmph.
Speed limits

Traffic on the main road – which is indicated by a yellow rectangle edged with black and white – has priority, but at junctions or intersections of roads of equal importance you must give way to traffic coming from the right. Motor vehicles always have right of way over non-motorised traffic.
Priority

The legal limit for alcohol in the blood is 0.5 per millilitre.
Alcohol limit

The wearing of seat-belts is generally compulsory.
Seat-belts

To hire a car in Portugal the driver must be 21 or over and have held a driving licence for at least a year.
Car hire

Motoring

Avis	Faro. Airport: tel. 089/81 86 25
	Lagos. Largo das Portas de Portugal 11; tel. 082/76 36 91
	Also agents in Albufeira, Praia da Rocha and Quarteira
Budget	Faro. Airport: tel. 089/81 88 88
	Also agents in Albufeira and Praia da Rocha
Europcar	Faro Av. da República 2; tel. 089/82 37 78 Airport: tel. 089/81 87 26
	Lagos Estrada Nacional (N)120; tel. 082/76 32 03
	Also agents in Albufeira, Monte Gordo, Praia da Rocha and Vilamoura
Hertz	Faro Airport: tel. 089/81 82 48
	Lagos Rossio de S. João, Edificio Panorama, Loja 3; tel. 082/76 98 09
	Also agents in Albufeira, Armação de Pêra, Praia da Rocha and Vilamoura
Car-share	Car-share within Portugal and in various European countries can be arranged through the central car-share exchange in Portimão (tel./fax 082/41 71 10).

Nightlife

Most of the nightlife in the Algarve is in the bars and discos of the big hotels. Albufeira in particular is full of bars and pubs and, like other resorts in the middle part of the Algarve, also has plenty of discos but the "in place" varies from year to year.

Other entertainment after dark can be found in casinos (see entry) and at fado nights (see Fado) where you can dine to the accompaniment of Portugal's own distinctive folk ballads.

Opening Times

Shops	Most shops are open Mon.–Fri. from 9am to 1pm and from 3 to 7pm, and Sat. from 9am to 1pm, but many of the smaller shops stay open longer in the evening and at weekends. The big shopping centres often open from 10am to midnight even at weekends.
Chemists	Opening hours for chemists are normally Mon.–Fri. 9am–1pm and 3–7pm, Sat. 9am–1pm. Lists of chemists on duty outside opening hours are posted in chemist shop windows.
Banks	Banking hours are Mon.–Fri. 8.30am–3pm. Some banks close for lunch between noon and 1pm.
Post offices	Post offices are generally open Mon.–Fri. 9am–noon and 2.30–6pm.
Filling stations	Filling stations normally open from 7am to 8pm, but some open round the clock in larger places, tourist resorts and on the N125.
Restaurants	Restaurants open for lunch between noon and 2pm and from 7 in the evening. Orders will usually be taken up to 10pm.

Most churches are closed during the day and only open for services on Sunday mornings or around 6pm during the week.

Churches

Post

Ordinary letters and postcards to the rest of Europe usually take between three and seven days. Airmail (correio azul) will get there faster but is quite a lot more expensive.

Mail

The postage for ordinary letters (cartas) and postcards (postais) within Europe is 85 Esc., and the airmail rate is 350 Esc. Stamps (selos) can be bought in post offices (correios) and in shops with the sign "CTT Selos".

Postage

Letter boxes for ordinary mail are red and can be either pillar-boxes or mailboxes on walls, while the mailboxes for correio azul are blue.

Letter boxes

Poste restante mail should be marked "posta restante" and sent to the appropriate post office. A passport or other form of personal identification is necessary when collecting mail.

Poste restante

Telegrams (telegrama) can be sent from post offices and hotel front desks or by phone (tel. 10).

Telegrams

Pousadas

Pousadas are state-run hotels in converted castles, palaces, and monasteries, or modern buildings located in places of outstanding natural beauty or historic interest. The interior, whether ancient or modern, is always attractive and furnished to a very high standard. As a rule the maximum stay is five days. Since the number of rooms tends to be very limited it is advisable to book well in advance. Room rates are relatively high, at between 18,000 and 30,000 Esc. for a double room, depending on the grading and the season. Pousadas normally have their own restaurants with very good food and wine.

There are only two pousadas in the Algarve:

Local pousadas

Pousada do Infante
Sagres; tel. 082/6 42 22–3, fax 082/6 42 25
Middle-ranking pousada, with 39 rooms; lovely view over the rocky coast; the attractive amenities include restaurant and swimming pool.

Pousada de São Brás
São Brás de Alportel; tel. 089/84 23 05–6, fax 089/84 17 26
Unpretentious pousada with 25 rooms in quiet location; swimming pool, tennis court and restaurant.

Pousada in the southern Alentejo:

Pousada de Santa Clara
Santa-Clara-a-Velha; tel. 083/9 82 50, fax 083/9 84 02
This pousada on the Santa-Clara-a-Velha barrage only has six rooms. Not the height of luxury but good service, absolute peace and quiet, parkland with ancient trees, and terrace with wonderful views of the lake and mountain scenery.

Public Holidays

| January 1st | New Year |
| February | Mardi Gras/Carnival |

Public Holidays

March/April	Good Friday
April 25th	Liberation Day (national holiday commemorating the Carnation Revolution on April 25th 1974)
May 1st	Labour Day
May/June	Corpus Christi
June 10th	Portugal Day (national holiday on anniversary of the death of poet Luís de Camões on June 10th 1580)
August 15th	Assumption Day
October 5th	Republic Day (national holiday commemorating the fall of the monarchy on October 5th 1910)
November 1st	All Saints Day
December 1st	Restoration Day (national holiday commemorating the restoration of Portugal's independence from Spain on December 1st 1640)
December 8th	Immaculate Conception
December 25th	Christmas

Public Transport

By bus

The Algarve has good bus links between the larger places, with several buses a day. These often include express services ("expressos") and are mostly operated by Eva Transportes. Along the coast, between Lagos and Ayamonte in Spain, is the Linha Litoral which links all the main resorts. The smaller towns and villages further inland can also be reached by bus but these run less frequently. The bus stations (estação rodoviária) are usually right in the centre of town. There are also expressos to Lisbon and the rest of Portugal.

Bus stations

Albufeira: Av. da Liberdade; tel. 089/51 36 50
Armação de Pêra: Av. da Liberdade; tel. 082/31 24 94
Faro: Av. da República; tel. 089/80 37 92
Lagos: Rossio S. João; tel. 082/76 29 44
Olhão: Av. General Humberto Delgado; tel. 089/70 21 57
Portimão: Largo do Dique; tel. 082/2 32 11
Quarteira: Av. Project. Apart. Golfo Mar; tel. 089/38 91 43
Tavira: Praça da República; tel. 081/2 25 46
Vilamoura: Aldeia do Mar; tel. 089/30 26 35
Vila Real de Santo António: Av. da República; tel. 081/4 31 95

By train

In the south of the Algarve a railway line runs almost parallel to the coast connecting all the places, large and small, between Vila Real de Santo António and Lagos. The trains are none too frequent and very slow, but railway enthusiasts will find it a trip worth making, especially given the beautiful scenery along parts of the track. There are good, fast rail connections to Lisbon and further north.

By boat

Apart from sightseeing boats the only regular public transport by boat is the ferry over the Guadiana between Vila Real de Santo António in Portugal and Ayamonte in Spain (daily between 9am and 7.30pm). This is less important than it was, however, since the bridge carrying the IP1 was built.

Restaurants

Although the Algarve is well supplied with restaurants what is usually found in the tourist resorts is a mix of Portuguese and European cuisine or some form of international fare. For good typically Portuguese meals look for somewhere quite plain and simple since, as a rule, in the smaller, more homely places the food is very fresh and extremely palatable.

A popular snack between meals – sardines being grilled in the open air

Most Portuguese restaurants open for lunch between noon and 2pm, and again from 6 or 7pm, when they then carry on serving till at least 10pm.

Meal times

If just a snack is required, do as the Portuguese love to do, and get a roll, a toastie or some other typical local snack (see Food and Drink) in a bar or café.

Snacks

Vila Joya
6.5km out of town on the Praia da Galé road; tel. 089/59 17 95
Outstanding creative cuisine with prices to match, 5-course menu every day; up-market dining in a villa by the sea with a terrace.

Albufeira

Três Palmeiras
Areias de São João (about 2.5km east of Albufeira); tel. 089/58 63 53
Popular with tourists and locals.

O Montinho
Montechoro; tel. 089/54 19 59
French cuisine, country hotel with terrace, lovely view.

Clipper
Avenida Beira-Mar; tel. 082/31 41 08
Aimed solely at the tourist trade, menu not large but good.

Armação de Pêra

O Serol
Rua Portas do Mar 24; tel. 082/31 21 46
One of the best fish restaurants on the Algarve, almost always full.

A Roda
Avenida 28 de Maio; tel. 081/2 02 39
Simple place with terrace alongside the road, but lovely sea view; large portions at reasonable prices.

Cabanas

Restaurants

Cacela	**Costa** Fábrica at Cacela, east of Tavira; tel. 081/95 14 67 Very pretty setting off the beaten track on the edge of the lagoon (closed part of the year).
Caldas de Monchique	**Restaurante Central**; tel. 082/9 22 03 Restaurant with fin-de-siècle charm in keeping with the little hill town. **Paraíso da Montanha**; tel. 082/9 21 50 Specialities: air-dried ham, piri-piri chicken.
Faro	**Café Aliança** Praça D. Francisco Gomes 26; tel. 089/80 16 21 Café rich in tradition, you get coffee, cakes and snacks. **Dois Irmãos** Largo Terreiro do Bispo; tel. 089/80 39 12 Traditional restaurant (opened 1925) with little courtyard, good Portuguese food. **Kappra** Rua Brites de Almeida 45; tel. 089/82 33 66 Pleasant civilised ambience. **Cidade Velha** Rua Domingo Guieiro 19; tel. 089/2 71 45 Superior Portuguese cuisine, intimate stylish restaurant in historic heart of Faro. **Camané** Av. Nascente (Praia de Faro, left of the bridge); tel. 089/81 75 39 Out of town on Faro beach, highly rated; specialises in fish and seafood.
Lagos	**O Castelo** Rua 25 de Abril 47; tel. 082/76 09 57 Elegant restaurant in the centre; quality worth paying for. **O Galeão** Rua da Laranjeira 1; tel. 082/76 39 09 Highly rated restaurant. **Dom Sebastião** Rua 25 de Abril 20; tel. 082/76 27 95 Good food, not too expensive, rustic style.
Loulé	**Avenida** Av. José da Costa Mealha 13; tel. 089/6 21 06 Friendly service, good Portuguese cuisine. **Bica Velha** Rue Martim Moniz 17; tel. 089/6 33 76 Highly rated, rustic decor.
Monchique	**Paraíso da Montanha** Estrada de Fóia; tel. 082/9 21 31 2km outside Monchique, lovely dining on the terrace with a view of the mountains; medium price-range.
Portimão	**Taberna da Maré** Travessa da Barca 9; tel. 082/41 46 14 Family concern, very small, simple restaurant, good plain Portuguese cuisine; specialises in bacalhau dishes.

Lúcio, Largo Serpa Pinto
Very good seafood, has many Portuguese regulars.

A Casa de Jantar
Rua de Santa Isabel 14; tel. 082/2 20 72
International cuisine.

Falésia   Praia da Rocha
Avenida Tomás Cabreira; tel. 082/2 35 24
Restaurant in medium price-range, terrace.

Safari
Rua António Feu 8; tel. 082/2 35 40
Specialities: seafood and African dishes.

Fortaleza de Santa Catarina
In the castle at the eastern end of the promenade; tel. 082/2 20 66 fine
opportunity to sit outside in the castle courtyard, fish a speciality.

Romeu, Rua Gonçalo Velho 40; tel. 089/31 39 90   Quarteira
Fish specialities.

Fortaleza do Beliche   Sagres
on the road to Cabo de São Vicente; tel. 082/6 41 24
Elegant pousada restaurant in scenic setting overlooking the sea.

A Tasca
Praia do Baleeria; tel. 082/6 41 77
Popular with the Portuguese too, excellent seafood and fish dishes.

O Rui   Silves
On the Algoz road; tel. 082/6 41 06
Fine place with solid Portuguese cuisine; lovely view of river and castle
from the terrace.

Pronto a Comer   Tavira
Rua Alm. Cândido Reis 6; tel. 081/2 33 43
Typically Portuguese place with good plain food.

Beira Rio
Rua Borda de Água de Asseca; tel. 081/2 31 65
Good food at reasonable prices; on the side of the river.

Ponto de Encontro
Praça Dr. António Padinha 39; tel. 081/2 37 30
Simple place with homely atmosphere, fish specialities.

São Gabriel   Vale do Lobo
Road to Quinta do Lago; tel. 089/39 45 21
Smart restaurant with terrace, top category.

O Favo; tel. 089/39 46 53
Excellent wines.

O Cesteiro   Vilamoura
Marina de Vilamoura; tel. 089/31 29 61
Specialities: fish and seafood.

Edmundo   Vila Real de Santo
Avenida da República 55; tel. 081/4 46 89   António
Unpretentious place on the river bank.

Shopping

Good buys in Portugal include footwear, leather goods, and gold and silver items, although prices in the tourist resorts of the Algarve tend to be higher than elsewhere in the country. Lagos, Portimão and Faro are good places to shop. Sometimes simple items of clothing at bargain prices can be found in the markets held at regular intervals in many places (see Markets). Handicrafts are very popular as souvenirs.

Azulejos – hand-painted tiles – make a lovely, typically Portuguese souvenir. New mass-produced azulejos are on sale everywhere in souvenir shops and markets, but tiles in the old traditional patterns are more likely to be found in antique shops.

Azulejos

In Portugal many folk-art products are still items of everyday use. This is particularly true of pottery and ceramics which vary in form and style according to where they are made, and which range from the blackish ware for everyday use to brightly painted ornaments. The best-known of these is the multi-hued Barcelos cockerel, originally from the North, which has come to symbolise Portugal as a whole. The Algarve specialises in miniature chimney places modelled on the famous local stoves.

Pottery

Beautiful embroidered tablecloths, hand-woven fabrics, wickerwork, and cork and wood carvings are sold in local markets and in specialist shops in the larger places.

Other handicrafts

Fado CDs and tapes make a good souvenir of a holiday in the Algarve. They can be bought at bargain prices in the markets, but for really good fado it is better to go to record shops. Soloists whose recordings are worth recommending include the great Amália Rodrigues, best known of all the fadistas (some of her classic performances are now available on CD), Alfredo Marceneiro and Carlos Ramos. There are newer fado compositions by Carlos do Carmo and purely instrumental versions from Rão Kyão (flute and saxaphone), Carlos Paredes and Pedro Caldeira Cabral. Elements of Portuguese folk music are featured in pieces by the Madredeus group, which has recently shot to international fame. Also very popular is the music of the legendary José Afonso.

Music

Port, from the Douro region in the north of the country, is a popular souvenir of Portugal, and comes in a whole range of prices and vintages. Other souvenir drinks include ginjinha, the local cherry brandy, vinho verde, and medronho, the fiery spirit distilled from the arbutus which grows here in the Algarve (see Food and Drink).

Port, vinho verde, spirits

Spas

Of Portugal's 30 or so spas the only one in the Algarve is Caldas de Monchique (see A to Z, Monchique). It offers treatments for rheumatism and respiratory, liver, stomach and intestinal disorders.

Direcção-Geral do Turismo
Avenida António Augusto de Aguiar 86, 1004 Lisboa Codex
Tel. 01/57 50 15

Information

Sport

Angling and big-game fishing are favourite pastimes of the Algarvios. Boats can be chartered for deep sea fishing from the main centres of

Angling

◀ *A display of ceramic ware outside a shop in Porches*

Sport

Vilamoura, Portimão and Lagos, and no licence is needed provided you are fishing on an amateur basis. The same applies to fishing from the beach, but you will need a licence for lake and river angling inland. This is obtainable from: Direcção Geral das Florestas, Av. da República 72, Faro.

Cycling   See entry

Golf   See entry

Horse-riding   The Algarve is ideal for anyone who wants a riding holiday or just to spend a few hours on horseback. It has about 20 riding centres (where you can also get tuition) so those listed below are just a selection.

Albufeira region:
Centro de Equitação Vale Navio, Estrada da Branqueira; tel. 089/58 65 59

Aljezur region:
Herdade do Serrão, Parque de Campismo do Serrão, Aldeia Velha, Aljezur; tel. 082/9 85 94

Faro region:
Centro Hípico e Escola de Equitação Gambelas, Faro; tel. 0931/81 27 94

Lagoa region:
Casa Agrícola Solear, Areias de Porches; tel. 082/5 24 40

Lagos region:
Quinta dos Almarjães, Burgau; tel. 082/6 91 52

Loulé region:
Centro Hípico Pinetrees Almansil, between Quinta do Lago and Vale do Lobo; tel. 089/39 43 69

Portimão region:
Centro Hípico da Penina, Hotel da Penina, Montes de Alvor; tel. 082/41 54 15

Silves region:
Centro Hípico de Silves, Sítio da Cruz de Portugal, Silves; tel. 082/44 41 20

Tavira region:
Centro de Equitação Quinta das Oliveiras, N125; tel. 081/2 21 07

Sailing   The Algarve's finest marina, with the best facilities for boats and crews, is at Vilamoura but there are a number of smaller harbours and anchorages all along the coast. The best places to stay on a sailing holiday are Albufeira, Armação de Pêra, Alvor, Lagos, Monte Gordo, Portimão, Praia da Falésia, Praia da Oura, Praia da Rocha, Quinta do Lago, Tavira, Vale do Lobo, and of course, Vilamoura. There are also many places where it is possible to hire sailing dinghies and get tuition.

Scuba-diving   The rocky south-west of the Algarve coast is great for scuba diving, and at depths between 5 and 30m you can find excellent and in some cases still relatively untouched diving grounds. To hire equipment or get diving lessons try one of the many diving centres in Albufeira, Alvor, Lagos, Monte Gordo, Praia da Falésia and Vilamoura.

Surfing   The surfing conditions are excellent along many different parts of the Algarve coastline. There are many places for learning how to surf and hiring surfboards (see Beaches).

Tennis   Almost all the Algarve's big hotels have their own tennis courts. There are also plenty of public tennis clubs. Among the best are Roger Taylor's Tennis Centre at Vale do Lobo and David Lloyd's at Rocha Brava.

The yacht harbour at Vilamoura

See entry

Walking

There are water-skiing facilities at all the Algarve's main tourist resorts.

Water-skiing

Taxis

The classic Portuguese taxis are black with a green roof, but white taxis are also becoming more common. Almost all taxis have meters. Out of town there are set rates and up to 50% extra is charged for night journeys and luggage. For longer one-way cross-country journeys the passenger may have to pay the full return fare. If engaging a taxi for an outing negotiate the price in advance. As a general rule Portuguese taxis are relatively cheap. The normal tip is 10–15%.

Telephone

Local and international calls can be made from post offices and private telephone companies (eg Telecom) where it is possible to pay after making the call, and from public phoneboxes. These take 10, 20 or 50 Esc. coins or a phonecard (cartão para telefonar). There are two different phonecard systems using different apparatus, so be sure to use the correct phonebox. There are no cheap rates for international calls.

For international calls from Portugal via the operator dial 099 for Europe and 098 for elsewhere. For direct dialling, the country codes are as follows:

International calls

To Portugal
00 351 then the area code, minus the first 0 – eg. 81 (Tavira), 82 (Lagos, Portimão), 89 (Faro) – then the number

Time

From Portugal
Canada: 00 1 (then as for calls to Portugal)
United Kingdom: 00 44
United States: 00 1

Time

Portugal is on Greenwich Mean Time (GMT) plus one hour in winter and GMT plus two hours in summer i.e from April to November.

Tipping

In hotels and restaurants service is included, but waiters, hotel maids and porters normally expect a tip of about 10%. An appropriate tip is also in order for tourist guides, hairdressers, and taxi drivers, and it is customary to tip the person who shows you to your seat at concerts and the theatre as well.

Travel Documents

Personal documents

Visitors to Portugal from EU countries, including Ireland and the UK, and Australia, Canada, New Zealand and the United States only require a valid passport and can stay for up to 60 days without a visa. Children must either have their own passport or be entered in one of their parent's passports.

Car documents

Drivers of their own cars will need to have their national driving licence, the vehicle's registration documents, and a Green Card for their insurance. Visitors driving a car which is not their own must be able to produce proof that they are doing so with the owner's permission.

Walking

Walking and hiking in the Algarve is gaining in popularity, and quite a few tour operators offer walking holidays as a safe way of exploring its truly beautiful countryside, including the lovely hill country of the Serra de Monchique.

Guided walks

Guided walks worth recommending include those offered by:

Tempo Passa
Kiosk Praça Teixeira Gomes, Portimão; tel. 082/41 71 10, 47 12 41

Turinfo
Tourist information office, Sagres; tel. 082/6 45 20

Walking holidays

Bahia Biketours
Rua Prof. Luíz de Azevedo 53, Lagos; tel. 082/76 77 10

When To Go

At the height of summer the visitor can expect packed roads, fully-booked hotels and crowded beaches, and although temperatures from June to September are never too much to bear it can get very hot. Hence the best time to visit the Algarve is either in spring (from mid-March to early June), or autumn (from early September to early November), when the temperatures are very pleasant, the weather as a whole is relatively settled and swimming is still possible. Early spring has the added bonus of lush greenery and a host of flowers. Even in winter temperatures only briefly drop below 10°C and there are usually a few warm or at least mild days between December and March.

Water temperatures in the Atlantic are generally lower than in the Mediterranean, hardly getting above 20°C in summer and falling to 15°C in winter. Sea temperatures in the east of the Algarve are around two degrees higher than in the west.

Water temperatures

Youth Hostels

The Algarve has four youth hostels (pousadas de juventude). Visitors must have an international youth hostelling permit obtainable from their own national YHA. Maximum stay is eight nights. Prices are between 1100 and 2000 Esc. per person per day.

Youth hostel places can be booked in advance at the central YHA office in Lisbon. In summer this is something to be highly recommended:
Associação Portuguesa de Pousada de Juventude
Avenida Duque de Ávila 137, 1000 Lisboa; tel. 01/355 90 81

Reservations

Pousada de Juventude de Alcoutim
8970 Alcoutim; tel./fax 081/4 60 04

Addresses

Pousada de Juventude de Lagos
Rue de Lancerote de Freitas 50
8600 Lagos; tel./fax 082/76 19 70

Pousada de Juventude de Portimão
Lugar do Coca Maravilhas
8500 Portimão; tel./fax 082/49 18 04

Pousada de Juventude de Vila Real de Santo António
Rua Dr. Sousa Martins 40
8900 Vila Real de Santo António; tel./fax 081/4 45 65

Index

Principal Sights of Tourist Interest

Note: The places listed above are merely a selection of the principal places of interest in themselves, or for attractions in the surrounding area. There are, of course, innumerable other places worth visiting, to which attention is drawn by one or more stars.

Imprint

88 colour photographs, 3 ground plans, 1 drawing, 1 large map at end of book

Text: Eva Missler

Editorial work: Baedeker-Redaktion (Birgit Borowski)

General direction: Reiner Eisenschmid, Baedeker Stuttgart

Cartography: Franz Huber, Munich
Large map: Karto + Grafik Verlagsgesellschaft

Source of photographs: Archiv für Kunst und Geschichte (2), Bildagenture Schapo-walow (2), Bildagenture Schuster (5), Borowski (31), Fotoaguntur Helga Lade (9), Friedrichsmeier (2), HB Verlag, Hamburg (2), Historia-Photo (2), IFA-Bilderteam (8), Missler (24).

English Translation: Wendy Bell, David Cocking, Brenda Ferris

Editorial work: Margaret Court